AR

FRED VAN LENTE ★ RYAN DUNLAVEY

ACTION PRESIDENTS

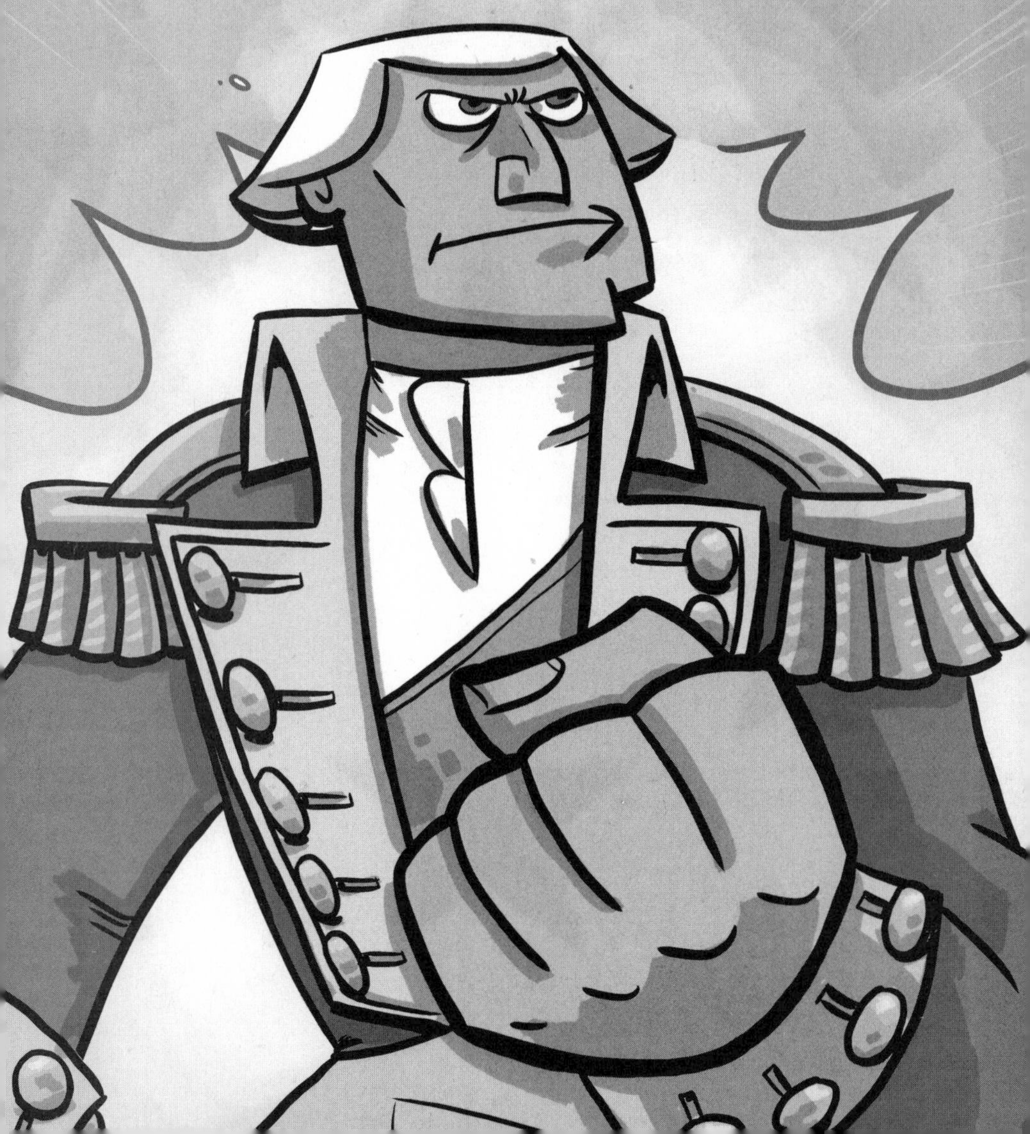

FRED VAN LENTE ★ RYAN DUNLAVEY

ACTION PRESIDENTS

REAL HISTORY!
FAKE JOKES!

GEORGE WASHINGTON!

HARPER
An Imprint of HarperCollinsPublishers

Action Presidents #1: George Washington!

For information address HarperCollins Children's Books, a division of HarperCollins Publishers, 195 Broadway, New York, NY 10007.
www.harpercollinschildrens.com

Library of Congress Control Number: 2017950229
ISBN 978-0-06-239405-7 (trade bdg.)

The artist used Adobe Photoshop, a Wacom Cintiq tablet, and insomnia to create the digital illustrations for this book.

17 18 19 20 21 CG / LSCH 10 9 8 7 6 5 4 3 2 1

❖

First Edition

For Dad, who taught me to love (and make fun of) history.
—FVL

In memory of Jim Dunlavey, my dad, who dragged me to
Mount Vernon too many times to count. It was worth it!
—Ryan

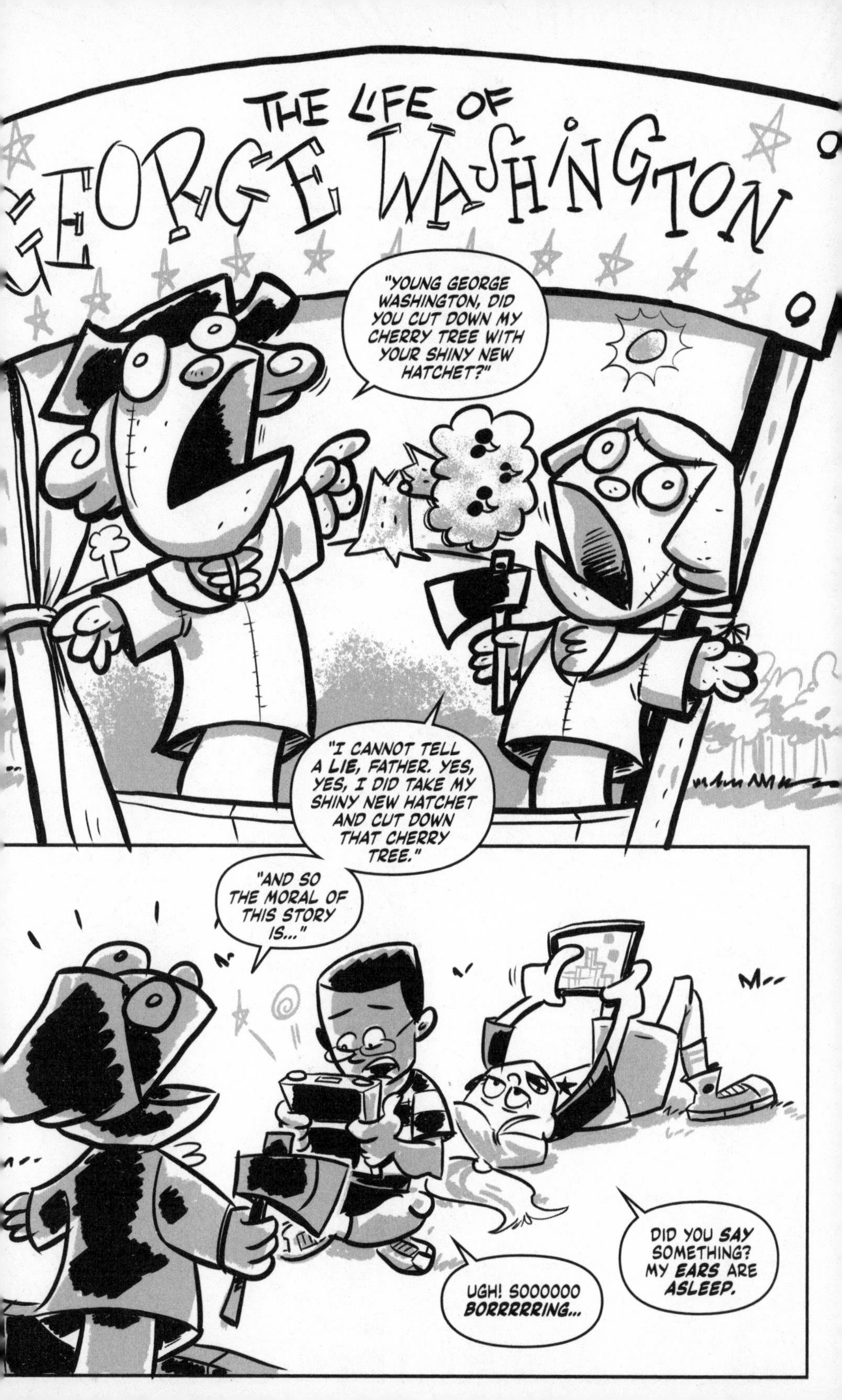
THE LIFE OF GEORGE WASHINGTON
"YOUNG GEORGE WASHINGTON, DID YOU CUT DOWN MY CHERRY TREE WITH YOUR SHINY NEW HATCHET?"
"I CANNOT TELL A LIE, FATHER. YES, YES, I DID TAKE MY SHINY NEW HATCHET AND CUT DOWN THAT CHERRY TREE."
"AND SO THE MORAL OF THIS STORY IS..."
UGH! SOOOOOO BORRRRRING...
DID YOU SAY SOMETHING? MY EARS ARE ASLEEP.

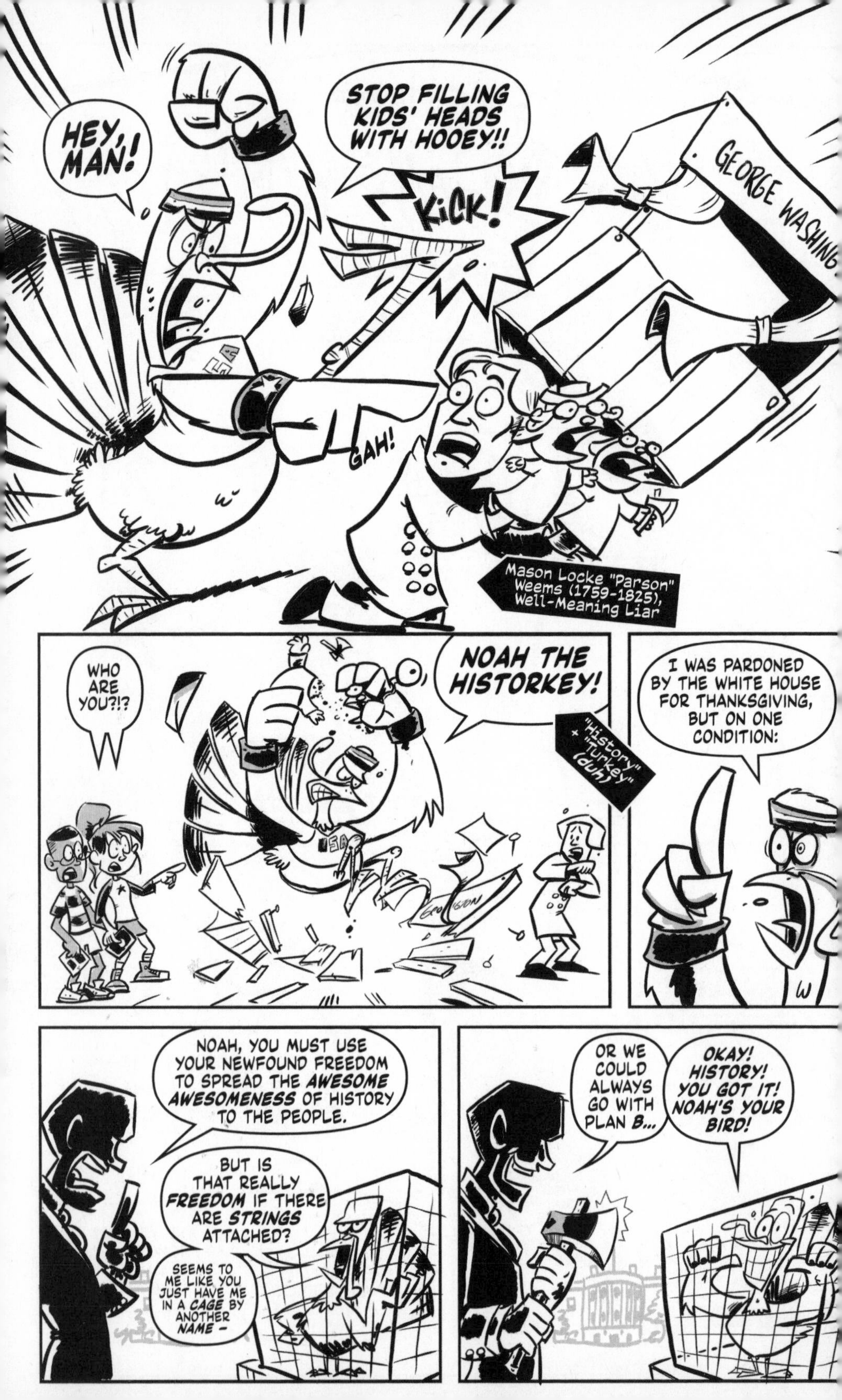
HEY, MAN!
STOP FILLING KIDS' HEADS WITH HOOEY!!
KICK!
GEORGE WASHING
GAH!
Mason Locke "Parson" Weems (1759-1825), Well-Meaning Liar
WHO ARE YOU?!?
NOAH THE HISTORKEY!
"History" + "Turkey" (duh)
I WAS PARDONED BY THE WHITE HOUSE FOR THANKSGIVING, BUT ON ONE CONDITION:
NOAH, YOU MUST USE YOUR NEWFOUND FREEDOM TO SPREAD THE AWESOME AWESOMENESS OF HISTORY TO THE PEOPLE.
BUT IS THAT REALLY FREEDOM IF THERE ARE STRINGS ATTACHED?
SEEMS TO ME LIKE YOU JUST HAVE ME IN A CAGE BY ANOTHER NAME –
OR WE COULD ALWAYS GO WITH PLAN B...
OKAY! HISTORY! YOU GOT IT! NOAH'S YOUR BIRD!

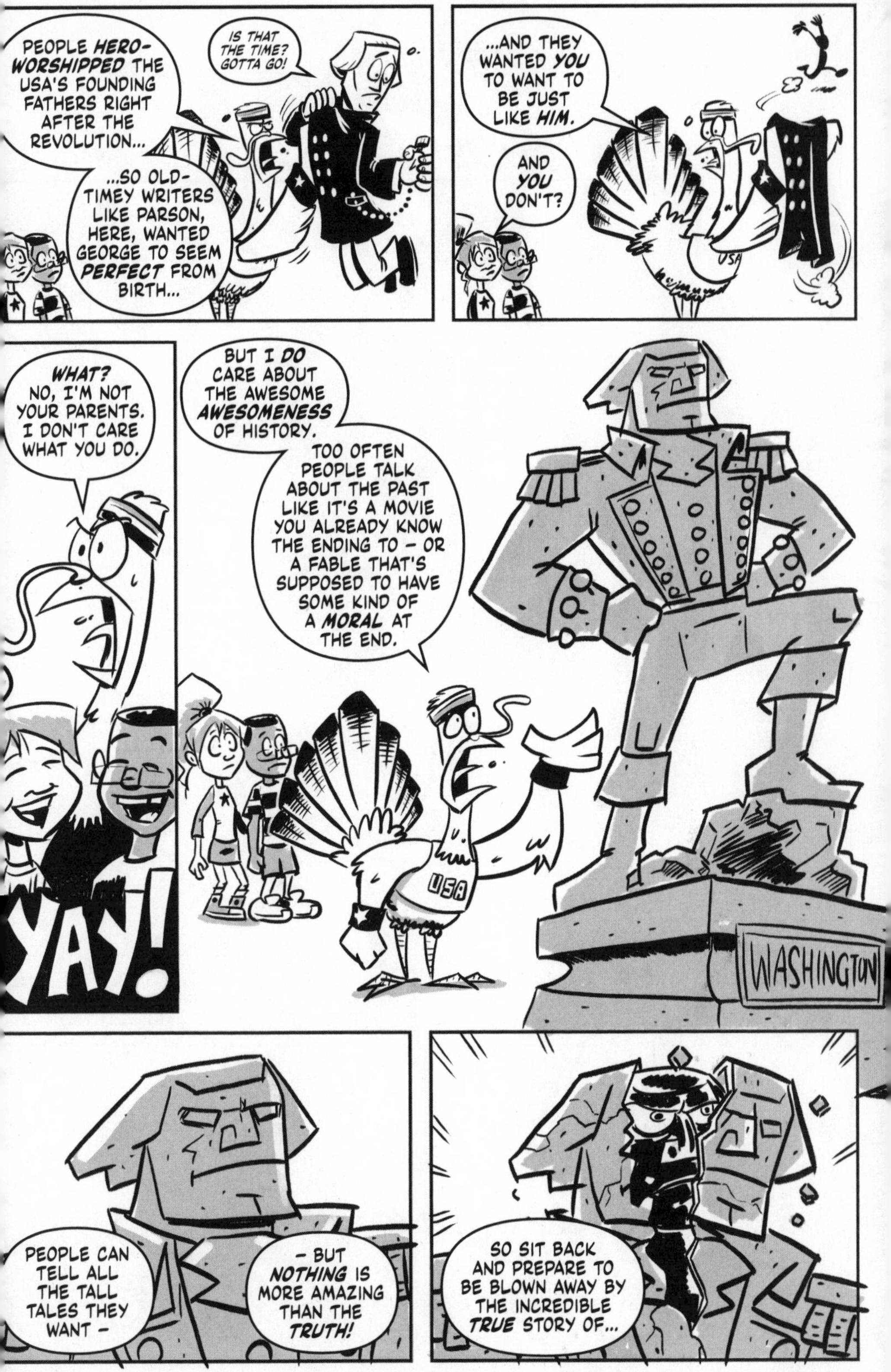

PEOPLE HERO-WORSHIPPED THE USA'S FOUNDING FATHERS RIGHT AFTER THE REVOLUTION...
IS THAT THE TIME? GOTTA GO!
...SO OLD-TIMEY WRITERS LIKE PARSON, HERE, WANTED GEORGE TO SEEM PERFECT FROM BIRTH...
...AND THEY WANTED YOU TO WANT TO BE JUST LIKE HIM.
AND YOU DON'T?
WHAT? NO, I'M NOT YOUR PARENTS. I DON'T CARE WHAT YOU DO.
YAY!
BUT I DO CARE ABOUT THE AWESOME AWESOMENESS OF HISTORY.
TOO OFTEN PEOPLE TALK ABOUT THE PAST LIKE IT'S A MOVIE YOU ALREADY KNOW THE ENDING TO – OR A FABLE THAT'S SUPPOSED TO HAVE SOME KIND OF A MORAL AT THE END.
USA
WASHINGTON
PEOPLE CAN TELL ALL THE TALL TALES THEY WANT –
– BUT NOTHING IS MORE AMAZING THAN THE TRUTH!
SO SIT BACK AND PREPARE TO BE BLOWN AWAY BY THE INCREDIBLE TRUE STORY OF...

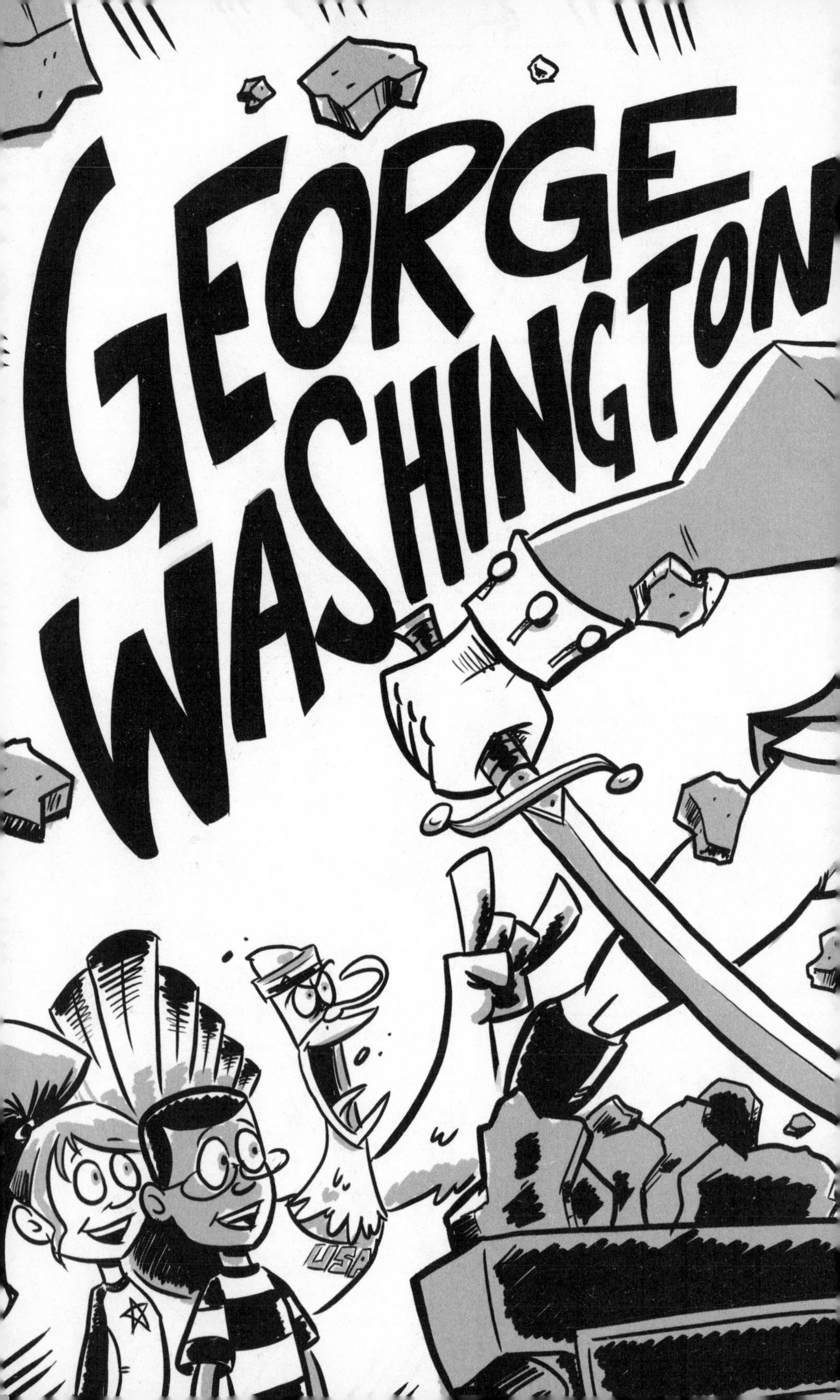
GEORGE WASHINGTON
USA

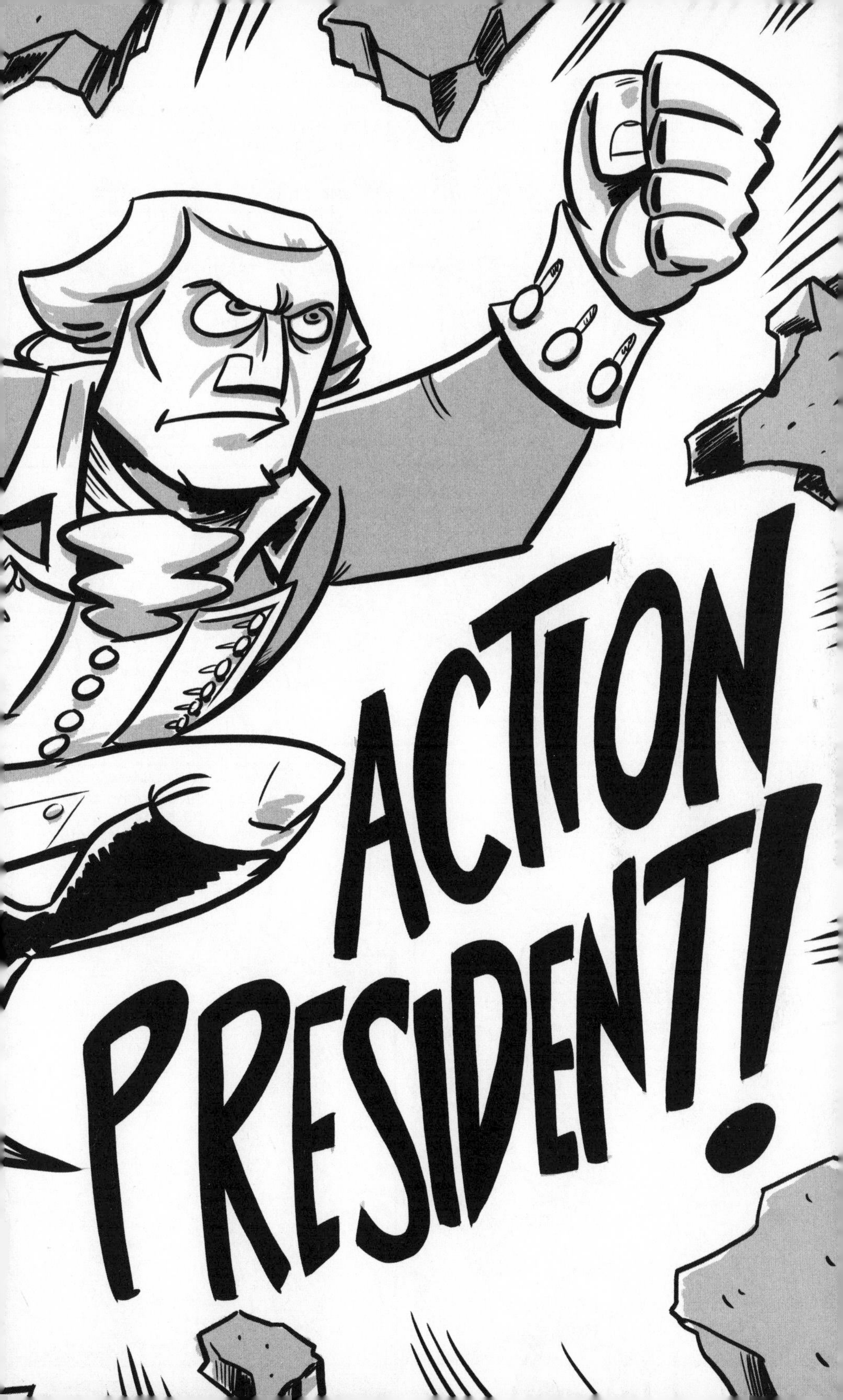
ACTION PRESIDENT!

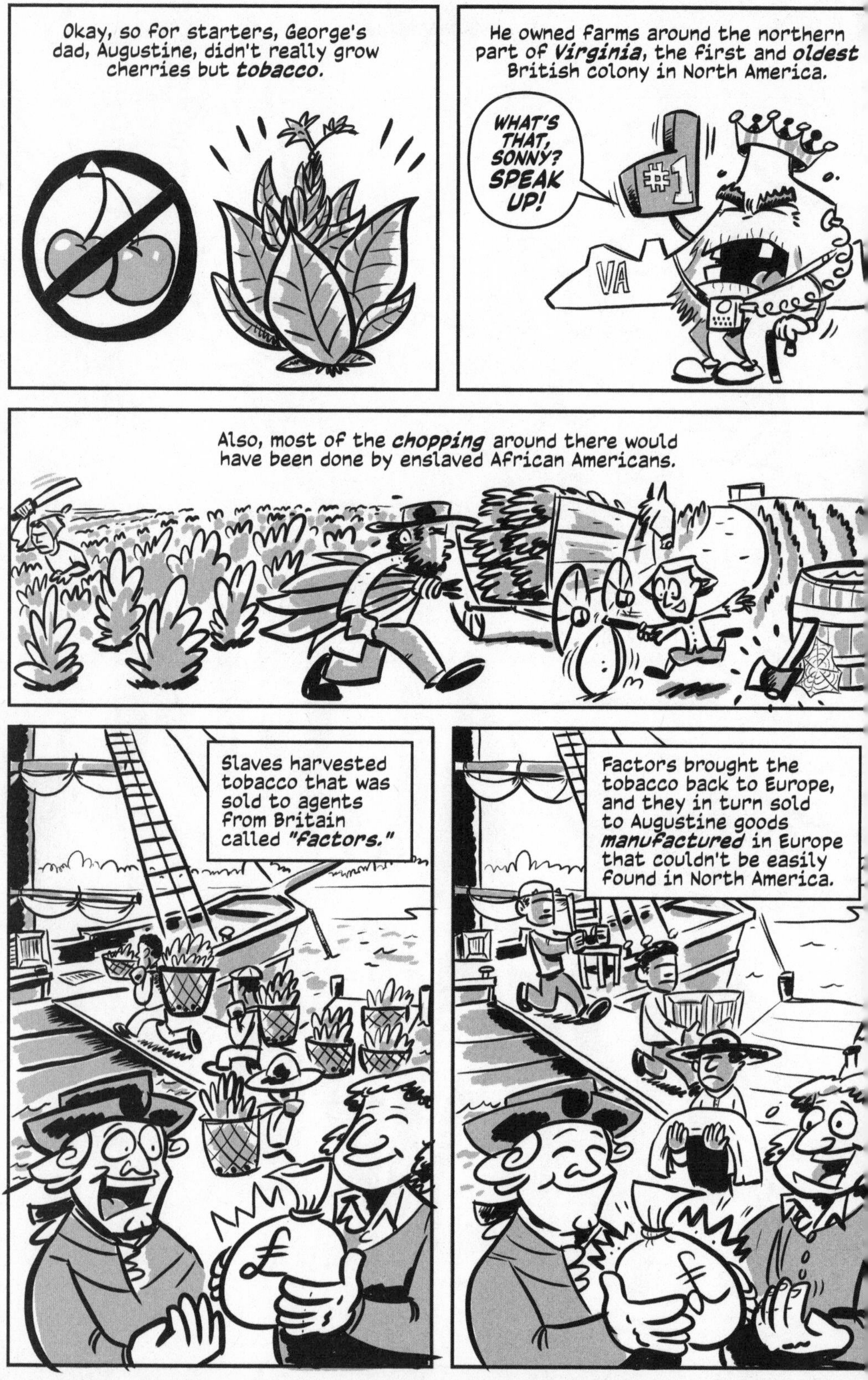

Okay, so for starters, George's dad, Augustine, didn't really grow cherries but *tobacco.*
He owned farms around the northern part of *Virginia*, the first and *oldest* British colony in North America.
WHAT'S THAT, SONNY? SPEAK UP!
#1
VA
Also, most of the *chopping* around there would have been done by enslaved African Americans.
Slaves harvested tobacco that was sold to agents from Britain called *"factors."*
Factors brought the tobacco back to Europe, and they in turn sold to Augustine goods *manufactured* in Europe that couldn't be easily found in North America.

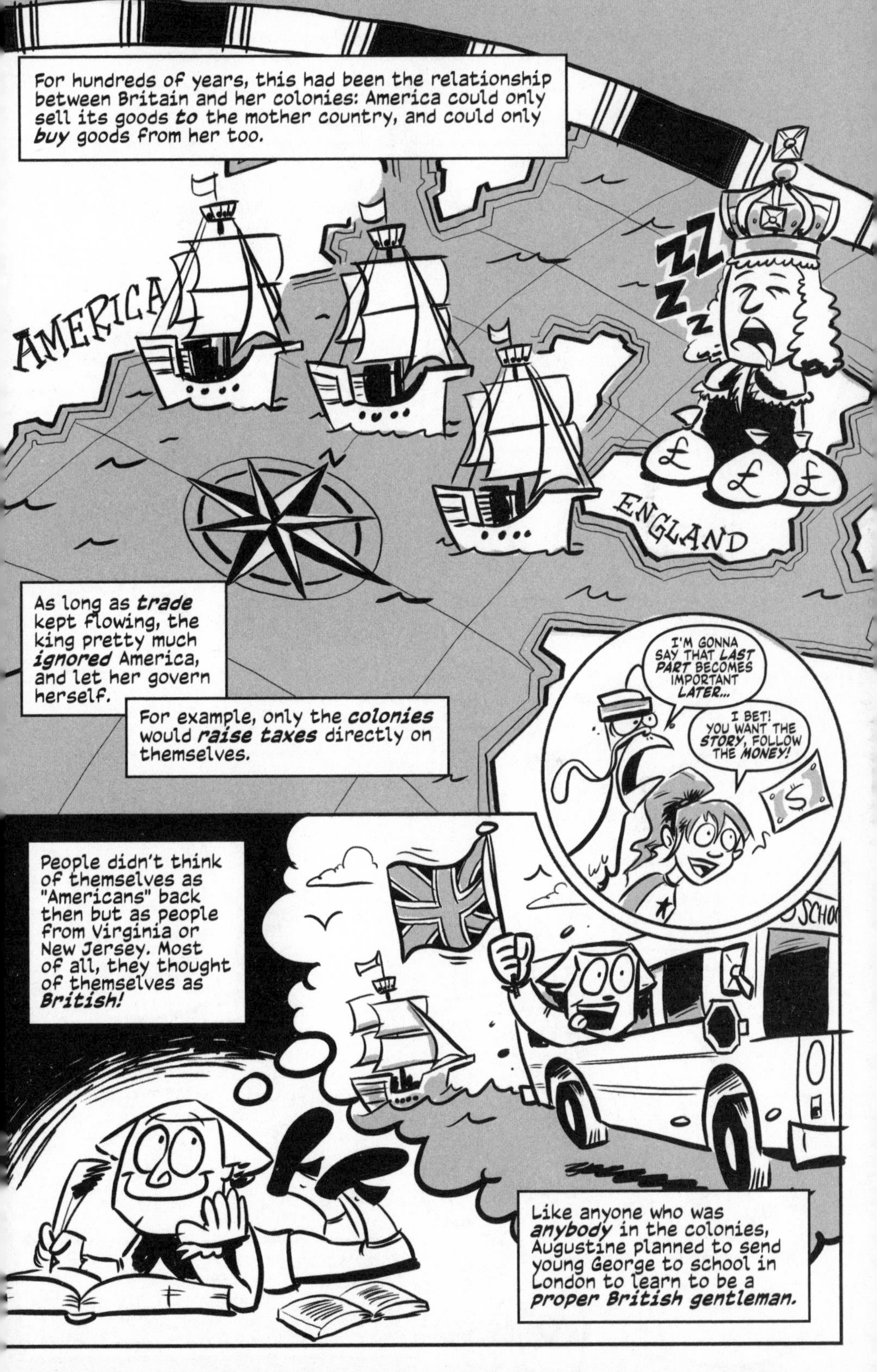
For hundreds of years, this had been the relationship between Britain and her colonies: America could only sell its goods *to* the mother country, and could only *buy* goods from her too.
AMERICA
ZZZ
ENGLAND
As long as *trade* kept flowing, the king pretty much *ignored* America, and let her govern herself.
For example, only the *colonies* would *raise taxes* directly on themselves.
I'M GONNA SAY THAT *LAST PART* BECOMES IMPORTANT *LATER...*
I BET! YOU WANT THE *STORY*, FOLLOW THE *MONEY!*
People didn't think of themselves as "Americans" back then but as people from Virginia or New Jersey. Most of all, they thought of themselves as *British!*
Like anyone who was *anybody* in the colonies, Augustine planned to send young George to school in London to learn to be a *proper British gentleman.*

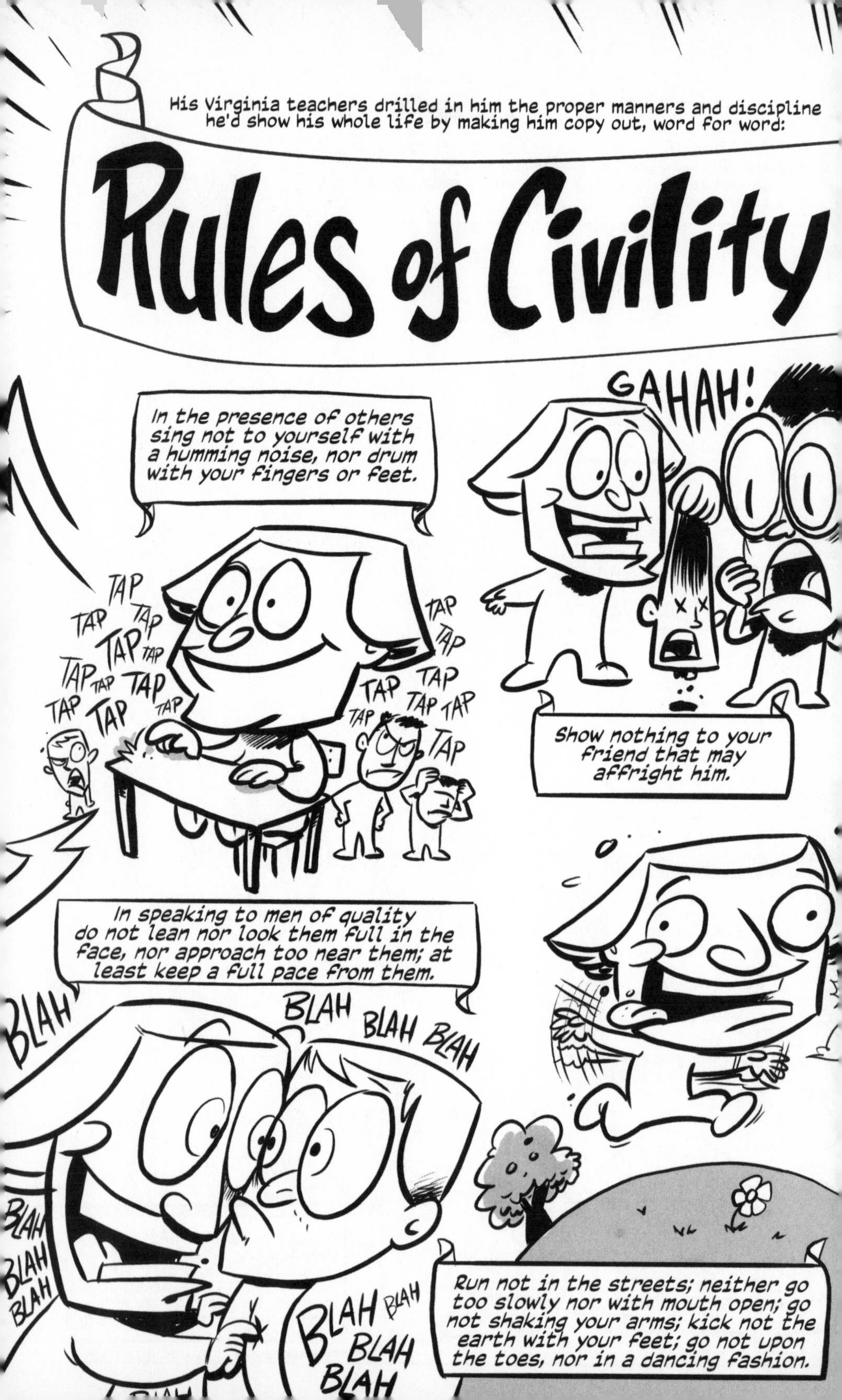

His Virginia teachers drilled in him the proper manners and discipline he'd show his whole life by making him copy out, word for word:
Rules of Civility
In the presence of others sing not to yourself with a humming noise, nor drum with your fingers or feet.
TAP TAP TAP TAP TAP TAP TAP TAP TAP TAP TAP TAP TAP TAP TAP TAP TAP TAP TAP TAP
GAHAH!
Show nothing to your friend that may affright him.
In speaking to men of quality do not lean nor look them full in the face, nor approach too near them; at least keep a full pace from them.
BLAH BLAH BLAH BLAH BLAH BLAH BLAH BLAH BLAH BLAH BLAH
Run not in the streets; neither go too slowly nor with mouth open; go not shaking your arms; kick not the earth with your feet; go not upon the toes, nor in a dancing fashion.

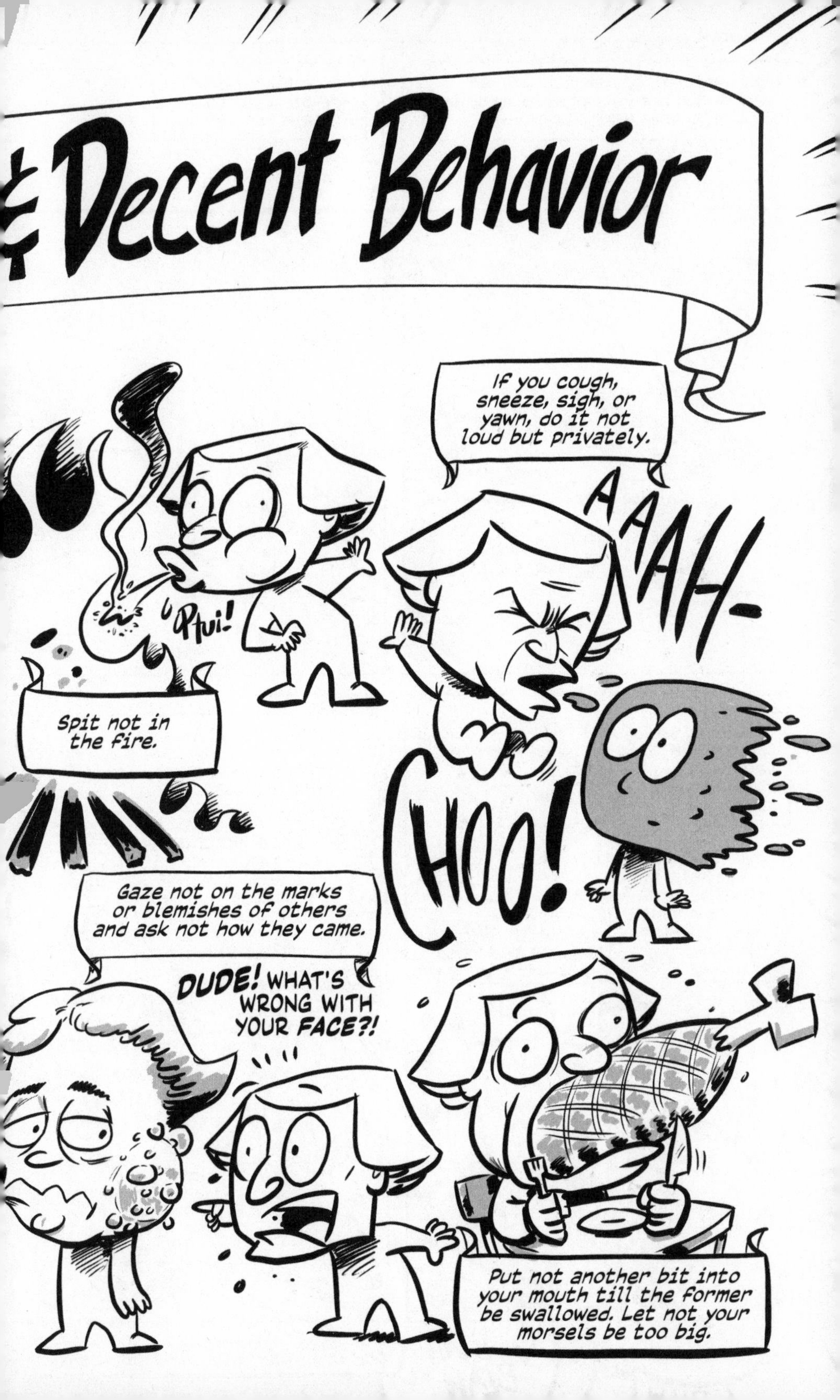

& Decent Behavior
If you cough, sneeze, sigh, or yawn, do it not loud but privately.
Ptui!
Spit not in the fire.
AAAAH-
CHOO!
Gaze not on the marks or blemishes of others and ask not how they came.
DUDE! WHAT'S WRONG WITH YOUR FACE?!
Put not another bit into your mouth till the former be swallowed. Let not your morsels be too big.

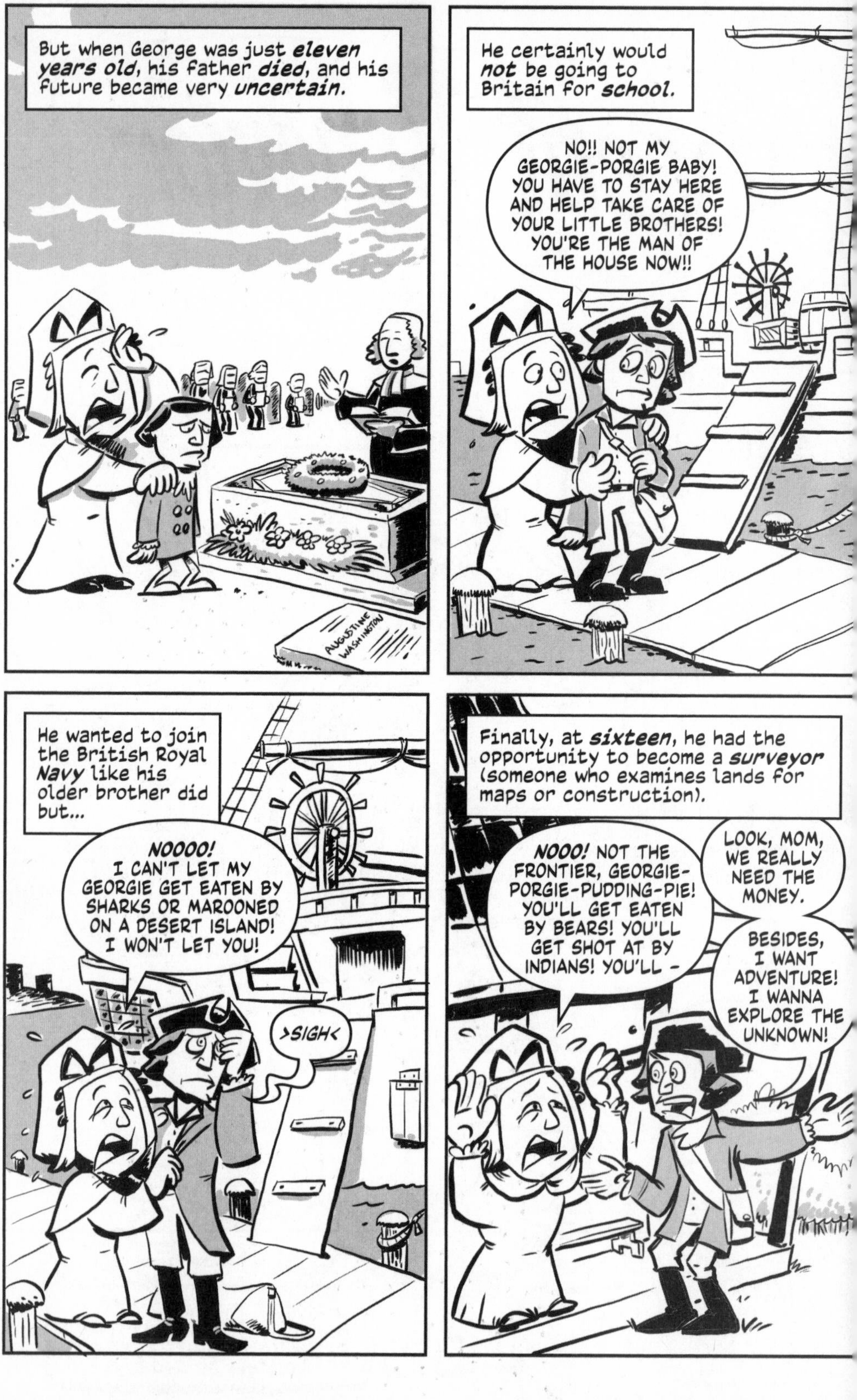
But when George was just eleven years old, his father died, and his future became very uncertain.
AUGUSTINE WASHINGTON
He certainly would not be going to Britain for school.
NO!! NOT MY GEORGIE-PORGIE BABY! YOU HAVE TO STAY HERE AND HELP TAKE CARE OF YOUR LITTLE BROTHERS! YOU'RE THE MAN OF THE HOUSE NOW!!
He wanted to join the British Royal Navy like his older brother did but...
NOOOO! I CAN'T LET MY GEORGIE GET EATEN BY SHARKS OR MAROONED ON A DESERT ISLAND! I WON'T LET YOU!
>SIGH<
Finally, at sixteen, he had the opportunity to become a surveyor (someone who examines lands for maps or construction).
NOOO! NOT THE FRONTIER, GEORGIE-PORGIE-PUDDING-PIE! YOU'LL GET EATEN BY BEARS! YOU'LL GET SHOT AT BY INDIANS! YOU'LL –
LOOK, MOM, WE REALLY NEED THE MONEY.
BESIDES, I WANT ADVENTURE! I WANNA EXPLORE THE UNKNOWN!

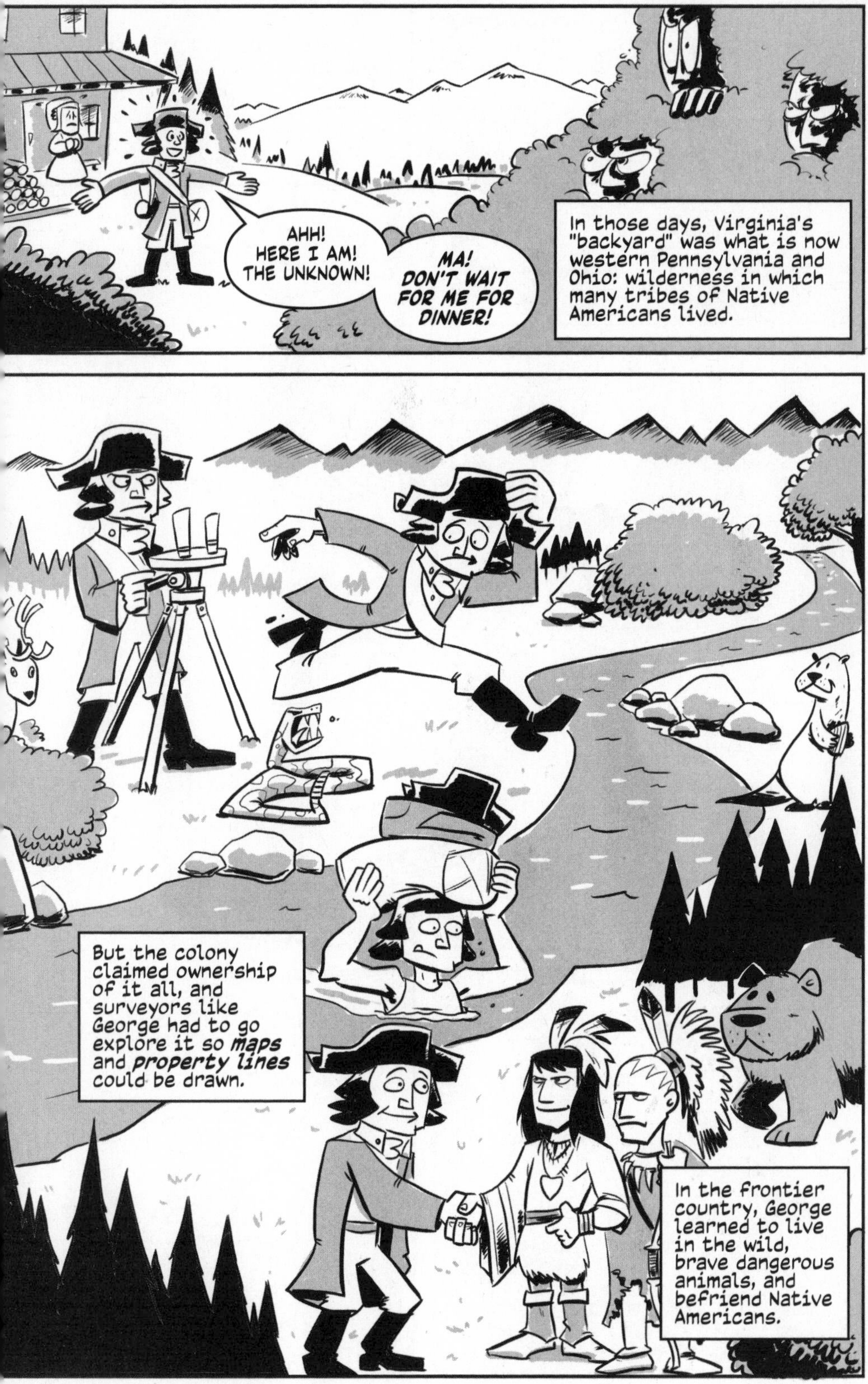

AHH!
HERE I AM!
THE UNKNOWN!
MA!
DON'T WAIT
FOR ME FOR
DINNER!
In those days, Virginia's "backyard" was what is now western Pennsylvania and Ohio: wilderness in which many tribes of Native Americans lived.
But the colony claimed ownership of it all, and surveyors like George had to go explore it so *maps* and *property lines* could be drawn.
In the frontier country, George learned to live in the wild, brave dangerous animals, and befriend Native Americans.

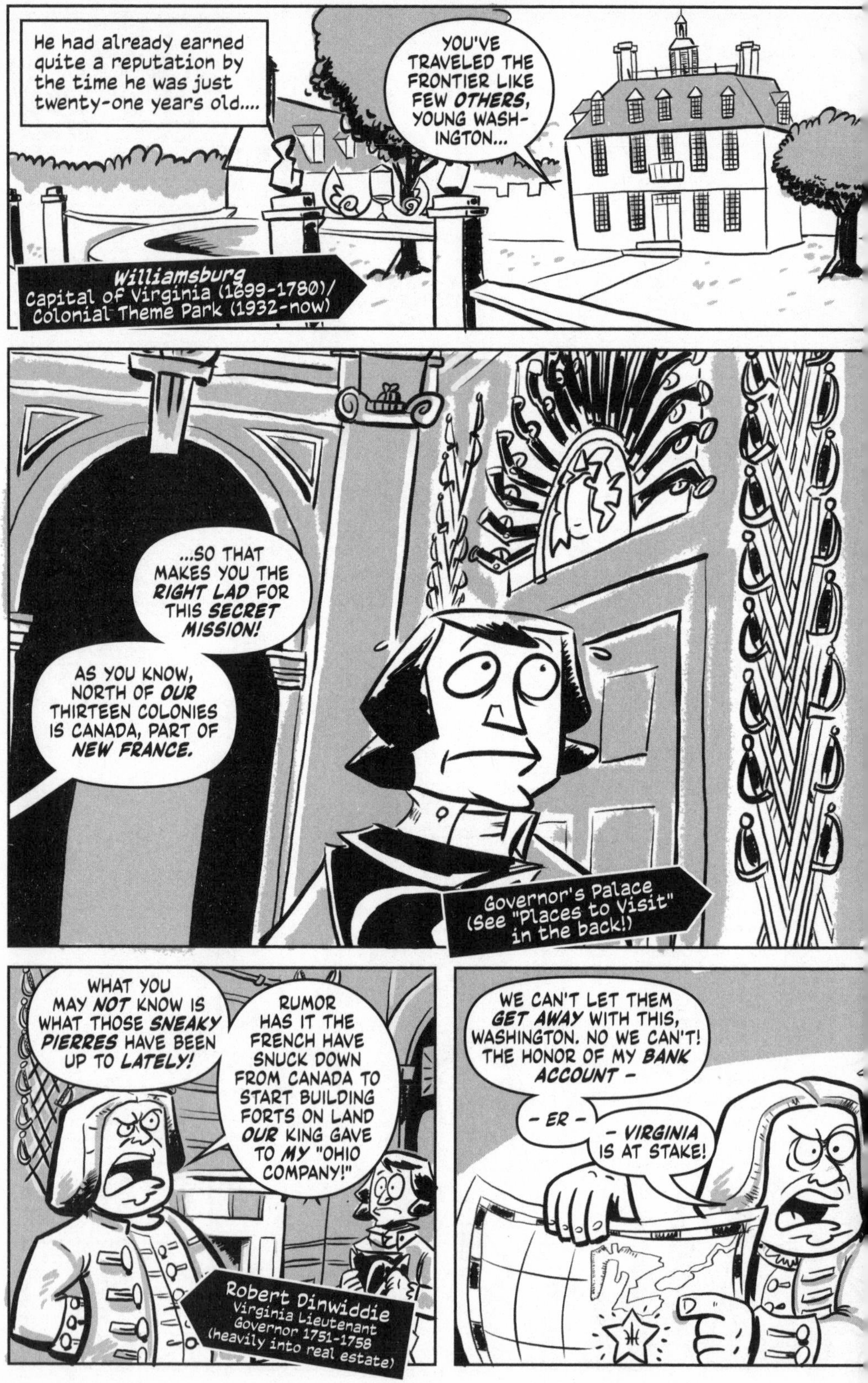

He had already earned quite a reputation by the time he was just twenty-one years old....
YOU'VE TRAVELED THE FRONTIER LIKE FEW OTHERS, YOUNG WASHINGTON...
Williamsburg
Capital of Virginia (1699-1780)/
Colonial Theme Park (1932-now)
...SO THAT MAKES YOU THE RIGHT LAD FOR THIS SECRET MISSION!
AS YOU KNOW, NORTH OF OUR THIRTEEN COLONIES IS CANADA, PART OF NEW FRANCE.
Governor's Palace
(See "Places to Visit" in the back!)
WHAT YOU MAY NOT KNOW IS WHAT THOSE SNEAKY PIERRES HAVE BEEN UP TO LATELY!
RUMOR HAS IT THE FRENCH HAVE SNUCK DOWN FROM CANADA TO START BUILDING FORTS ON LAND OUR KING GAVE TO MY "OHIO COMPANY!"
Robert Dinwiddie
Virginia Lieutenant Governor 1751-1758
(heavily into real estate)
WE CAN'T LET THEM GET AWAY WITH THIS, WASHINGTON. NO WE CAN'T! THE HONOR OF MY BANK ACCOUNT –
– ER –
– VIRGINIA IS AT STAKE!

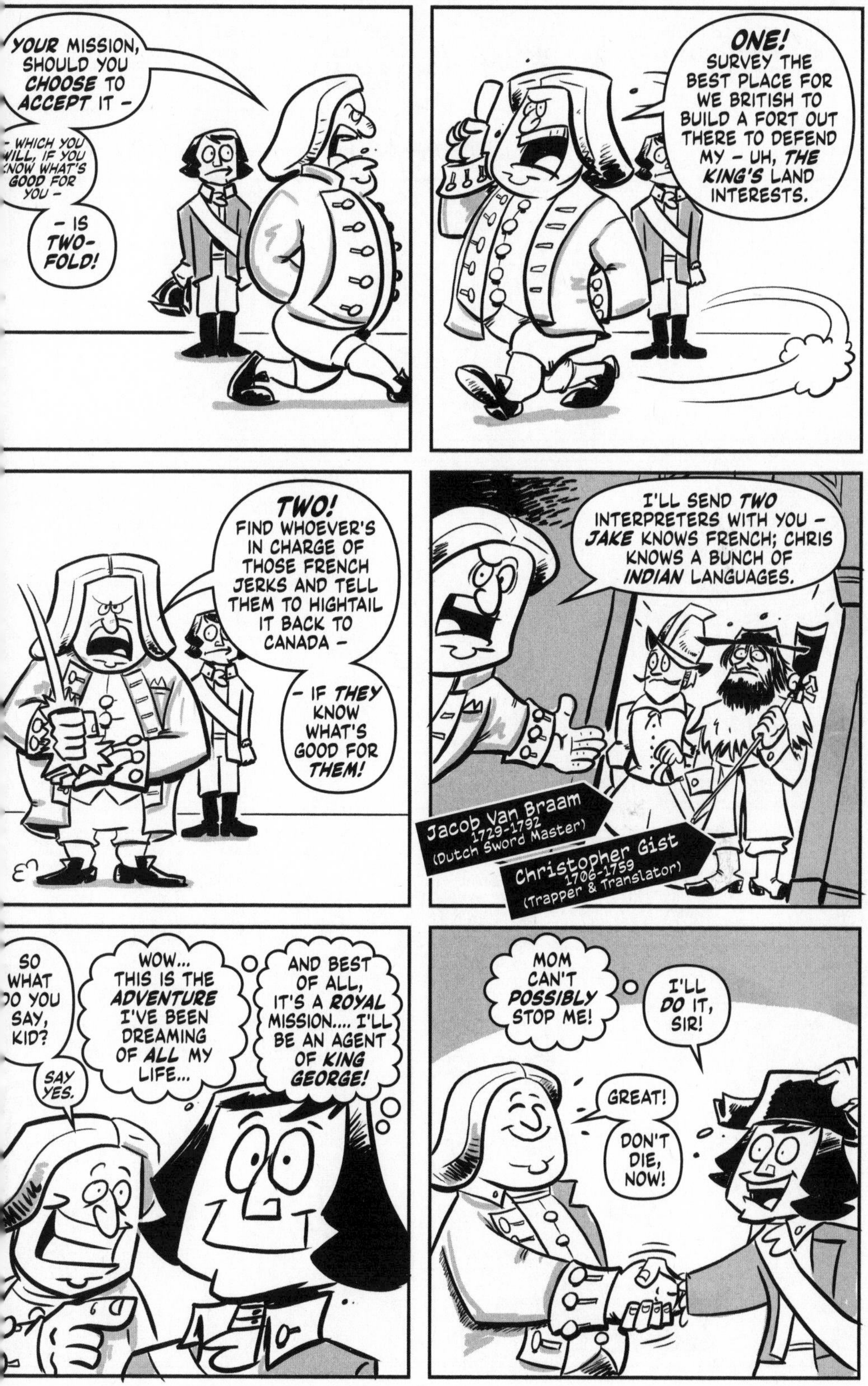

YOUR MISSION, SHOULD YOU CHOOSE TO ACCEPT IT –
– WHICH YOU WILL, IF YOU KNOW WHAT'S GOOD FOR YOU –
– IS TWO-FOLD!
ONE! SURVEY THE BEST PLACE FOR WE BRITISH TO BUILD A FORT OUT THERE TO DEFEND MY – UH, THE KING'S LAND INTERESTS.
TWO! FIND WHOEVER'S IN CHARGE OF THOSE FRENCH JERKS AND TELL THEM TO HIGHTAIL IT BACK TO CANADA –
– IF THEY KNOW WHAT'S GOOD FOR THEM!
I'LL SEND TWO INTERPRETERS WITH YOU – JAKE KNOWS FRENCH; CHRIS KNOWS A BUNCH OF INDIAN LANGUAGES.
Jacob Van Braam 1729-1792 (Dutch Sword Master)
Christopher Gist 1706-1759 (Trapper & Translator)
SO WHAT DO YOU SAY, KID?
SAY YES.
WOW... THIS IS THE ADVENTURE I'VE BEEN DREAMING OF ALL MY LIFE...
AND BEST OF ALL, IT'S A ROYAL MISSION.... I'LL BE AN AGENT OF KING GEORGE!
MOM CAN'T POSSIBLY STOP ME!
I'LL DO IT, SIR!
GREAT!
DON'T DIE, NOW!

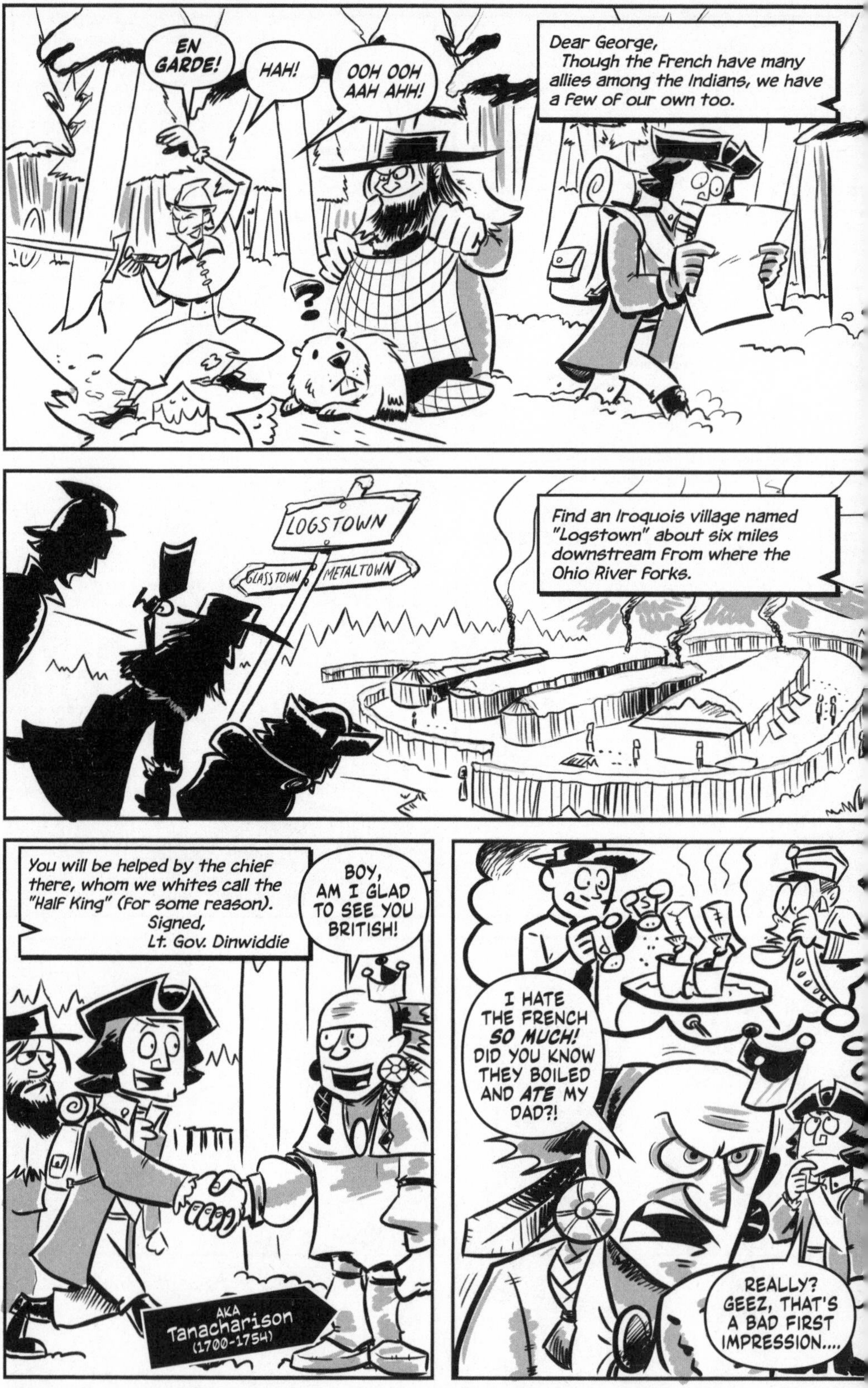

EN GARDE!
HAH!
OOH OOH AAH AHH!
Dear George,
Though the French have many allies among the Indians, we have a few of our own too.
LOGSTOWN
GLASSTOWN
METALTOWN
Find an Iroquois village named "Logstown" about six miles downstream from where the Ohio River forks.
You will be helped by the chief there, whom we whites call the "Half King" (for some reason).
Signed,
Lt. Gov. Dinwiddie
BOY, AM I GLAD TO SEE YOU BRITISH!
AKA Tanacharison (1700-1754)
I HATE THE FRENCH SO MUCH! DID YOU KNOW THEY BOILED AND ATE MY DAD?!
REALLY? GEEZ, THAT'S A BAD FIRST IMPRESSION....

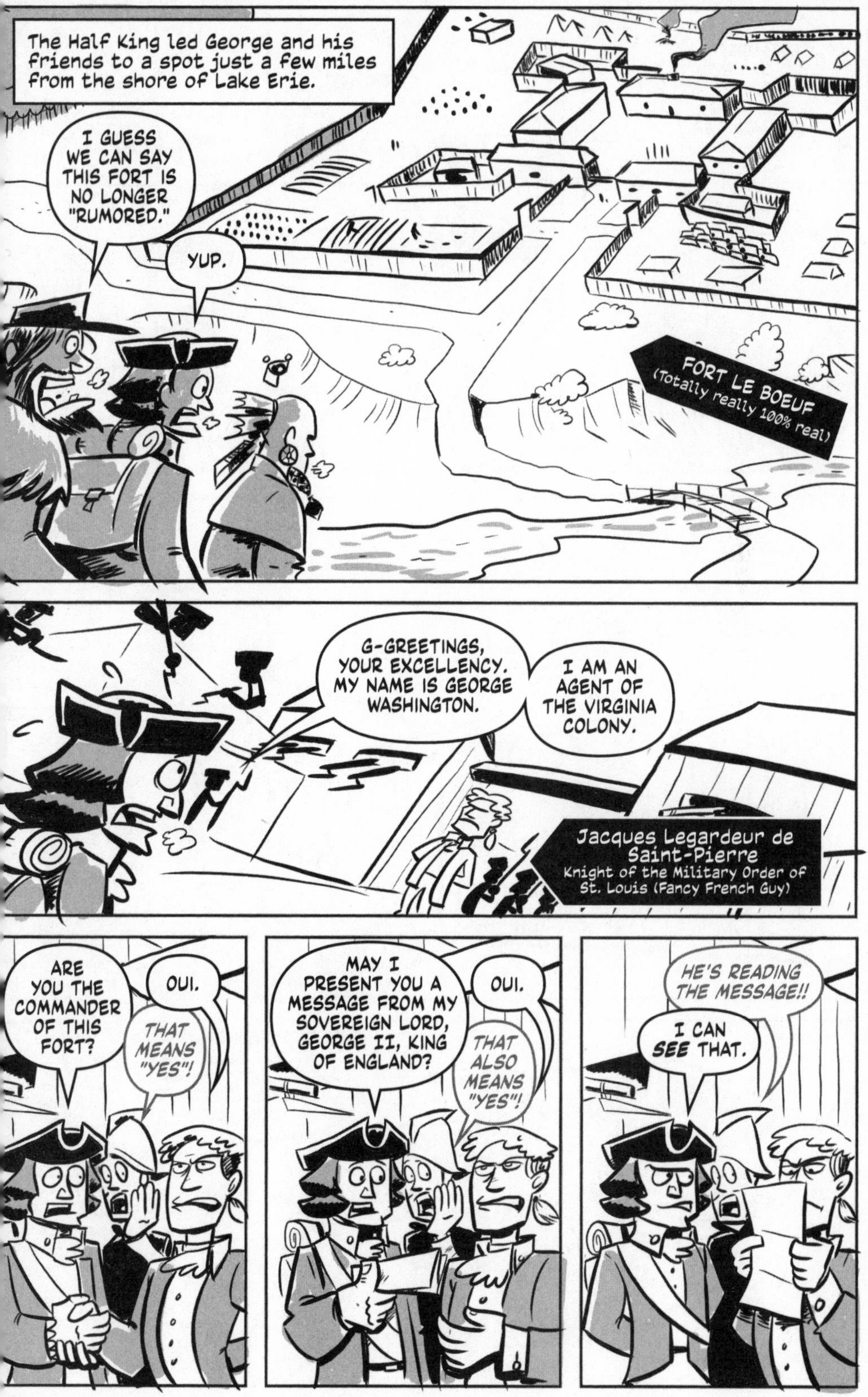

The Half King led George and his friends to a spot just a few miles from the shore of Lake Erie.
I GUESS WE CAN SAY THIS FORT IS NO LONGER "RUMORED."
YUP.
FORT LE BOEUF (Totally really 100% real)
G-GREETINGS, YOUR EXCELLENCY. MY NAME IS GEORGE WASHINGTON.
I AM AN AGENT OF THE VIRGINIA COLONY.
Jacques Legardeur de Saint-Pierre Knight of the Military Order of St. Louis (Fancy French Guy)
ARE YOU THE COMMANDER OF THIS FORT?
OUI.
THAT MEANS "YES"!
MAY I PRESENT YOU A MESSAGE FROM MY SOVEREIGN LORD, GEORGE II, KING OF ENGLAND?
OUI.
THAT ALSO MEANS "YES"!
HE'S READING THE MESSAGE!!
I CAN SEE THAT.

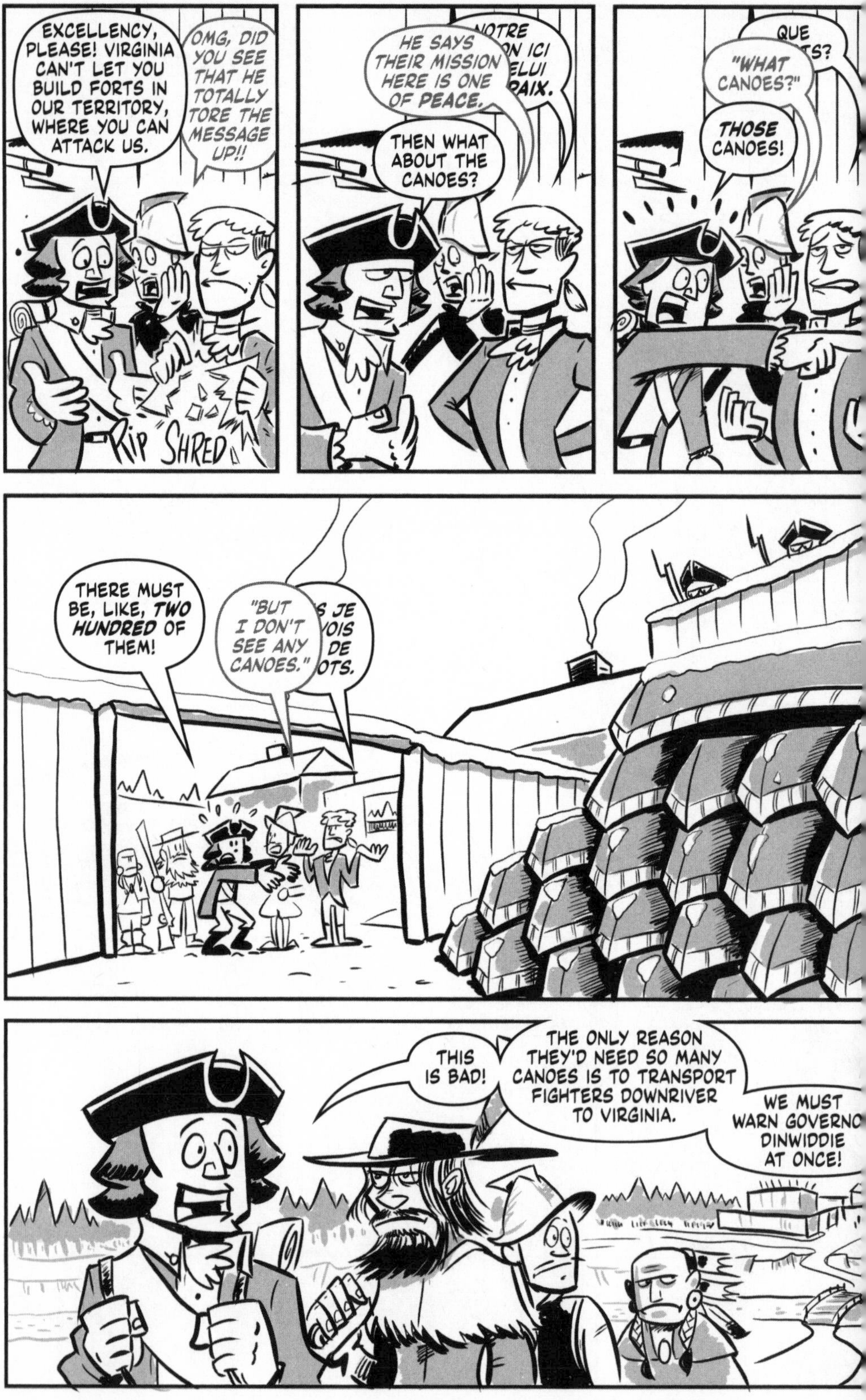

EXCELLENCY, PLEASE! VIRGINIA CAN'T LET YOU BUILD FORTS IN OUR TERRITORY, WHERE YOU CAN ATTACK US.
OMG, DID YOU SEE THAT HE TOTALLY TORE THE MESSAGE UP!!
RIP
SHRED
NOTRE
PAIX.
HE SAYS THEIR MISSION HERE IS ONE OF PEACE.
THEN WHAT ABOUT THE CANOES?
QUE
"WHAT CANOES?"
THOSE CANOES!
THERE MUST BE, LIKE, TWO HUNDRED OF THEM!
"BUT I DON'T SEE ANY CANOES."
JE
DE
THIS IS BAD!
THE ONLY REASON THEY'D NEED SO MANY CANOES IS TO TRANSPORT FIGHTERS DOWNRIVER TO VIRGINIA.
WE MUST WARN GOVERNO
DINWIDDIE AT ONCE!

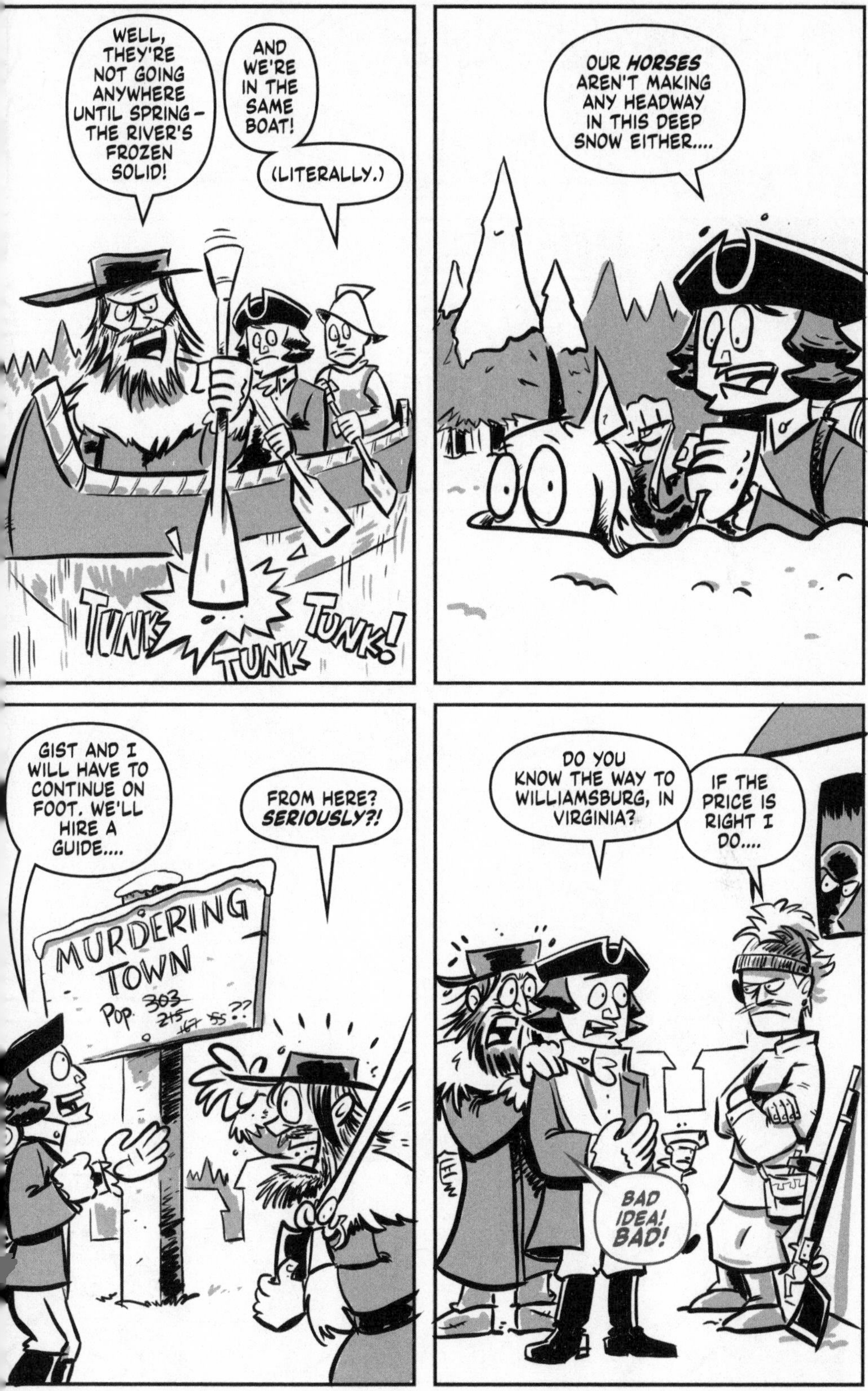

WELL, THEY'RE NOT GOING ANYWHERE UNTIL SPRING— THE RIVER'S FROZEN SOLID!
AND WE'RE IN THE SAME BOAT!
(LITERALLY.)
TUNK TUNK TUNK!
OUR HORSES AREN'T MAKING ANY HEADWAY IN THIS DEEP SNOW EITHER....
GIST AND I WILL HAVE TO CONTINUE ON FOOT. WE'LL HIRE A GUIDE....
FROM HERE? SERIOUSLY?!
MURDERING TOWN
Pop. 303 215 167 55 ??
DO YOU KNOW THE WAY TO WILLIAMSBURG, IN VIRGINIA?
IF THE PRICE IS RIGHT I DO....
BAD IDEA! BAD!

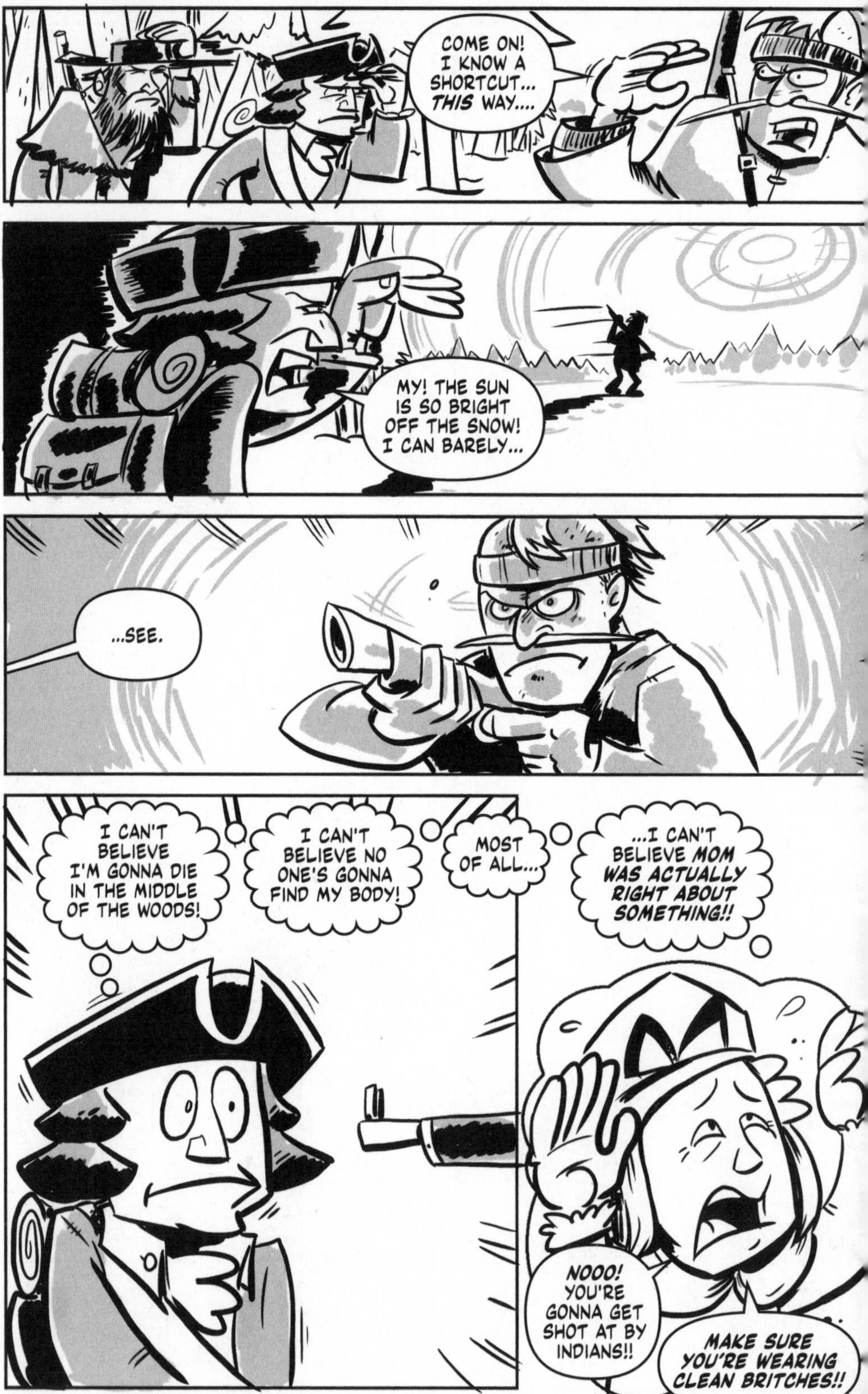

COME ON! I KNOW A SHORTCUT... THIS WAY....
MY! THE SUN IS SO BRIGHT OFF THE SNOW! I CAN BARELY...
...SEE.
I CAN'T BELIEVE I'M GONNA DIE IN THE MIDDLE OF THE WOODS!
I CAN'T BELIEVE NO ONE'S GONNA FIND MY BODY!
MOST OF ALL...
...I CAN'T BELIEVE MOM WAS ACTUALLY RIGHT ABOUT SOMETHING!!
NOOO! YOU'RE GONNA GET SHOT AT BY INDIANS!!
MAKE SURE YOU'RE WEARING CLEAN BRITCHES!!

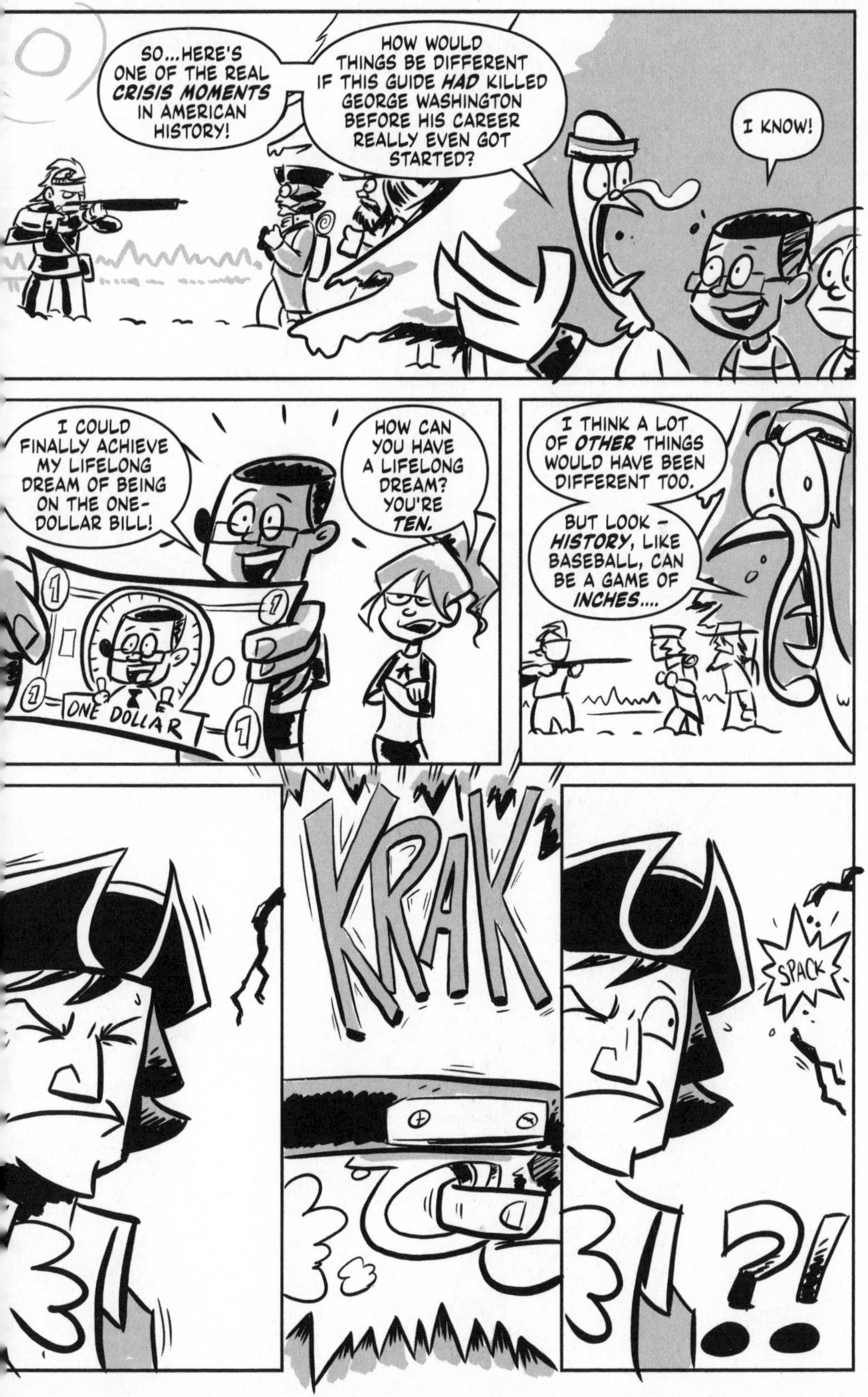
SO...HERE'S ONE OF THE REAL CRISIS MOMENTS IN AMERICAN HISTORY!
HOW WOULD THINGS BE DIFFERENT IF THIS GUIDE HAD KILLED GEORGE WASHINGTON BEFORE HIS CAREER REALLY EVEN GOT STARTED?
I KNOW!
I COULD FINALLY ACHIEVE MY LIFELONG DREAM OF BEING ON THE ONE-DOLLAR BILL!
ONE DOLLAR
HOW CAN YOU HAVE A LIFELONG DREAM? YOU'RE TEN.
I THINK A LOT OF OTHER THINGS WOULD HAVE BEEN DIFFERENT TOO.
BUT LOOK – HISTORY, LIKE BASEBALL, CAN BE A GAME OF INCHES....
KRAK
SPACK
?!

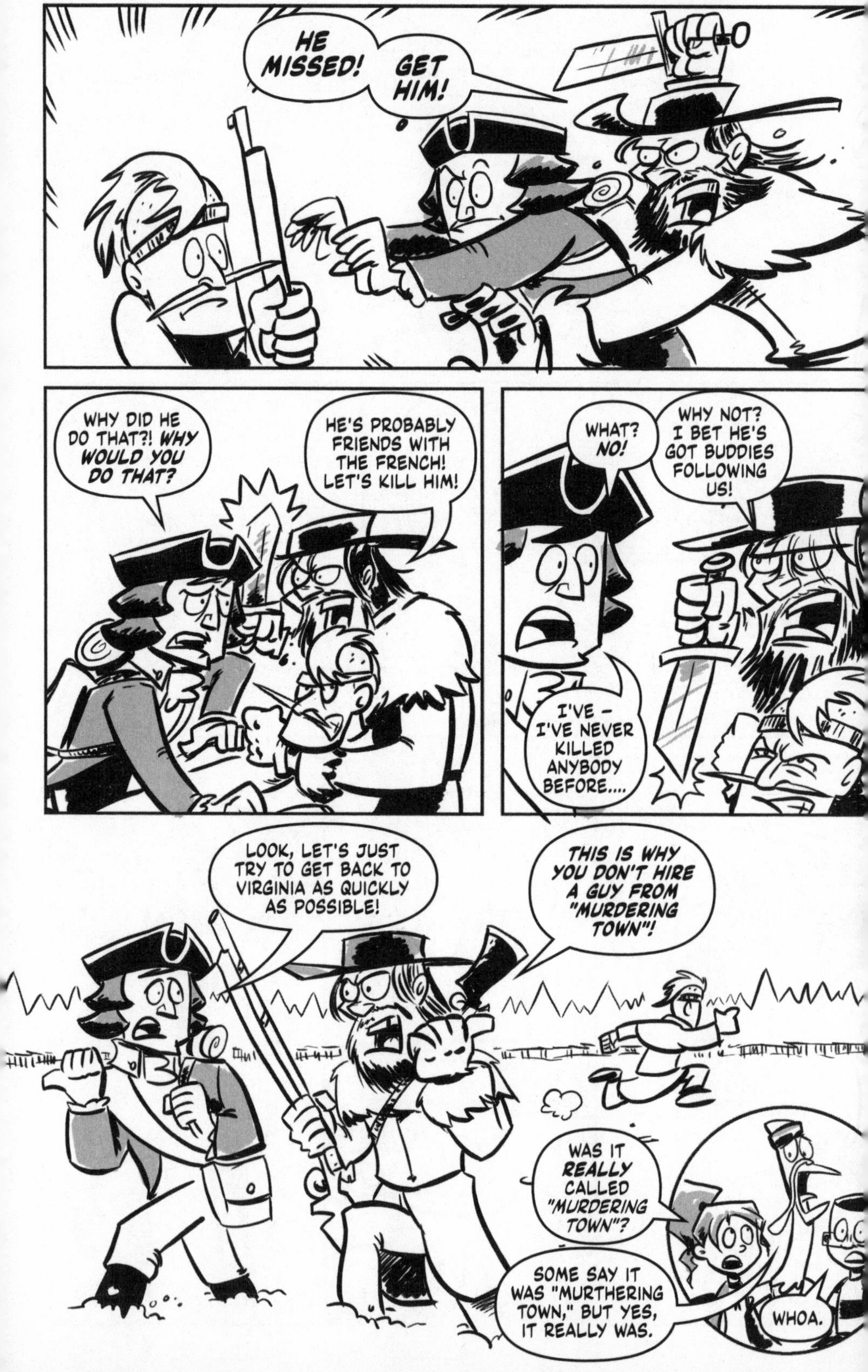
HE MISSED!
GET HIM!
WHY DID HE DO THAT?! WHY WOULD YOU DO THAT?
HE'S PROBABLY FRIENDS WITH THE FRENCH! LET'S KILL HIM!
WHAT? NO!
WHY NOT? I BET HE'S GOT BUDDIES FOLLOWING US!
I'VE – I'VE NEVER KILLED ANYBODY BEFORE....
LOOK, LET'S JUST TRY TO GET BACK TO VIRGINIA AS QUICKLY AS POSSIBLE!
THIS IS WHY YOU DON'T HIRE A GUY FROM "MURDERING TOWN"!
WAS IT REALLY CALLED "MURDERING TOWN"?
SOME SAY IT WAS "MURTHERING TOWN," BUT YES, IT REALLY WAS.
WHOA.

George and Gist built a makeshift ***raft*** and barely made it down the freezing river to Williamsburg.

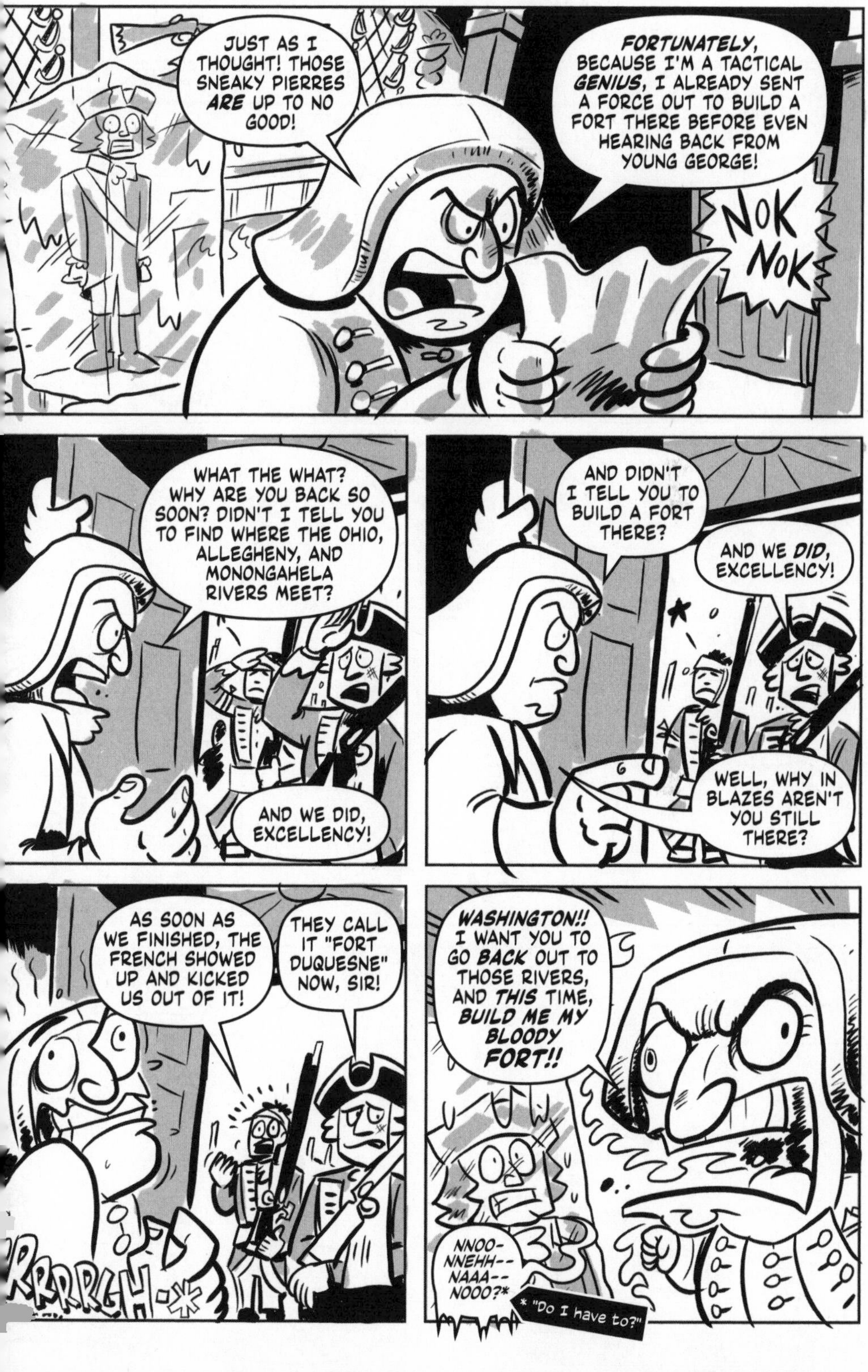

JUST AS I THOUGHT! THOSE SNEAKY PIERRES ARE UP TO NO GOOD!
FORTUNATELY, BECAUSE I'M A TACTICAL GENIUS, I ALREADY SENT A FORCE OUT TO BUILD A FORT THERE BEFORE EVEN HEARING BACK FROM YOUNG GEORGE!
NOK NOK
WHAT THE WHAT? WHY ARE YOU BACK SO SOON? DIDN'T I TELL YOU TO FIND WHERE THE OHIO, ALLEGHENY, AND MONONGAHELA RIVERS MEET?
AND WE DID, EXCELLENCY!
AND DIDN'T I TELL YOU TO BUILD A FORT THERE?
AND WE DID, EXCELLENCY!
WELL, WHY IN BLAZES AREN'T YOU STILL THERE?
AS SOON AS WE FINISHED, THE FRENCH SHOWED UP AND KICKED US OUT OF IT!
THEY CALL IT "FORT DUQUESNE" NOW, SIR!
RRRRGH-*
WASHINGTON!! I WANT YOU TO GO BACK OUT TO THOSE RIVERS, AND THIS TIME, BUILD ME MY BLOODY FORT!!
NNOO-NNEHH--NAAA--NOOO?*
* "Do I have to?"

George headed west again, this time with 159 men in his "Virginia Regimer

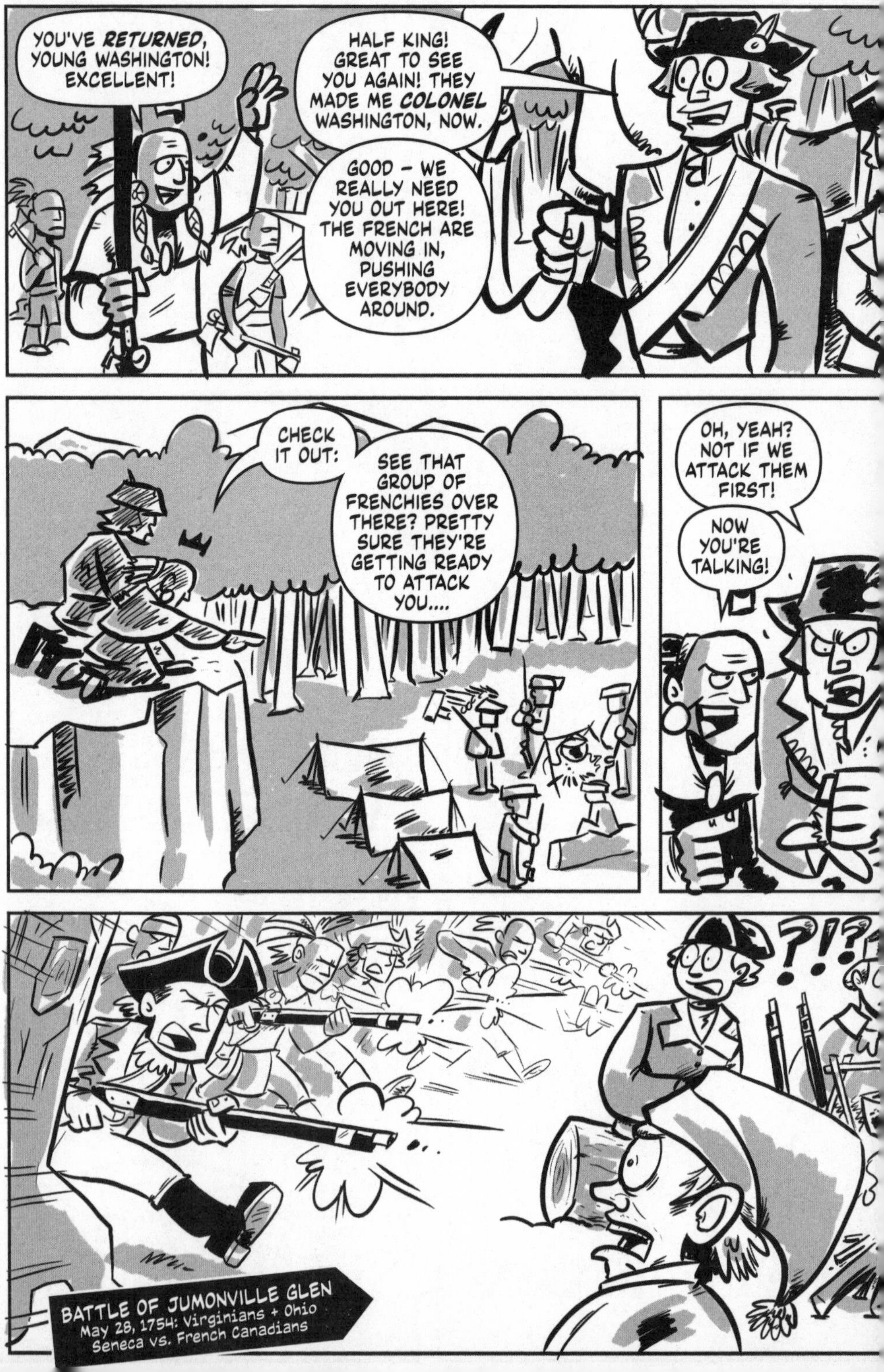

YOU'VE *RETURNED*, YOUNG WASHINGTON! EXCELLENT!
HALF KING! GREAT TO SEE YOU AGAIN! THEY MADE ME *COLONEL* WASHINGTON, NOW.
GOOD – WE REALLY NEED YOU OUT HERE! THE FRENCH ARE MOVING IN, PUSHING EVERYBODY AROUND.
CHECK IT OUT:
SEE THAT GROUP OF FRENCHIES OVER THERE? PRETTY SURE THEY'RE GETTING READY TO ATTACK YOU....
OH, YEAH? NOT IF WE ATTACK THEM FIRST!
NOW YOU'RE TALKING!
?!?
BATTLE OF JUMONVILLE GLEN
May 28, 1754: Virginians + Ohio Seneca vs. French Canadians

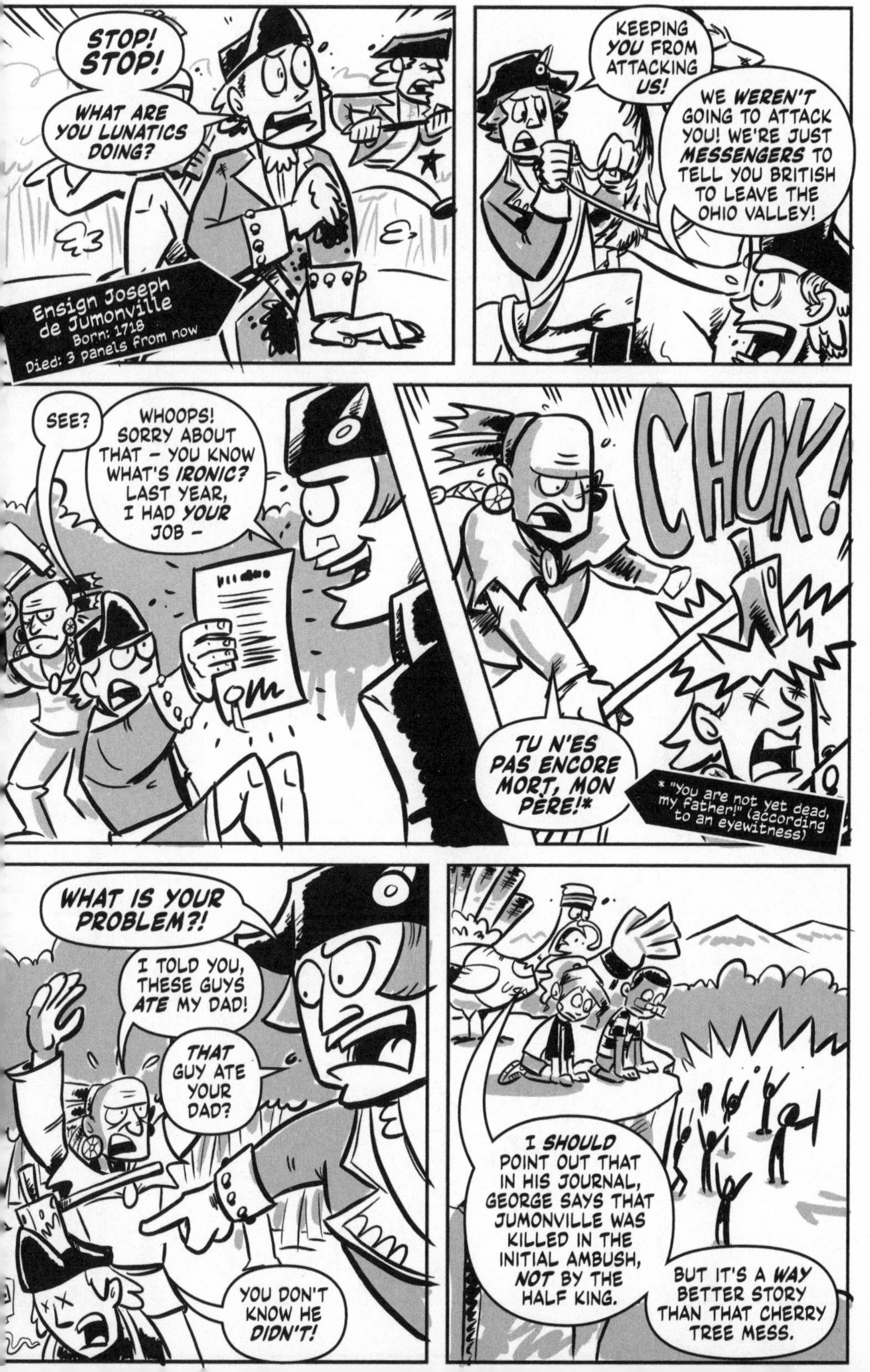

STOP! STOP!
WHAT ARE YOU LUNATICS DOING?
Ensign Joseph de Jumonville
Born: 1718
Died: 3 panels from now
KEEPING YOU FROM ATTACKING US!
WE WEREN'T GOING TO ATTACK YOU! WE'RE JUST MESSENGERS TO TELL YOU BRITISH TO LEAVE THE OHIO VALLEY!
SEE?
WHOOPS! SORRY ABOUT THAT – YOU KNOW WHAT'S IRONIC? LAST YEAR, I HAD YOUR JOB –
CHOK!
TU N'ES PAS ENCORE MORT, MON PÈRE!*
* "You are not yet dead, my father!" (according to an eyewitness)
WHAT IS YOUR PROBLEM?!
I TOLD YOU, THESE GUYS ATE MY DAD!
THAT GUY ATE YOUR DAD?
YOU DON'T KNOW HE DIDN'T!
I SHOULD POINT OUT THAT IN HIS JOURNAL, GEORGE SAYS THAT JUMONVILLE WAS KILLED IN THE INITIAL AMBUSH, NOT BY THE HALF KING.
BUT IT'S A WAY BETTER STORY THAN THAT CHERRY TREE MESS.

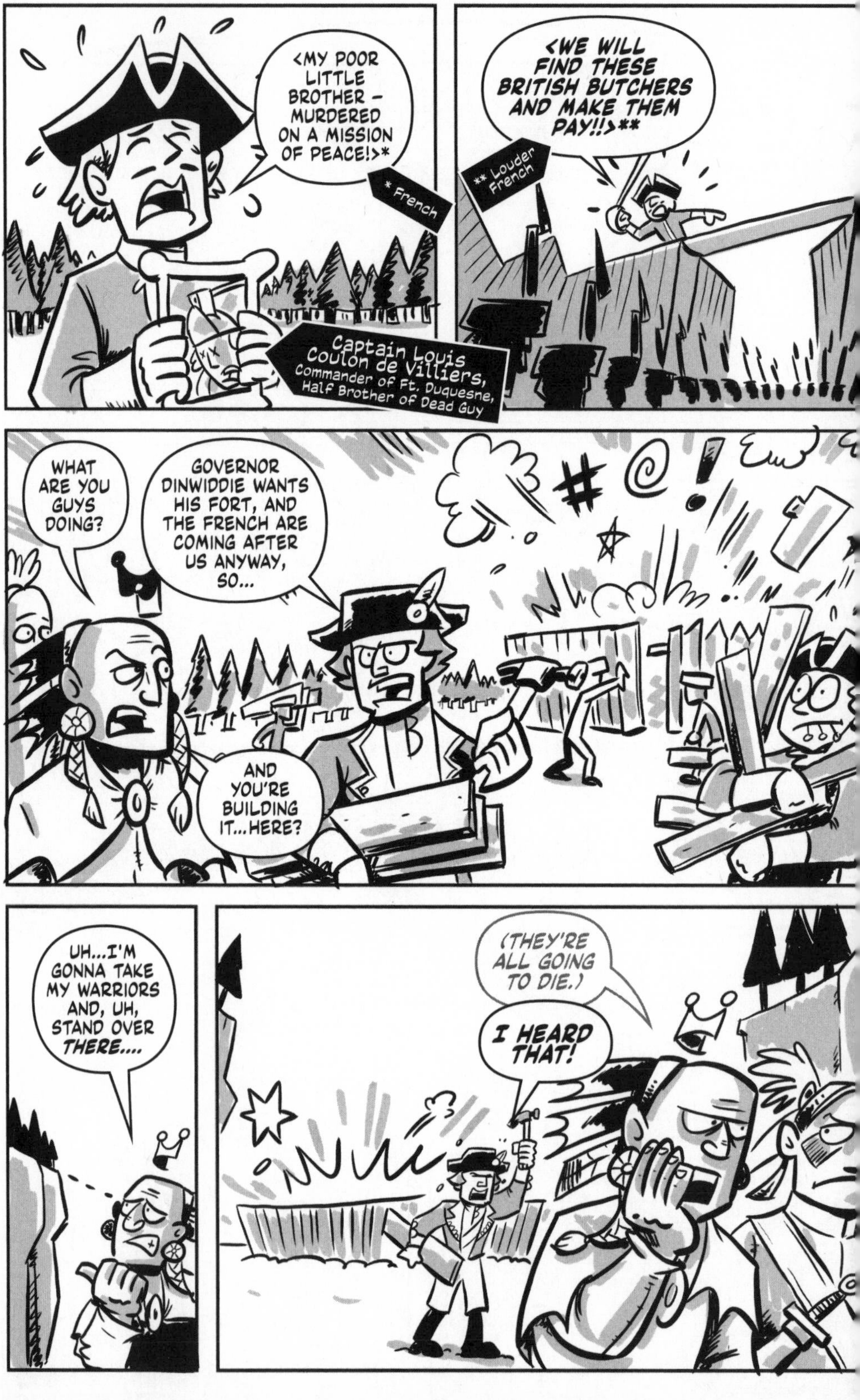

<MY POOR LITTLE BROTHER – MURDERED ON A MISSION OF PEACE!>*
* French
Captain Louis Coulon de Villiers, Commander of Ft. Duquesne, Half Brother of Dead Guy
<WE WILL FIND THESE BRITISH BUTCHERS AND MAKE THEM PAY!!>**
** Louder French
WHAT ARE YOU GUYS DOING?
GOVERNOR DINWIDDIE WANTS HIS FORT, AND THE FRENCH ARE COMING AFTER US ANYWAY, SO...
AND YOU'RE BUILDING IT...HERE?
UH...I'M GONNA TAKE MY WARRIORS AND, UH, STAND OVER *THERE*....
(THEY'RE ALL GOING TO DIE.)
I HEARD THAT!

The Battle of Fort Necessity

July 3, 1754:
French Canadians + Ottawas & Hurons vs. Virginians

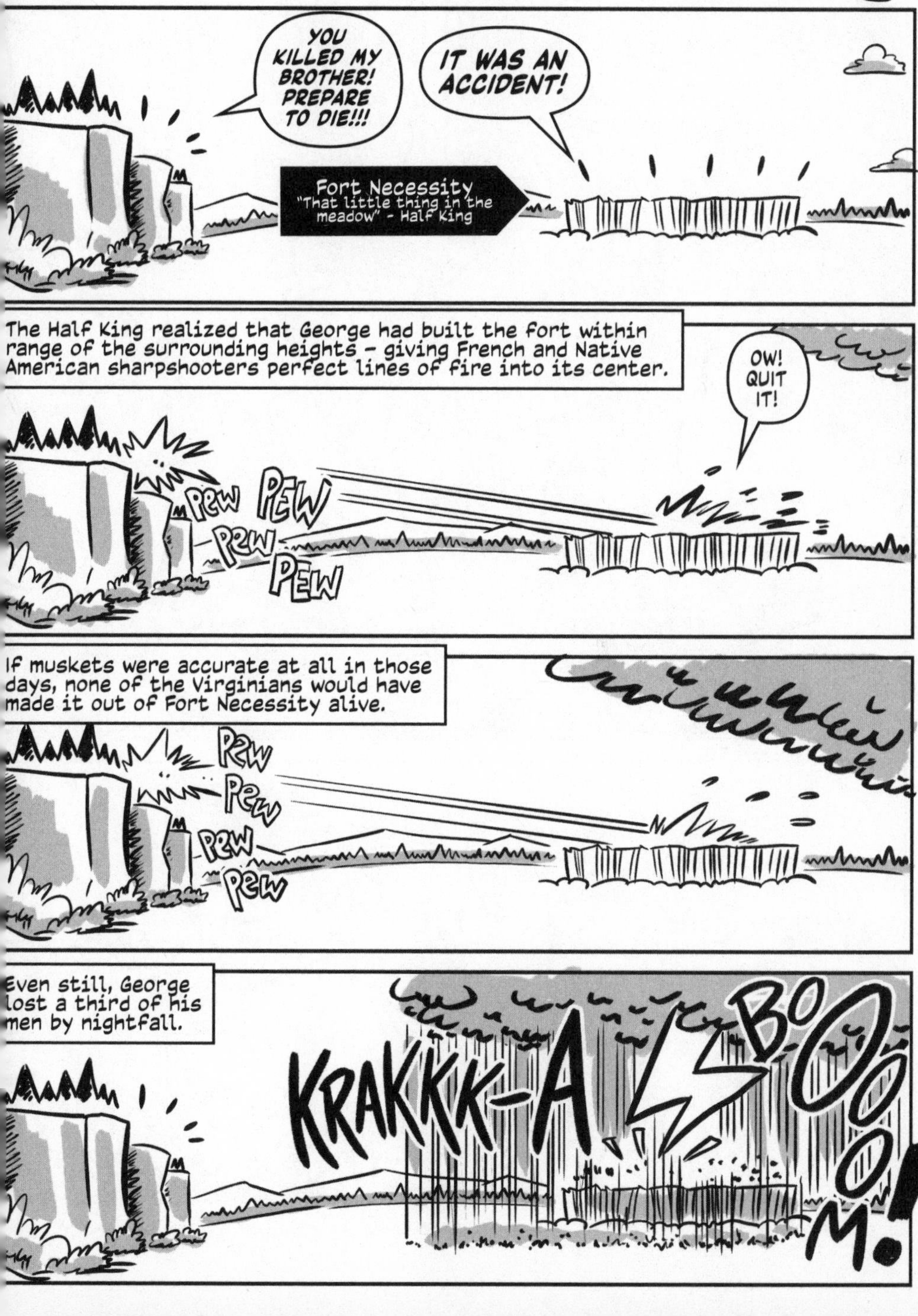
YOU KILLED MY BROTHER! PREPARE TO DIE!!!
IT WAS AN ACCIDENT!
Fort Necessity
"That little thing in the meadow" - Half King
The Half King realized that George had built the fort within range of the surrounding heights - giving French and Native American sharpshooters perfect lines of fire into its center.
OW! QUIT IT!
PEW PEW PEW PEW
If muskets were accurate at all in those days, none of the Virginians would have made it out of Fort Necessity alive.
PEW PEW PEW PEW
Even still, George lost a third of his men by nightfall.
KRAKKK-A-BOOOOOM!

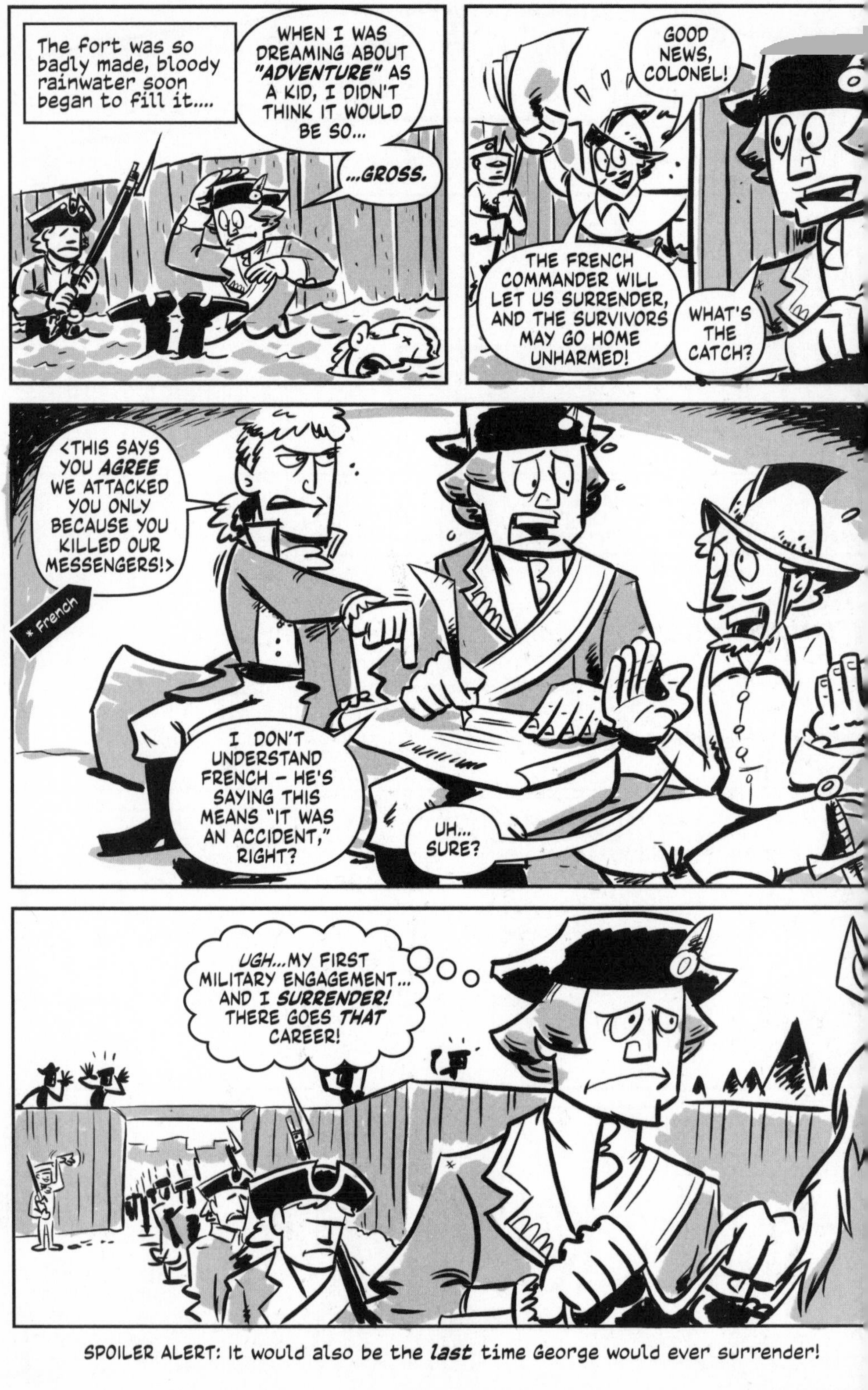

The fort was so badly made, bloody rainwater soon began to fill it....
WHEN I WAS DREAMING ABOUT "ADVENTURE" AS A KID, I DIDN'T THINK IT WOULD BE SO...
...GROSS.
GOOD NEWS, COLONEL!
THE FRENCH COMMANDER WILL LET US SURRENDER, AND THE SURVIVORS MAY GO HOME UNHARMED!
WHAT'S THE CATCH?
<THIS SAYS YOU AGREE WE ATTACKED YOU ONLY BECAUSE YOU KILLED OUR MESSENGERS!>
* French
I DON'T UNDERSTAND FRENCH – HE'S SAYING THIS MEANS "IT WAS AN ACCIDENT," RIGHT?
UH... SURE?
UGH...MY FIRST MILITARY ENGAGEMENT... AND I SURRENDER! THERE GOES THAT CAREER!

SPOILER ALERT: It would also be the *last* time George would ever surrender!

These two battles started what's known in the USA as

THE FRENCH & INDIAN WAR

In which Britain and France, each with their own Native American allies, struggled for the sole right to colonize the continent.

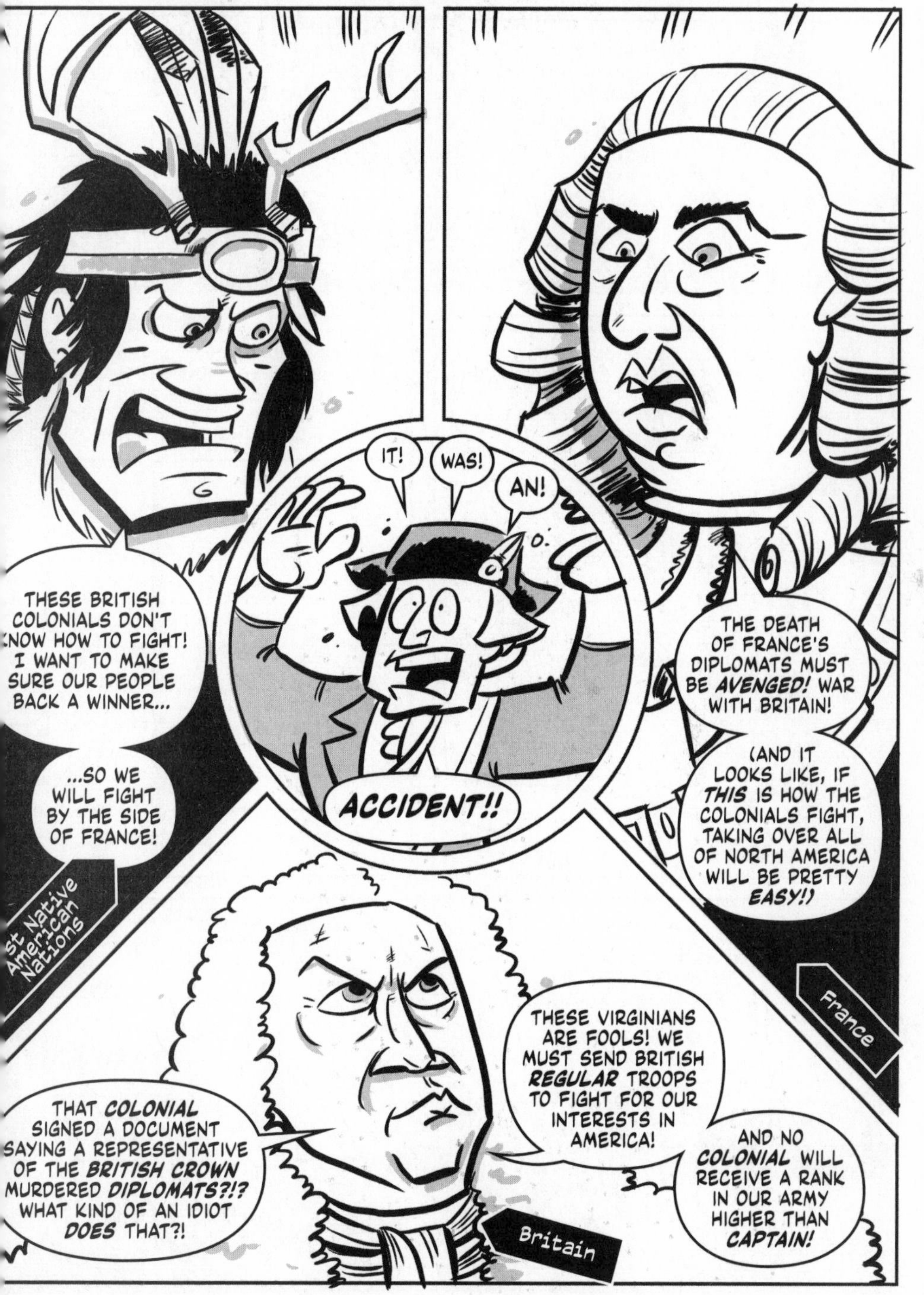

THESE BRITISH COLONIALS DON'T KNOW HOW TO FIGHT! I WANT TO MAKE SURE OUR PEOPLE BACK A WINNER...
...SO WE WILL FIGHT BY THE SIDE OF FRANCE!
st Native American Nations
THE DEATH OF FRANCE'S DIPLOMATS MUST BE AVENGED! WAR WITH BRITAIN!
(AND IT LOOKS LIKE, IF THIS IS HOW THE COLONIALS FIGHT, TAKING OVER ALL OF NORTH AMERICA WILL BE PRETTY EASY!)
France
IT!
WAS!
AN!
ACCIDENT!!
THAT COLONIAL SIGNED A DOCUMENT SAYING A REPRESENTATIVE OF THE BRITISH CROWN MURDERED DIPLOMATS?!? WHAT KIND OF AN IDIOT DOES THAT?!
THESE VIRGINIANS ARE FOOLS! WE MUST SEND BRITISH REGULAR TROOPS TO FIGHT FOR OUR INTERESTS IN AMERICA!
AND NO COLONIAL WILL RECEIVE A RANK IN OUR ARMY HIGHER THAN CAPTAIN!
Britain

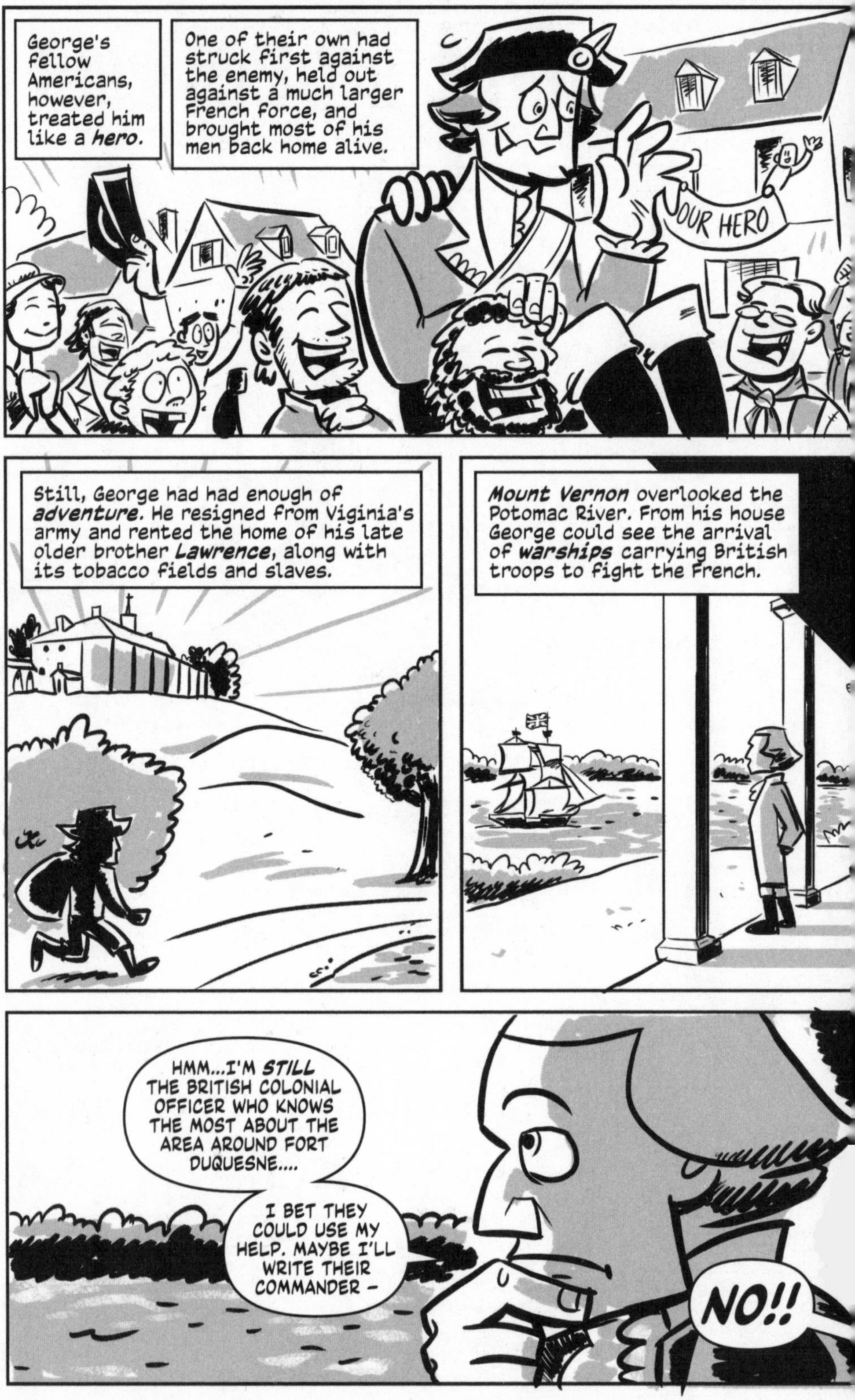

George's fellow Americans, however, treated him like a *hero.*
One of their own had struck first against the enemy, held out against a much larger French force, and brought most of his men back home alive.
OUR HERO
Still, George had had enough of *adventure.* He resigned from Viginia's army and rented the home of his late older brother *Lawrence*, along with its tobacco fields and slaves.
Mount Vernon overlooked the Potomac River. From his house George could see the arrival of *warships* carrying British troops to fight the French.
HMM...I'M *STILL* THE BRITISH COLONIAL OFFICER WHO KNOWS THE MOST ABOUT THE AREA AROUND FORT DUQUESNE....
I BET THEY COULD USE MY HELP. MAYBE I'LL WRITE THEIR COMMANDER –
NO!!

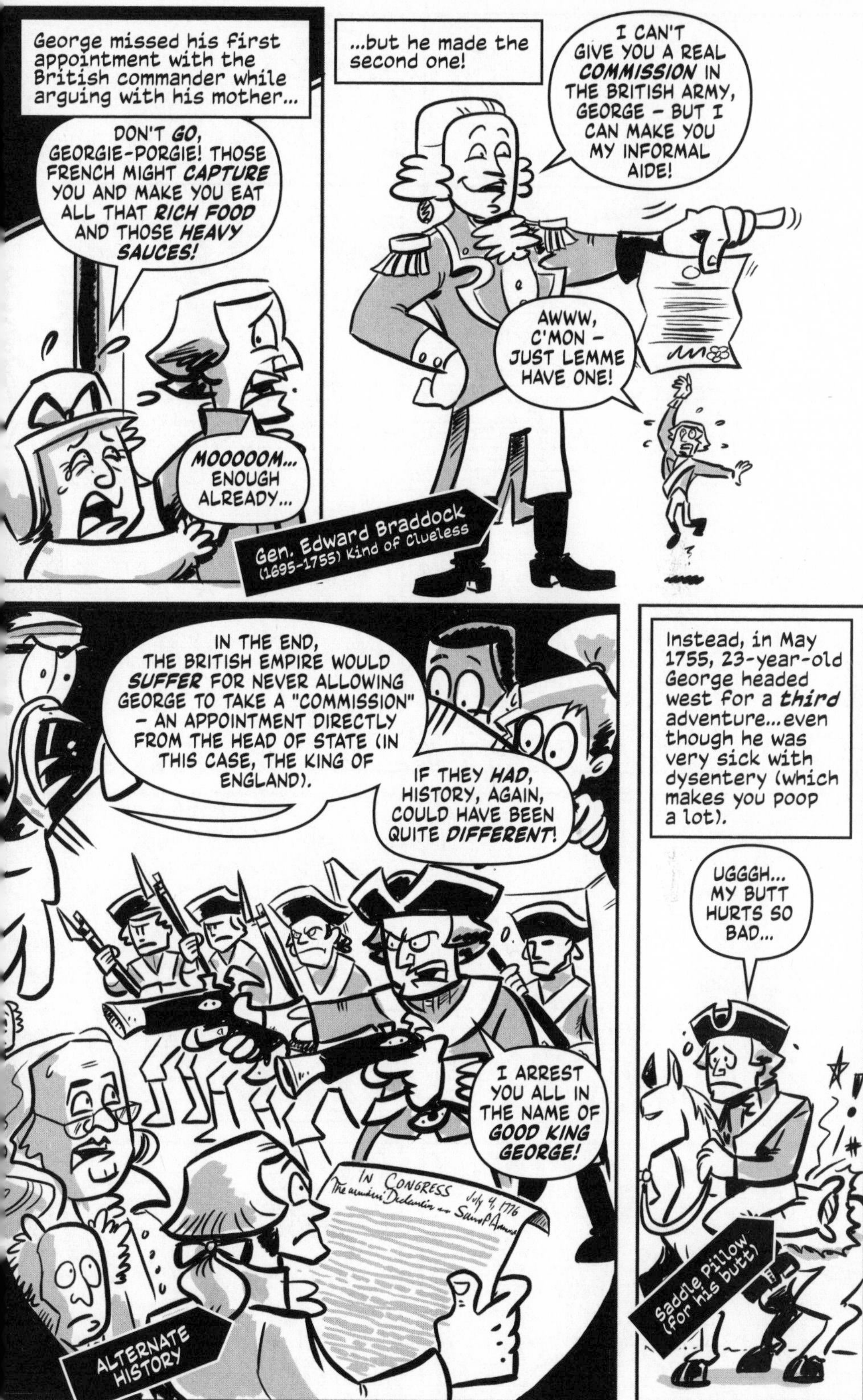

George missed his first appointment with the British commander while arguing with his mother...
DON'T GO, GEORGIE-PORGIE! THOSE FRENCH MIGHT CAPTURE YOU AND MAKE YOU EAT ALL THAT RICH FOOD AND THOSE HEAVY SAUCES!
MOOOOOM... ENOUGH ALREADY...
...but he made the second one!
I CAN'T GIVE YOU A REAL COMMISSION IN THE BRITISH ARMY, GEORGE - BUT I CAN MAKE YOU MY INFORMAL AIDE!
AWWW, C'MON - JUST LEMME HAVE ONE!
Gen. Edward Braddock (1695-1755) Kind of Clueless
IN THE END, THE BRITISH EMPIRE WOULD SUFFER FOR NEVER ALLOWING GEORGE TO TAKE A "COMMISSION" - AN APPOINTMENT DIRECTLY FROM THE HEAD OF STATE (IN THIS CASE, THE KING OF ENGLAND).
IF THEY HAD, HISTORY, AGAIN, COULD HAVE BEEN QUITE DIFFERENT!
I ARREST YOU ALL IN THE NAME OF GOOD KING GEORGE!
IN CONGRESS July 4, 1776
ALTERNATE HISTORY
Instead, in May 1755, 23-year-old George headed west for a third adventure...even though he was very sick with dysentery (which makes you poop a lot).
UGGGH... MY BUTT HURTS SO BAD...
Saddle Pillow (for his butt)

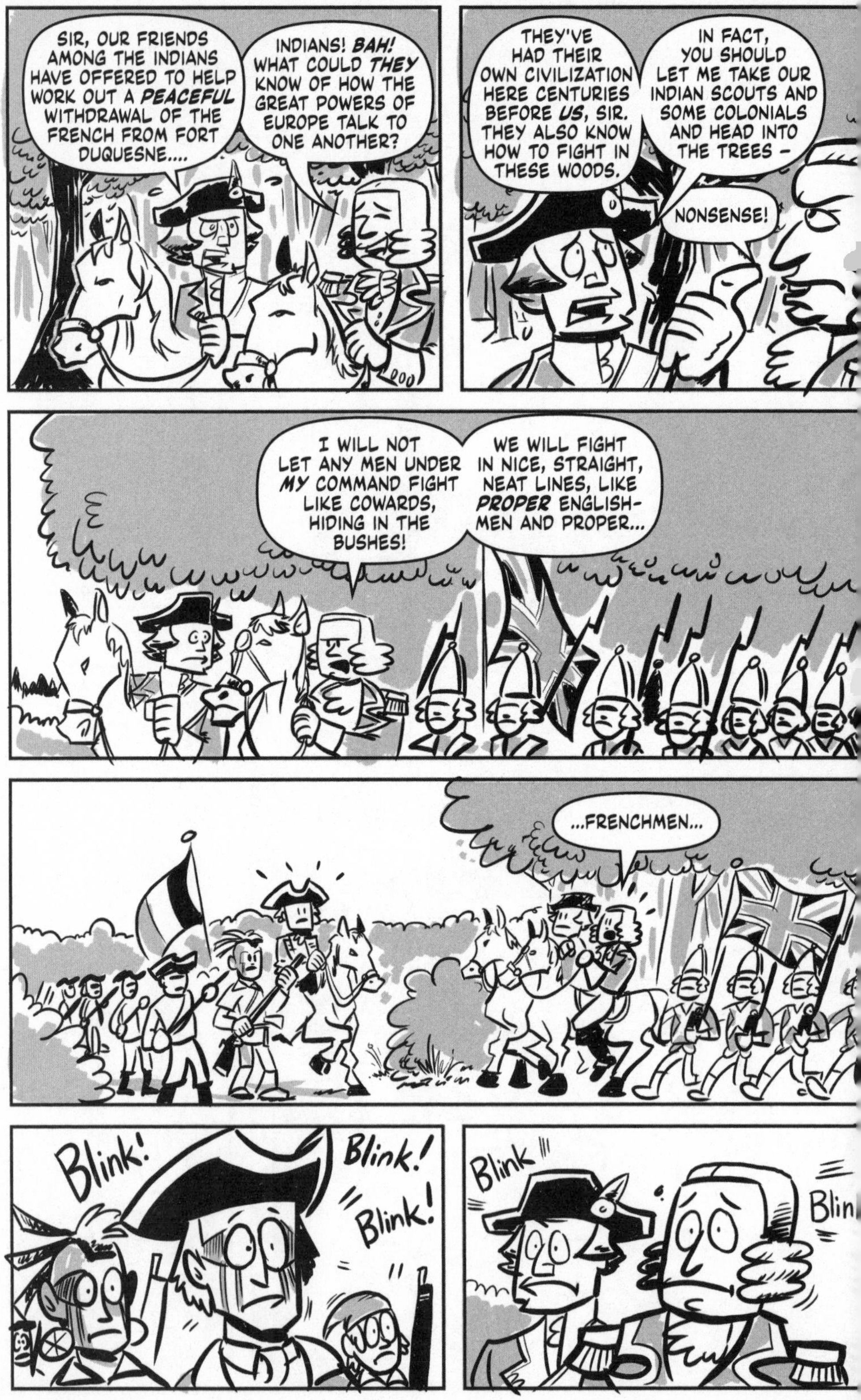
SIR, OUR FRIENDS AMONG THE INDIANS HAVE OFFERED TO HELP WORK OUT A PEACEFUL WITHDRAWAL OF THE FRENCH FROM FORT DUQUESNE....
INDIANS! BAH! WHAT COULD THEY KNOW OF HOW THE GREAT POWERS OF EUROPE TALK TO ONE ANOTHER?
THEY'VE HAD THEIR OWN CIVILIZATION HERE CENTURIES BEFORE US, SIR. THEY ALSO KNOW HOW TO FIGHT IN THESE WOODS.
IN FACT, YOU SHOULD LET ME TAKE OUR INDIAN SCOUTS AND SOME COLONIALS AND HEAD INTO THE TREES –
NONSENSE!
I WILL NOT LET ANY MEN UNDER MY COMMAND FIGHT LIKE COWARDS, HIDING IN THE BUSHES!
WE WILL FIGHT IN NICE, STRAIGHT, NEAT LINES, LIKE PROPER ENGLISHMEN AND PROPER...
...FRENCHMEN...
Blink!
Blink!
Blink!
Blink
Blin

THE BATTLE of the MONONGAHELA

July 9, 1755:
French Canadians + Ottawas + Potawatomis
vs. British Regulars + Colonials

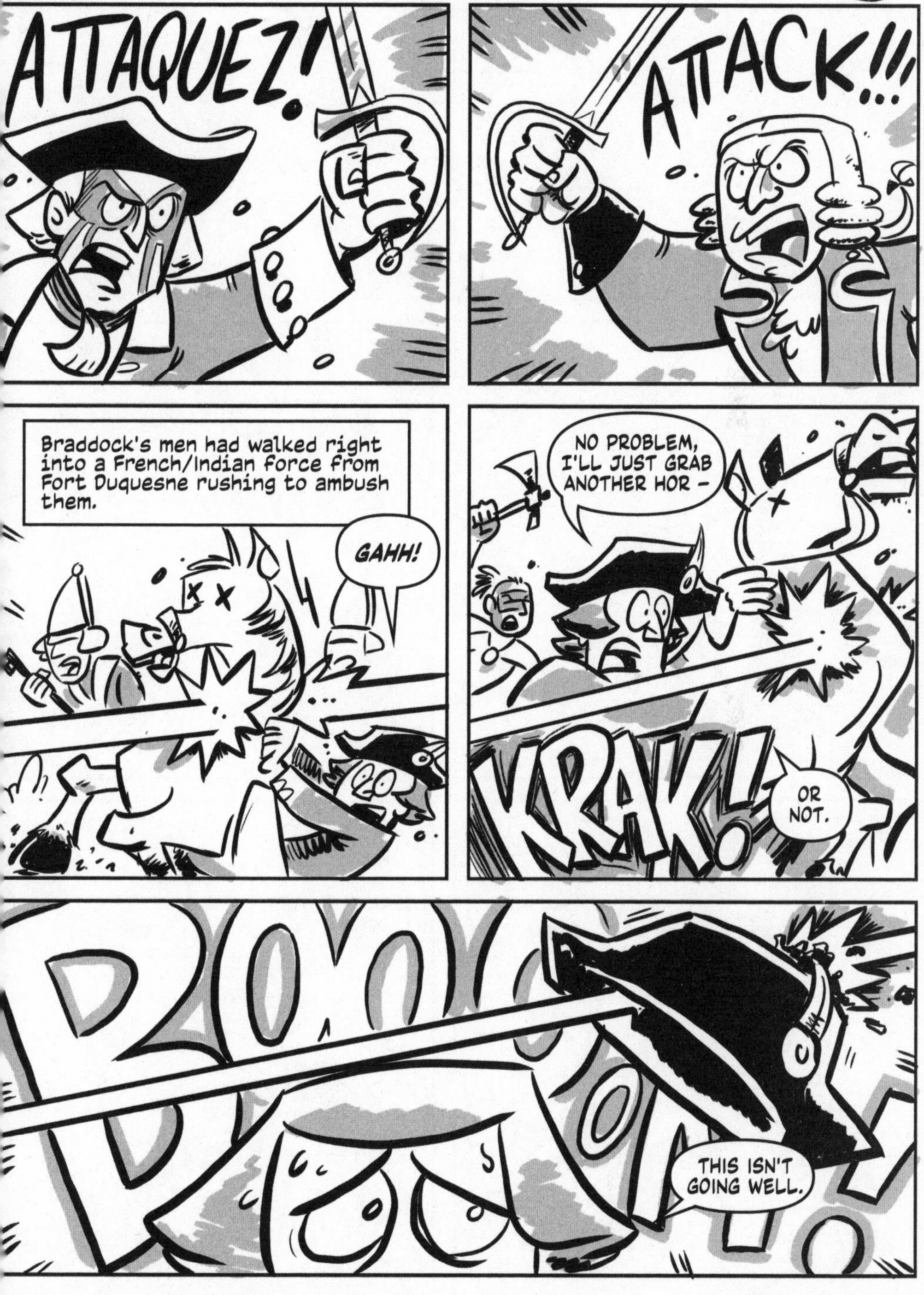
ATTAQUEZ!
ATTACK!!!
Braddock's men had walked right into a French/Indian force from Fort Duquesne rushing to ambush them.
GAHH!
NO PROBLEM, I'LL JUST GRAB ANOTHER HOR –
KRAK!
OR NOT.
THIS ISN'T GOING WELL.

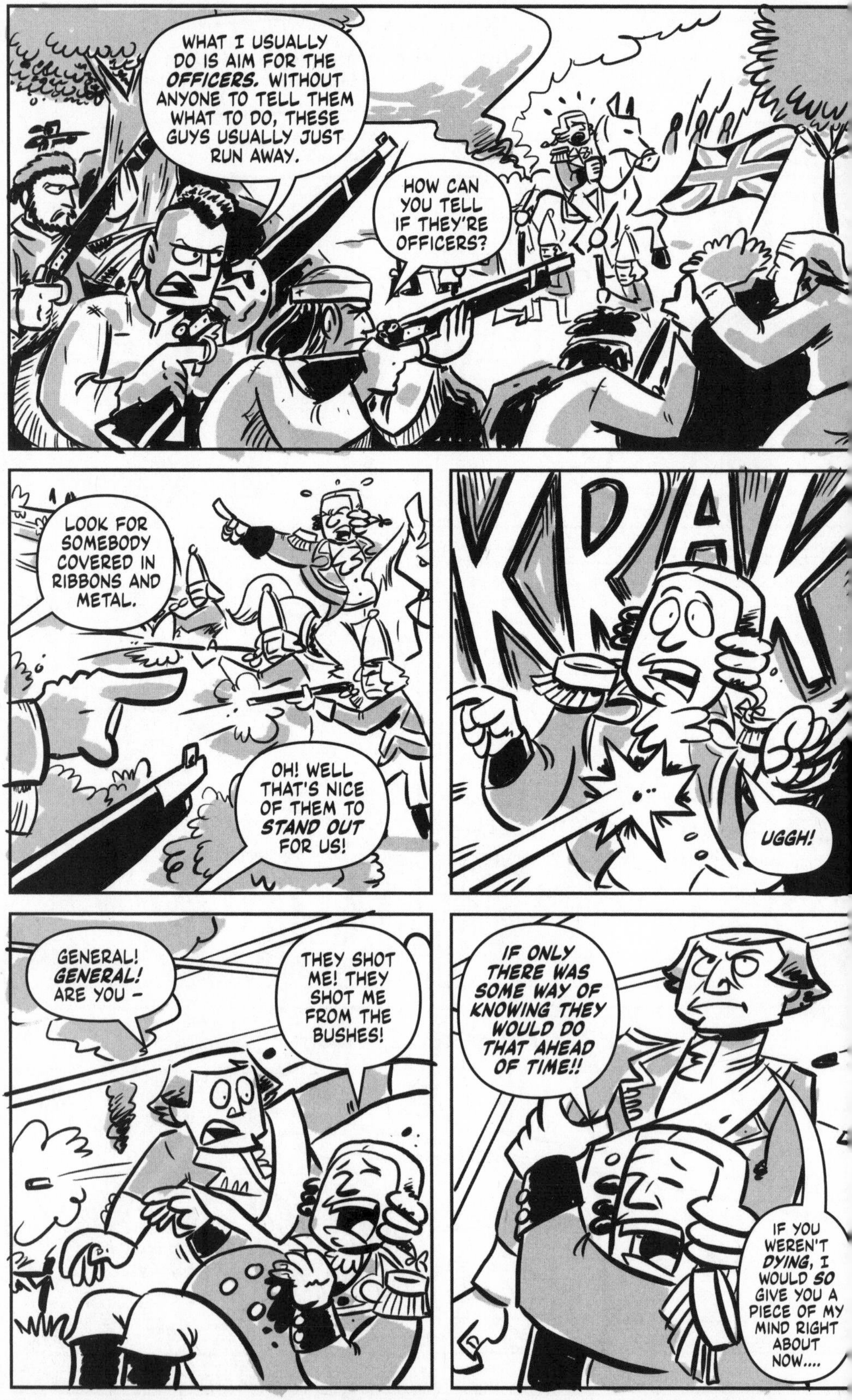
WHAT I USUALLY DO IS AIM FOR THE OFFICERS. WITHOUT ANYONE TO TELL THEM WHAT TO DO, THESE GUYS USUALLY JUST RUN AWAY.
HOW CAN YOU TELL IF THEY'RE OFFICERS?
LOOK FOR SOMEBODY COVERED IN RIBBONS AND METAL.
OH! WELL THAT'S NICE OF THEM TO STAND OUT FOR US!
KRAK
UGGH!
GENERAL! GENERAL! ARE YOU –
THEY SHOT ME! THEY SHOT ME FROM THE BUSHES!
IF ONLY THERE WAS SOME WAY OF KNOWING THEY WOULD DO THAT AHEAD OF TIME!!
IF YOU WEREN'T DYING, I WOULD SO GIVE YOU A PIECE OF MY MIND RIGHT ABOUT NOW....

Native American sharpshooters cut down the British officers until George (who, technically, was still just a civilian volunteer, after all) was the only one able to organize a retreat.

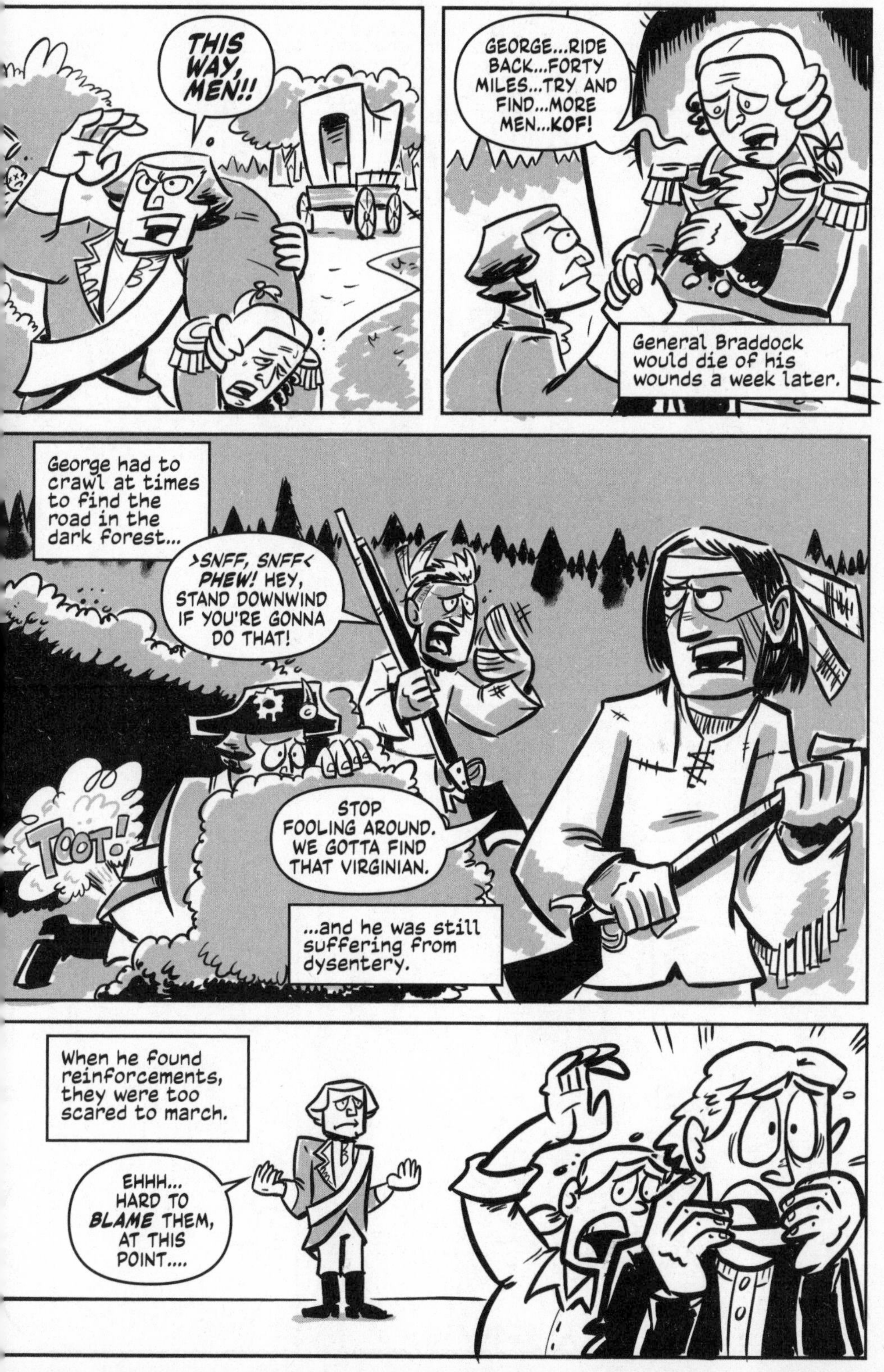

THIS WAY, MEN!!
GEORGE...RIDE BACK...FORTY MILES...TRY AND FIND...MORE MEN...KOF!
General Braddock would die of his wounds a week later.
George had to crawl at times to find the road in the dark forest...
>SNFF, SNFF< PHEW! HEY, STAND DOWNWIND IF YOU'RE GONNA DO THAT!
TOOT!
STOP FOOLING AROUND. WE GOTTA FIND THAT VIRGINIAN.
...and he was still suffering from dysentery.
When he found reinforcements, they were too scared to march.
EHHH... HARD TO BLAME THEM, AT THIS POINT....

British command unfairly blamed Braddock's defeat on colonial cowardice and stupidity.

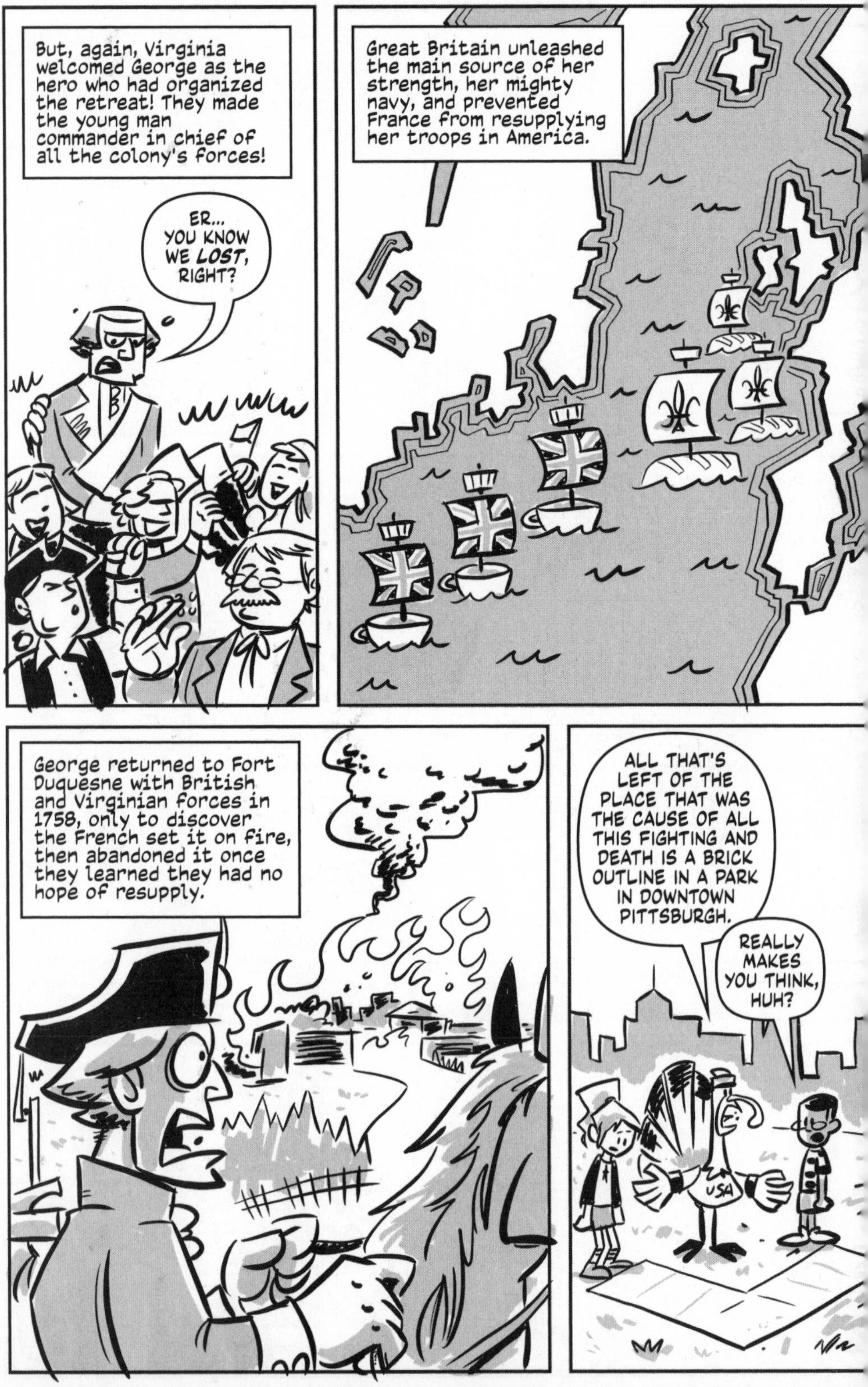
But, again, Virginia welcomed George as the hero who had organized the retreat! They made the young man commander in chief of all the colony's forces!
ER... YOU KNOW WE LOST, RIGHT?
Great Britain unleashed the main source of her strength, her mighty navy, and prevented France from resupplying her troops in America.
George returned to Fort Duquesne with British and Virginian forces in 1758, only to discover the French set it on fire, then abandoned it once they learned they had no hope of resupply.
ALL THAT'S LEFT OF THE PLACE THAT WAS THE CAUSE OF ALL THIS FIGHTING AND DEATH IS A BRICK OUTLINE IN A PARK IN DOWNTOWN PITTSBURGH.
REALLY MAKES YOU THINK, HUH?
USA

The War would go on for another five years and end in British victory, but the main fighting moved north. With *Virginia* safe, George resigned from the army and got married.

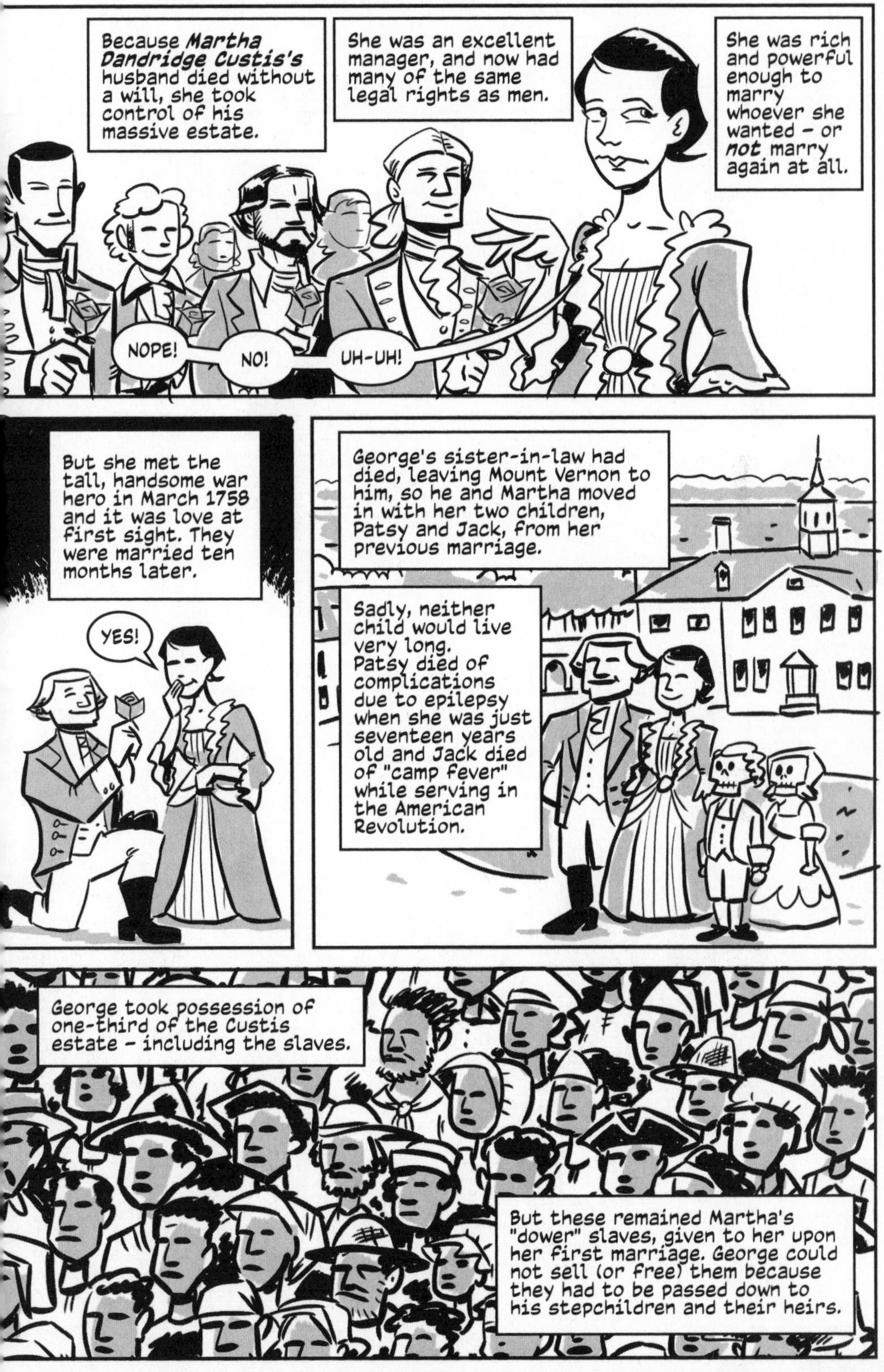

Because *Martha Dandridge Custis's* husband died without a will, she took control of his massive estate.
She was an excellent manager, and now had many of the same legal rights as men.
She was rich and powerful enough to marry whoever she wanted – or *not* marry again at all.
NOPE!
NO!
UH-UH!
But she met the tall, handsome war hero in March 1758 and it was love at first sight. They were married ten months later.
YES!
George's sister-in-law had died, leaving Mount Vernon to him, so he and Martha moved in with her two children, Patsy and Jack, from her previous marriage.
Sadly, neither child would live very long. Patsy died of complications due to epilepsy when she was just seventeen years old and Jack died of "camp fever" while serving in the American Revolution.
George took possession of one-third of the Custis estate – including the slaves.
But these remained Martha's "dower" slaves, given to her upon her first marriage. George could not sell (or free) them because they had to be passed down to his stepchildren and their heirs.

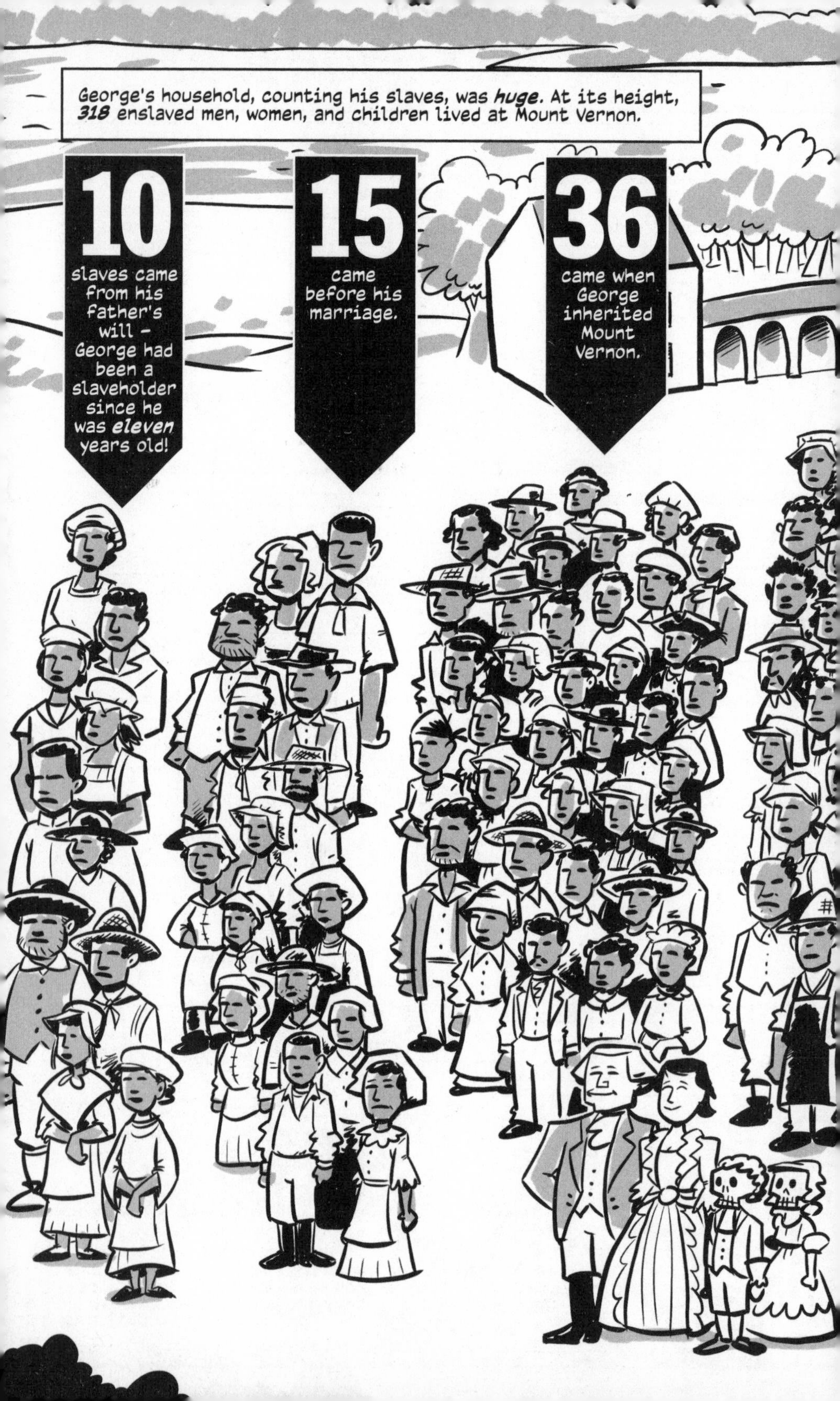
George's household, counting his slaves, was *huge.* At its height, *318* enslaved men, women, and children lived at Mount Vernon.
10
slaves came from his father's will – George had been a slaveholder since he was *eleven* years old!
15
came before his marriage.
36
came when George inherited Mount Vernon.

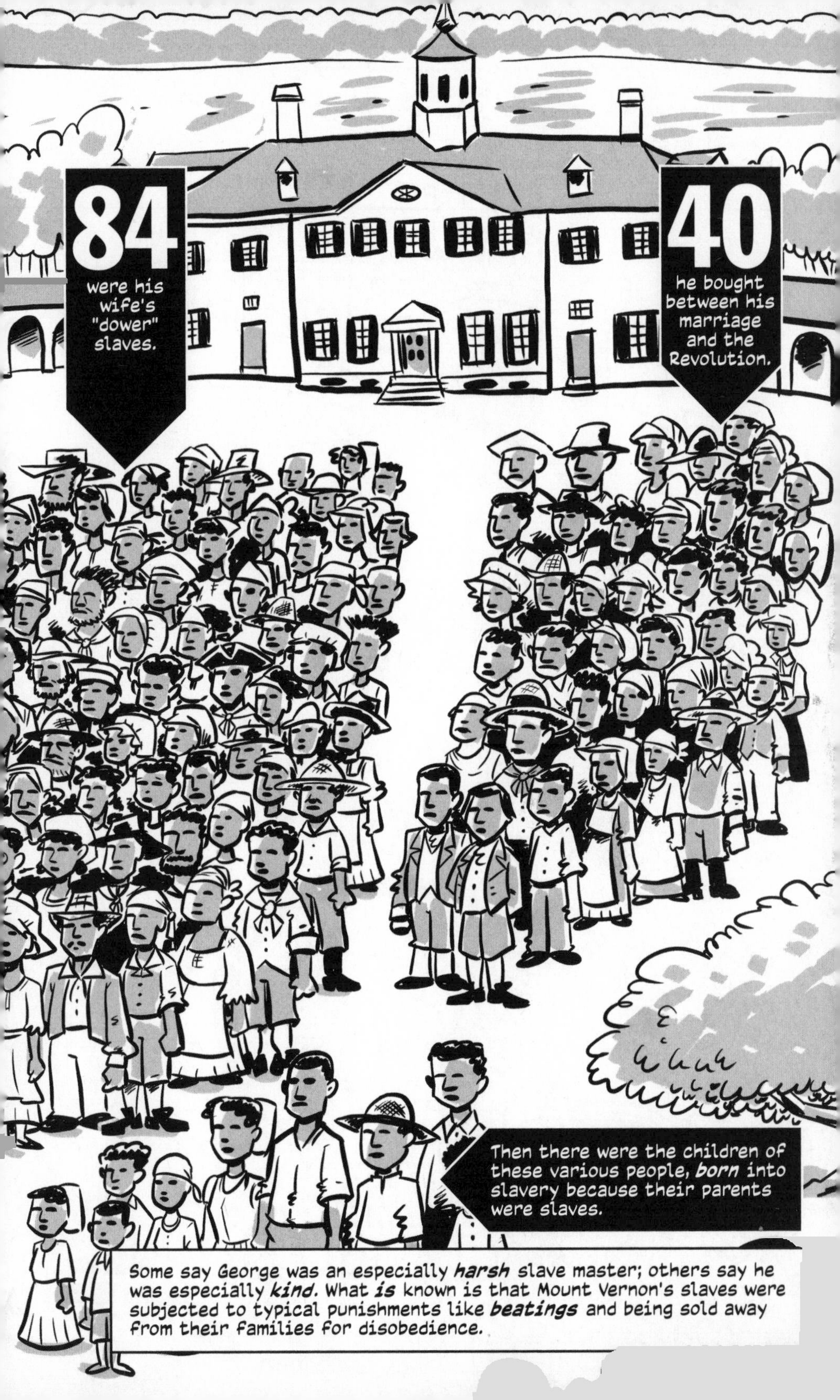
84
were his wife's "dower" slaves.
40
he bought between his marriage and the Revolution.
Then there were the children of these various people, *born* into slavery because their parents were slaves.
Some say George was an especially *harsh* slave master; others say he was especially *kind*. What *is* known is that Mount Vernon's slaves were subjected to typical punishments like *beatings* and being sold away from their families for disobedience.

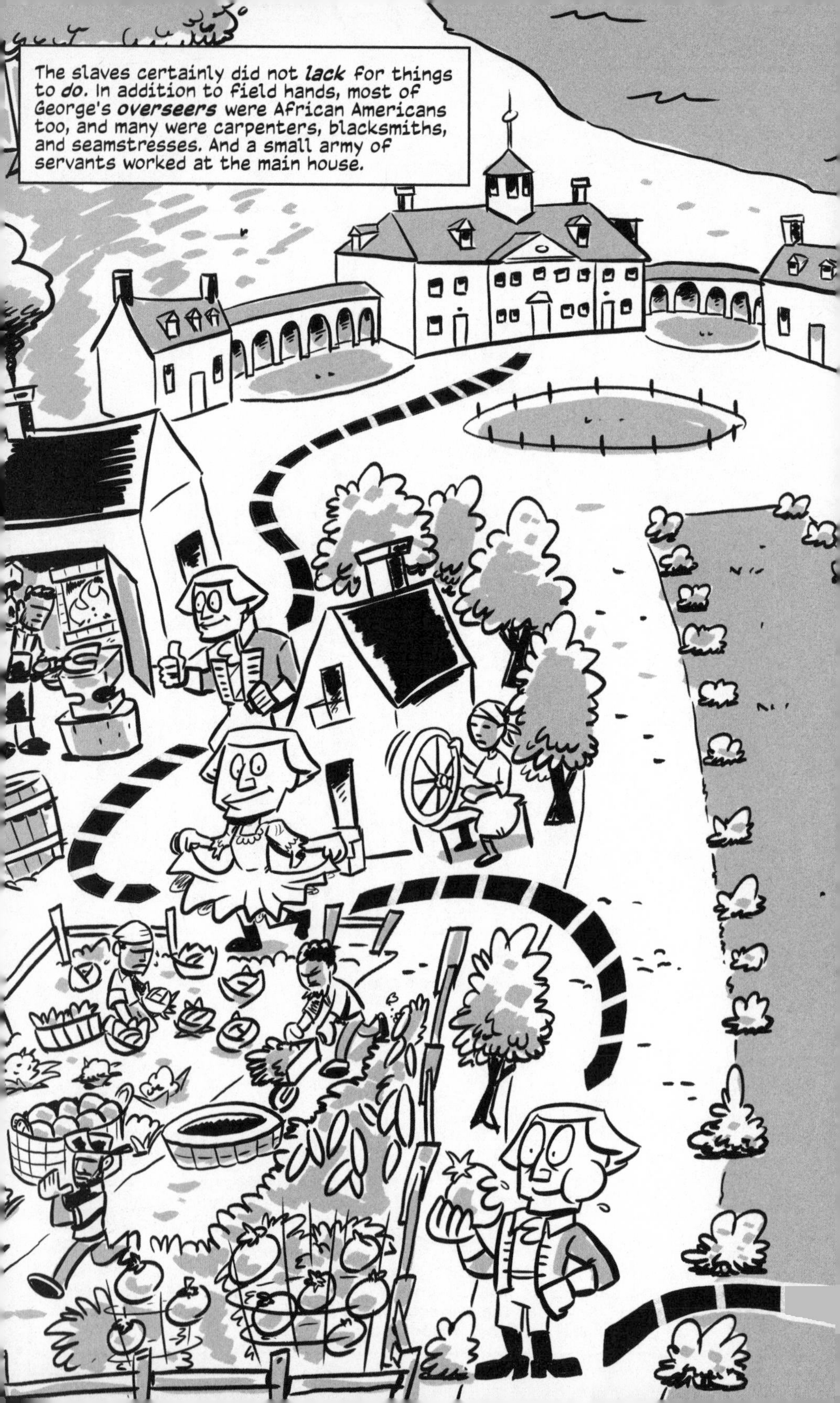
The slaves certainly did not *lack* for things to *do*. In addition to field hands, most of George's ***overseers*** were African Americans too, and many were carpenters, blacksmiths, and seamstresses. And a small army of servants worked at the main house.

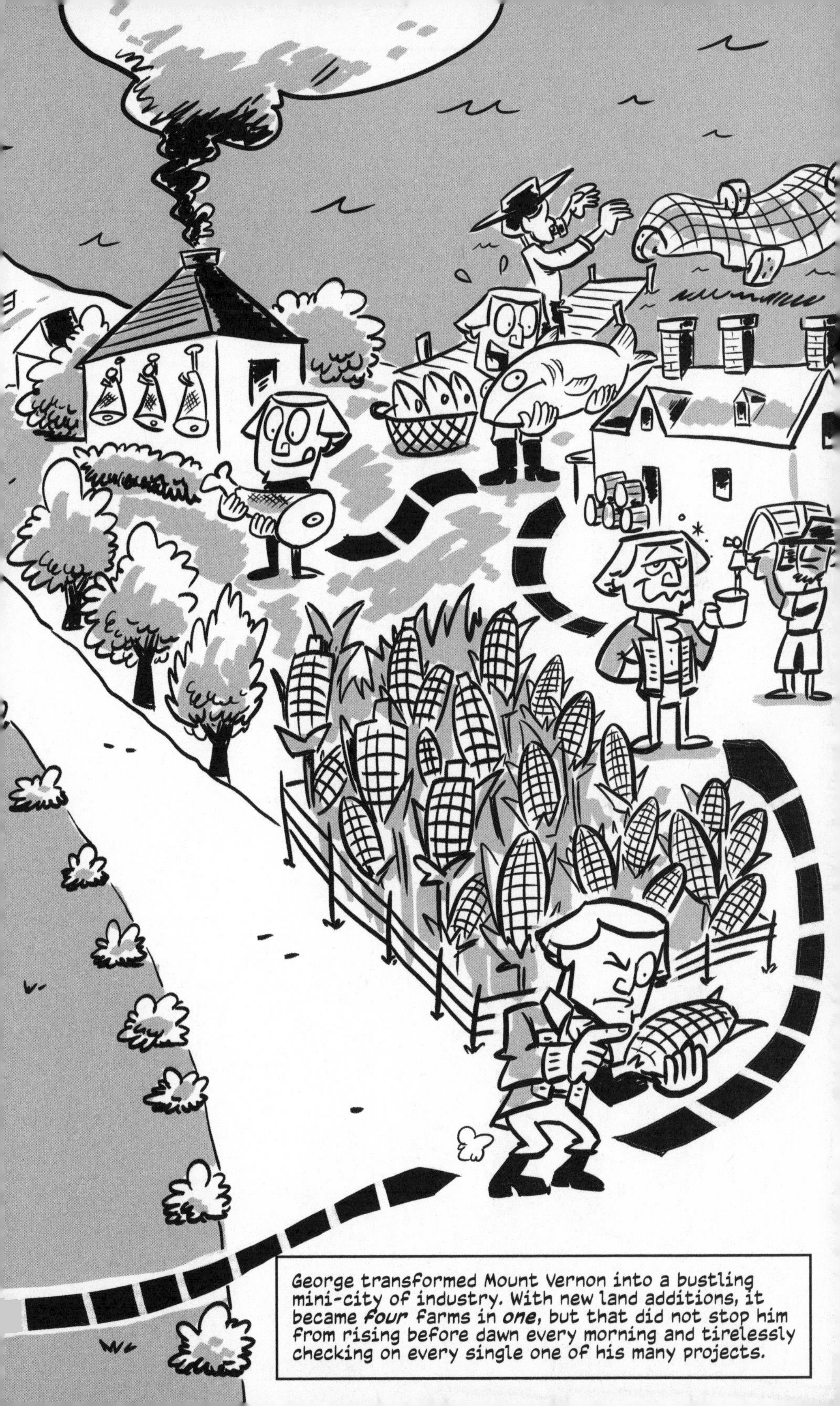
George transformed Mount Vernon into a bustling mini-city of industry. With new land additions, it became *four* farms in *one*, but that did not stop him from rising before dawn every morning and tirelessly checking on every single one of his many projects.

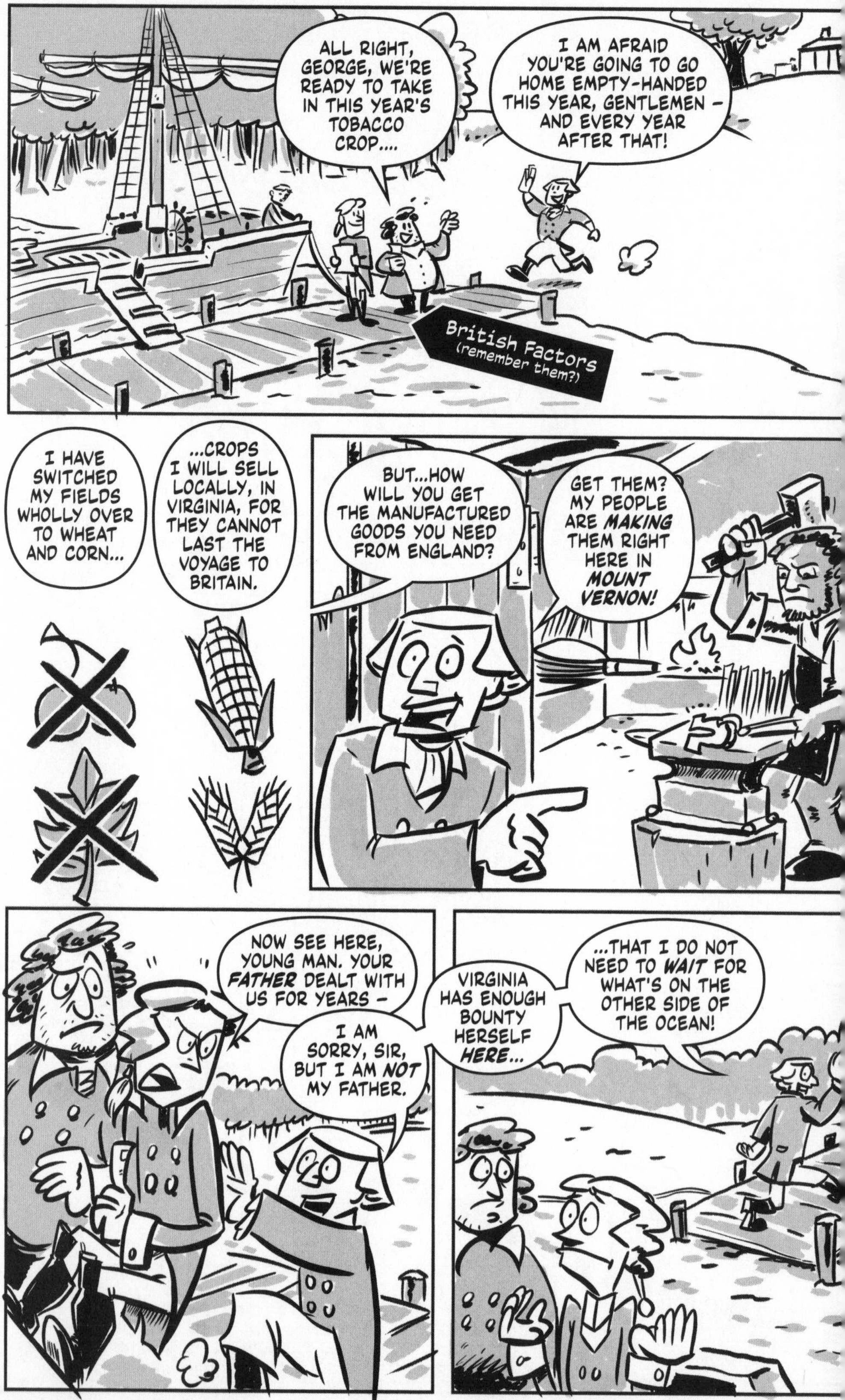

ALL RIGHT, GEORGE, WE'RE READY TO TAKE IN THIS YEAR'S TOBACCO CROP....
I AM AFRAID YOU'RE GOING TO GO HOME EMPTY-HANDED THIS YEAR, GENTLEMEN – AND EVERY YEAR AFTER THAT!
British Factors (remember them?)
I HAVE SWITCHED MY FIELDS WHOLLY OVER TO WHEAT AND CORN...
...CROPS I WILL SELL LOCALLY, IN VIRGINIA, FOR THEY CANNOT LAST THE VOYAGE TO BRITAIN.
BUT...HOW WILL YOU GET THE MANUFACTURED GOODS YOU NEED FROM ENGLAND?
GET THEM? MY PEOPLE ARE *MAKING* THEM RIGHT HERE IN *MOUNT VERNON!*
NOW SEE HERE, YOUNG MAN. YOUR *FATHER* DEALT WITH US FOR YEARS –
I AM SORRY, SIR, BUT I AM *NOT* MY FATHER.
VIRGINIA HAS ENOUGH BOUNTY HERSELF *HERE*...
...THAT I DO NOT NEED TO *WAIT* FOR WHAT'S ON THE OTHER SIDE OF THE OCEAN!

George was not the *only* colonial who felt this way.

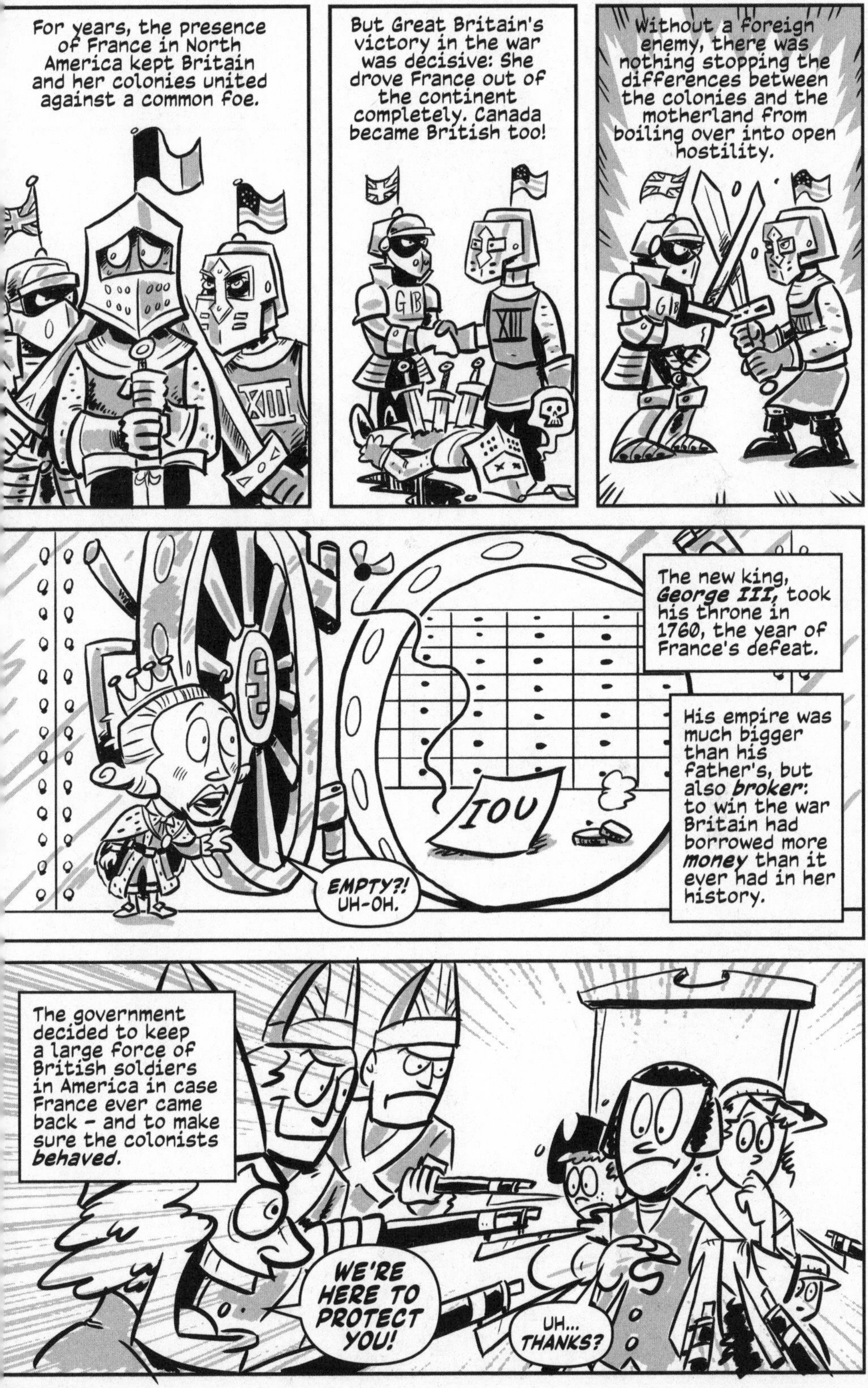
For years, the presence of France in North America kept Britain and her colonies united against a common foe.
But Great Britain's victory in the war was decisive: She drove France out of the continent completely. Canada became British too!
GB
XIII
Without a foreign enemy, there was nothing stopping the differences between the colonies and the motherland from boiling over into open hostility.
The new king, George III, took his throne in 1760, the year of France's defeat.
His empire was much bigger than his father's, but also broker: to win the war Britain had borrowed more money than it ever had in her history.
IOU
EMPTY?! UH-OH.
The government decided to keep a large force of British soldiers in America in case France ever came back – and to make sure the colonists behaved.
WE'RE HERE TO PROTECT YOU!
UH... THANKS?

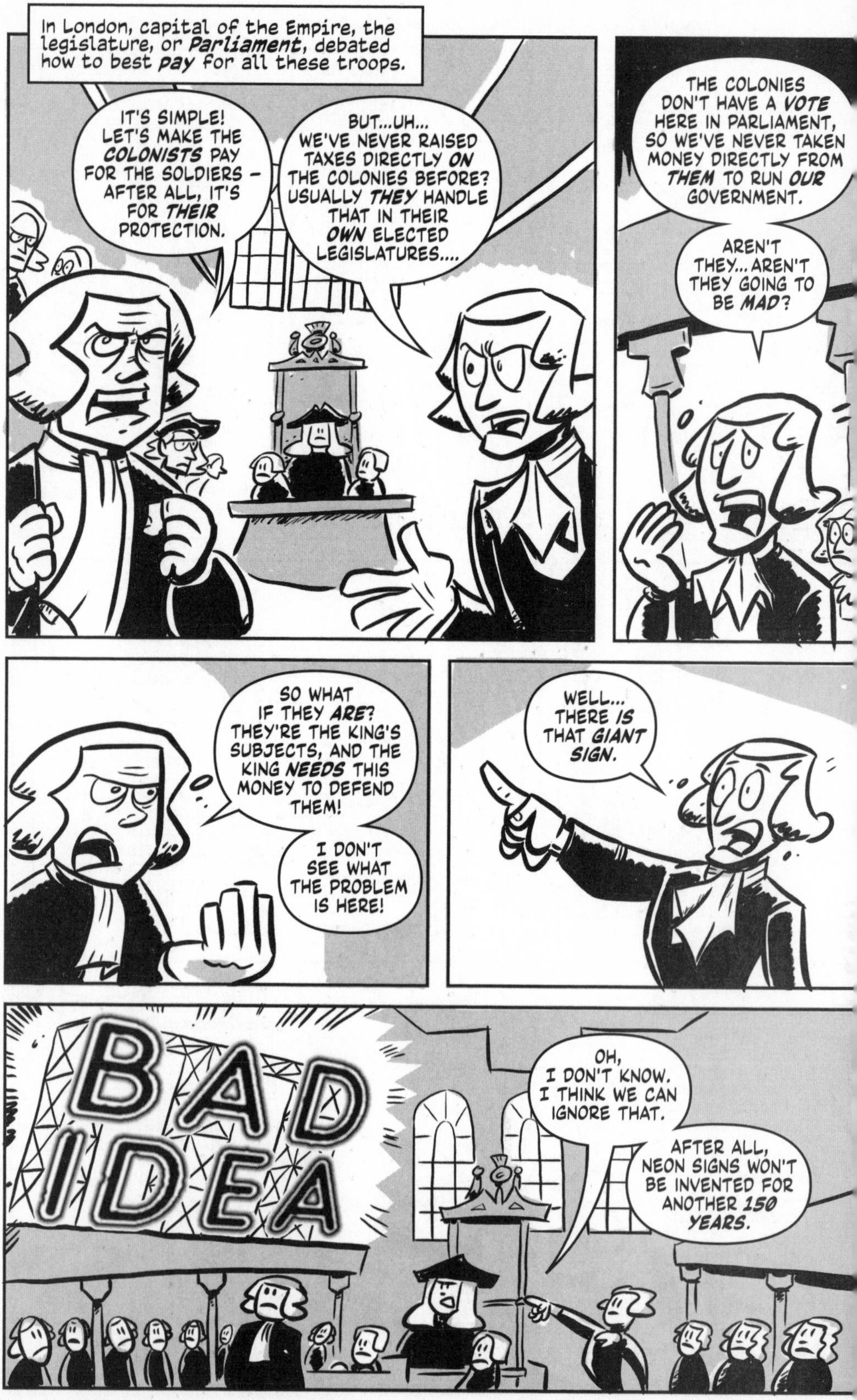
In London, capital of the Empire, the legislature, or *Parliament*, debated how to best *pay* for all these troops.
IT'S SIMPLE! LET'S MAKE THE *COLONISTS* PAY FOR THE SOLDIERS – AFTER ALL, IT'S FOR *THEIR* PROTECTION.
BUT...UH... WE'VE NEVER RAISED TAXES DIRECTLY *ON* THE COLONIES BEFORE? USUALLY *THEY* HANDLE THAT IN THEIR *OWN* ELECTED LEGISLATURES....
THE COLONIES DON'T HAVE A *VOTE* HERE IN PARLIAMENT, SO WE'VE NEVER TAKEN MONEY DIRECTLY FROM *THEM* TO RUN *OUR* GOVERNMENT.
AREN'T THEY... AREN'T THEY GOING TO BE *MAD*?
SO WHAT IF THEY *ARE*? THEY'RE THE KING'S SUBJECTS, AND THE KING *NEEDS* THIS MONEY TO DEFEND THEM!
I DON'T SEE WHAT THE PROBLEM IS HERE!
WELL... THERE *IS* THAT *GIANT SIGN*.
BAD IDEA
OH, I DON'T KNOW. I THINK WE CAN IGNORE THAT.
AFTER ALL, NEON SIGNS WON'T BE INVENTED FOR ANOTHER *150 YEARS*.

The colonial legislature in Virginia was called the ***House of Burgesses.***

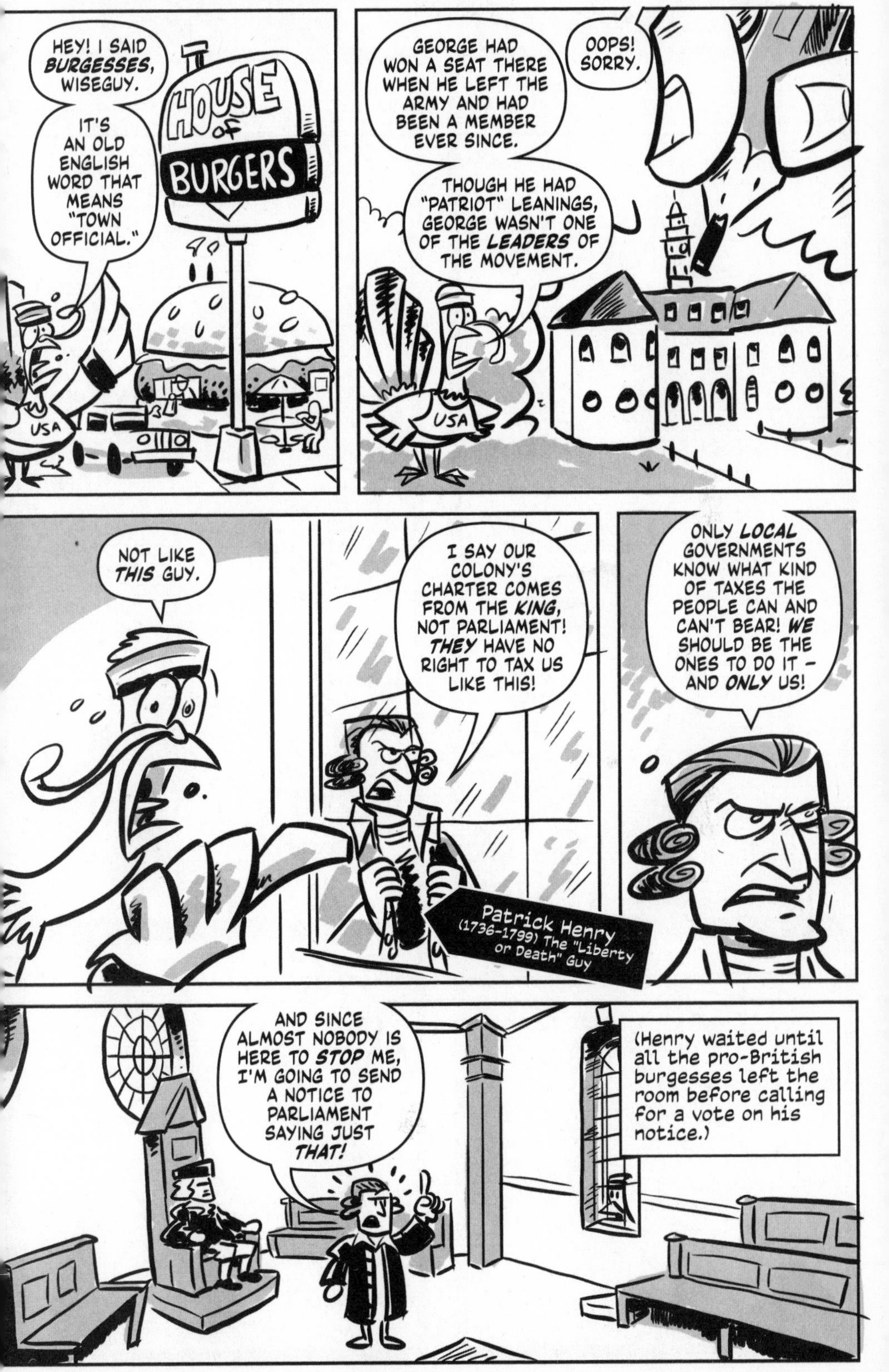
HEY! I SAID BURGESSES, WISEGUY.
IT'S AN OLD ENGLISH WORD THAT MEANS "TOWN OFFICIAL."
HOUSE of BURGERS
USA
GEORGE HAD WON A SEAT THERE WHEN HE LEFT THE ARMY AND HAD BEEN A MEMBER EVER SINCE.
OOPS! SORRY.
THOUGH HE HAD "PATRIOT" LEANINGS, GEORGE WASN'T ONE OF THE LEADERS OF THE MOVEMENT.
USA
NOT LIKE THIS GUY.
I SAY OUR COLONY'S CHARTER COMES FROM THE KING, NOT PARLIAMENT! THEY HAVE NO RIGHT TO TAX US LIKE THIS!
Patrick Henry (1736-1799) The "Liberty or Death" Guy
ONLY LOCAL GOVERNMENTS KNOW WHAT KIND OF TAXES THE PEOPLE CAN AND CAN'T BEAR! WE SHOULD BE THE ONES TO DO IT – AND ONLY US!
AND SINCE ALMOST NOBODY IS HERE TO STOP ME, I'M GOING TO SEND A NOTICE TO PARLIAMENT SAYING JUST THAT!
(Henry waited until all the pro-British burgesses left the room before calling for a vote on his notice.)

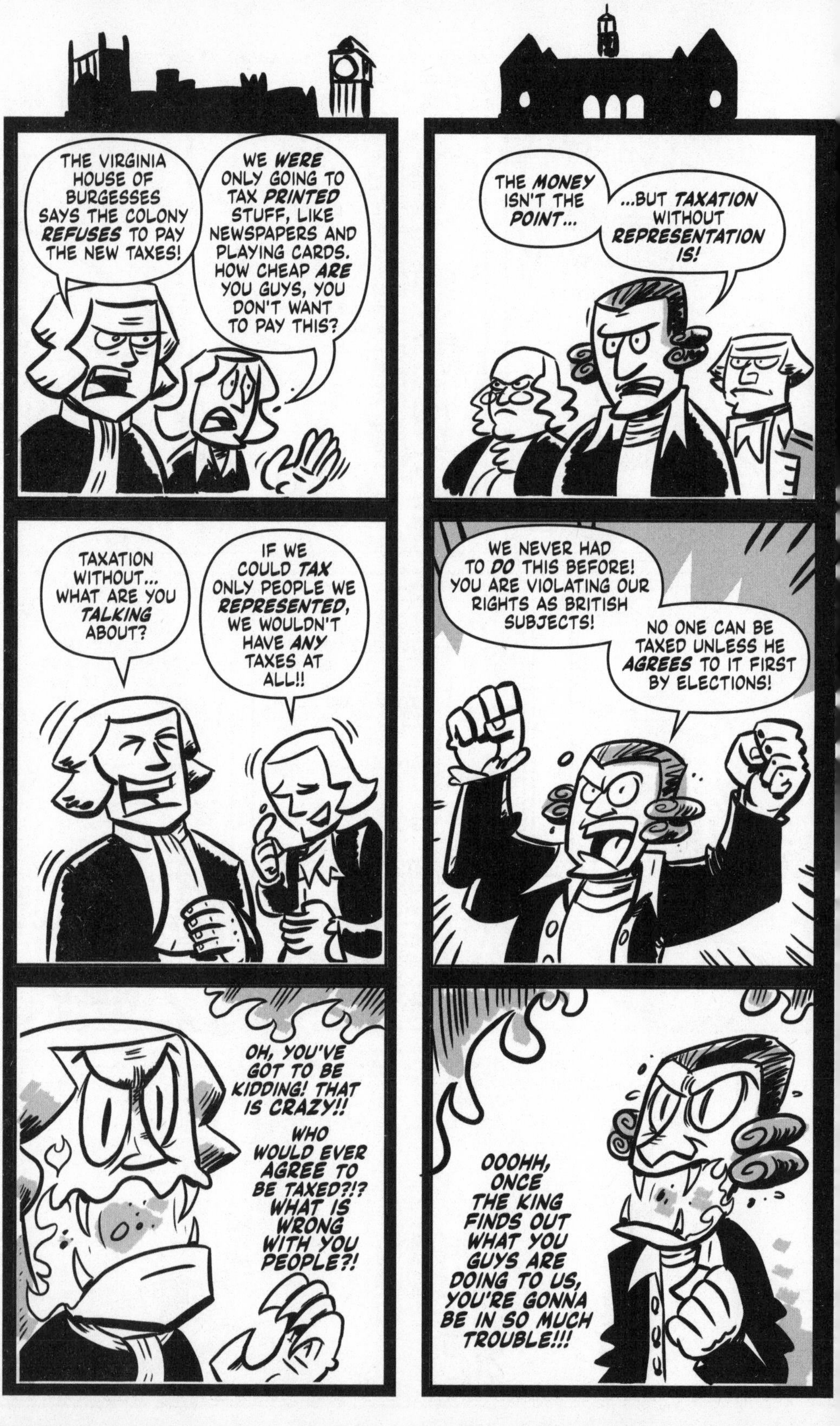
THE VIRGINIA HOUSE OF BURGESSES SAYS THE COLONY REFUSES TO PAY THE NEW TAXES!
WE WERE ONLY GOING TO TAX PRINTED STUFF, LIKE NEWSPAPERS AND PLAYING CARDS. HOW CHEAP ARE YOU GUYS, YOU DON'T WANT TO PAY THIS?
THE MONEY ISN'T THE POINT...
...BUT TAXATION WITHOUT REPRESENTATION IS!
TAXATION WITHOUT... WHAT ARE YOU TALKING ABOUT?
IF WE COULD TAX ONLY PEOPLE WE REPRESENTED, WE WOULDN'T HAVE ANY TAXES AT ALL!!
WE NEVER HAD TO DO THIS BEFORE! YOU ARE VIOLATING OUR RIGHTS AS BRITISH SUBJECTS!
NO ONE CAN BE TAXED UNLESS HE AGREES TO IT FIRST BY ELECTIONS!
OH, YOU'VE GOT TO BE KIDDING! THAT IS CRAZY!!
WHO WOULD EVER AGREE TO BE TAXED?!? WHAT IS WRONG WITH YOU PEOPLE?!
OOOHH, ONCE THE KING FINDS OUT WHAT YOU GUYS ARE DOING TO US, YOU'RE GONNA BE IN SO MUCH TROUBLE!!!

The relationship between Britain and her colonies just got worse and ***worse*** throughout the 1760s and early 1770s. Parliament would make taxes, America would protest, and Parliament would get rid of those taxes but then pass more.

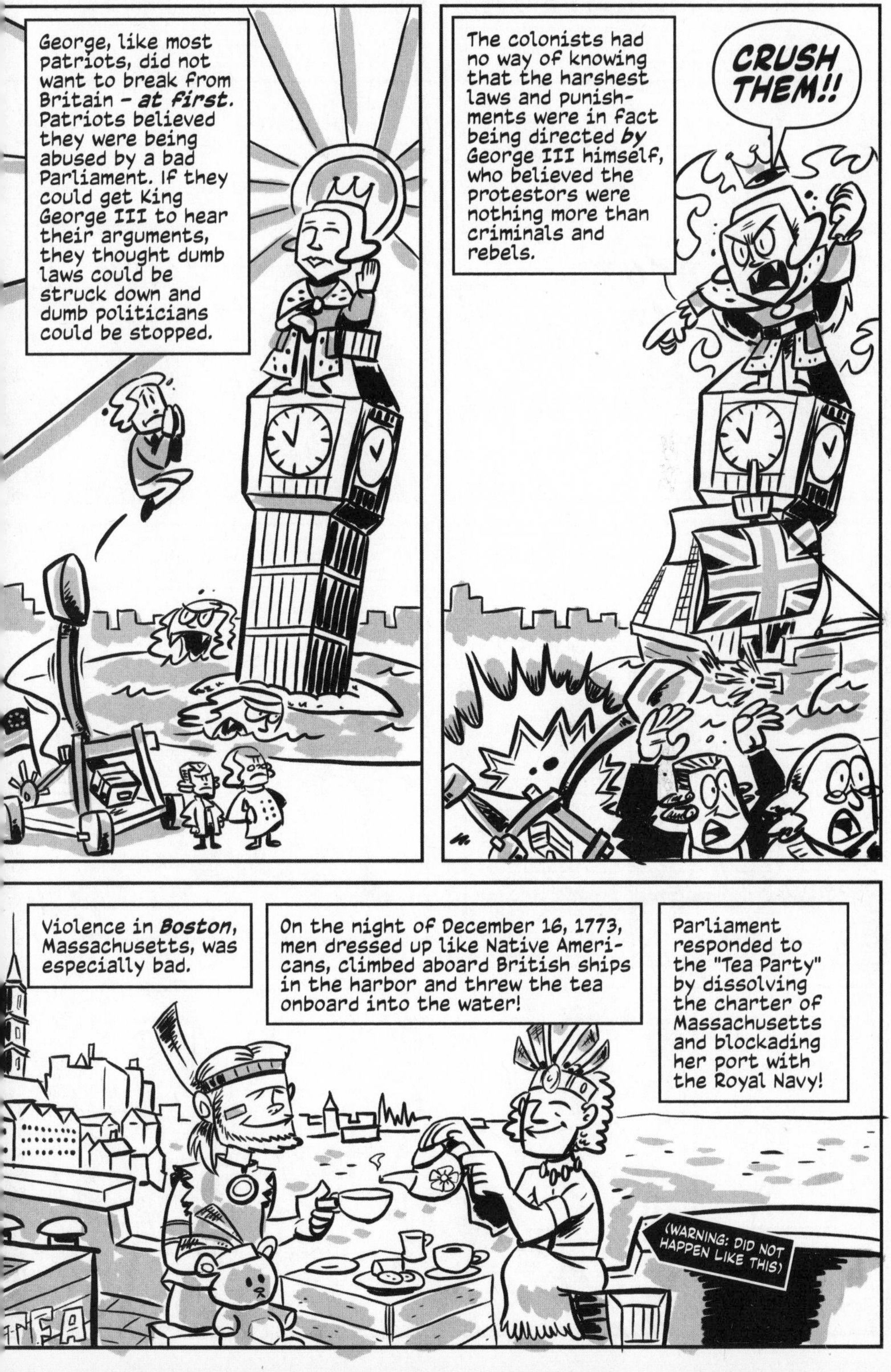
George, like most patriots, did not want to break from Britain – at first. Patriots believed they were being abused by a bad Parliament. If they could get King George III to hear their arguments, they thought dumb laws could be struck down and dumb politicians could be stopped.
The colonists had no way of knowing that the harshest laws and punishments were in fact being directed by George III himself, who believed the protestors were nothing more than criminals and rebels.
CRUSH THEM!!
Violence in Boston, Massachusetts, was especially bad.
On the night of December 16, 1773, men dressed up like Native Americans, climbed aboard British ships in the harbor and threw the tea onboard into the water!
Parliament responded to the "Tea Party" by dissolving the charter of Massachusetts and blockading her port with the Royal Navy!
(WARNING: DID NOT HAPPEN LIKE THIS)

George attended a meeting of the House of Burgesses that voted for Virginia to observe a ***Day of Prayer*** for the people of Boston.

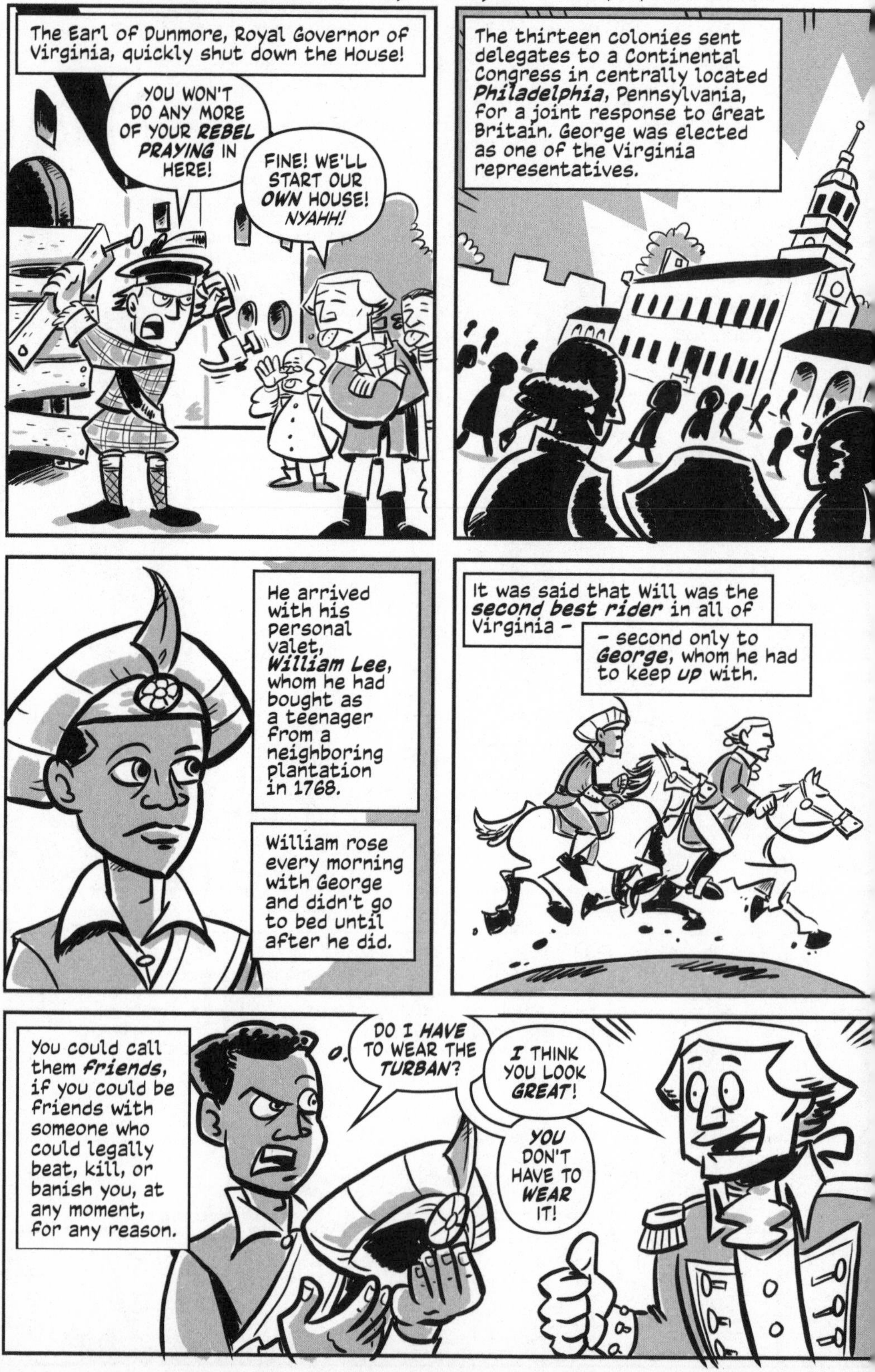

The Earl of Dunmore, Royal Governor of Virginia, quickly shut down the House!
YOU WON'T DO ANY MORE OF YOUR REBEL PRAYING IN HERE!
FINE! WE'LL START OUR OWN HOUSE! NYAHH!
The thirteen colonies sent delegates to a Continental Congress in centrally located Philadelphia, Pennsylvania, for a joint response to Great Britain. George was elected as one of the Virginia representatives.
He arrived with his personal valet, William Lee, whom he had bought as a teenager from a neighboring plantation in 1768.
William rose every morning with George and didn't go to bed until after he did.
It was said that Will was the second best rider in all of Virginia –
– second only to George, whom he had to keep up with.
You could call them friends, if you could be friends with someone who could legally beat, kill, or banish you, at any moment, for any reason.
DO I HAVE TO WEAR THE TURBAN?
I THINK YOU LOOK GREAT!
YOU DON'T HAVE TO WEAR IT!

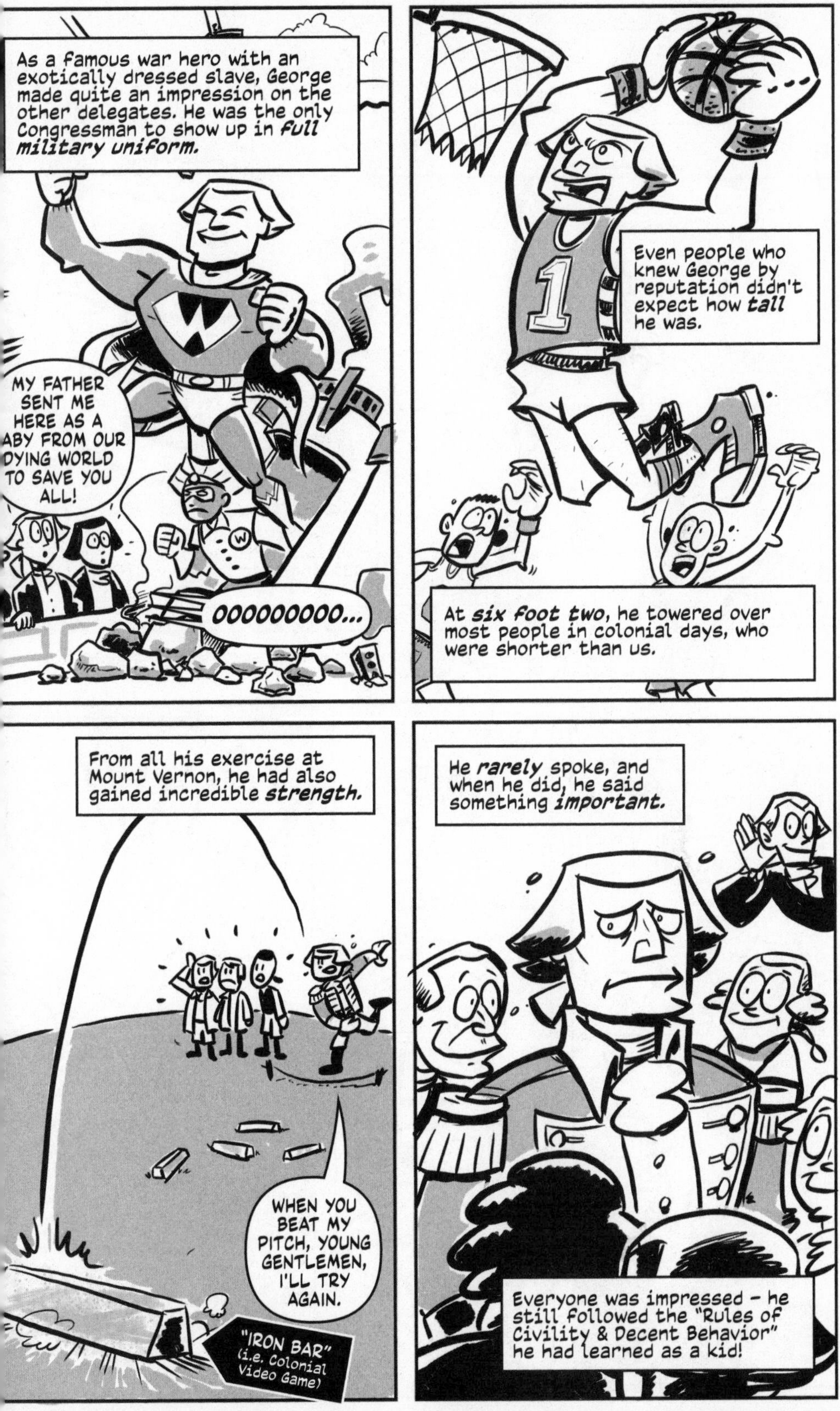

As a famous war hero with an exotically dressed slave, George made quite an impression on the other delegates. He was the only Congressman to show up in *full military uniform.*
MY FATHER SENT ME HERE AS A ABY FROM OUR DYING WORLD TO SAVE YOU ALL!
OOOOOOOOO...
Even people who knew George by reputation didn't expect how *tall* he was.
At *six foot two*, he towered over most people in colonial days, who were shorter than us.
From all his exercise at Mount Vernon, he had also gained incredible *strength.*
WHEN YOU BEAT MY PITCH, YOUNG GENTLEMEN, I'LL TRY AGAIN.
"IRON BAR" (i.e. Colonial Video Game)
He *rarely* spoke, and when he did, he said something *important.*
Everyone was impressed - he still followed the "Rules of Civility & Decent Behavior" he had learned as a kid!

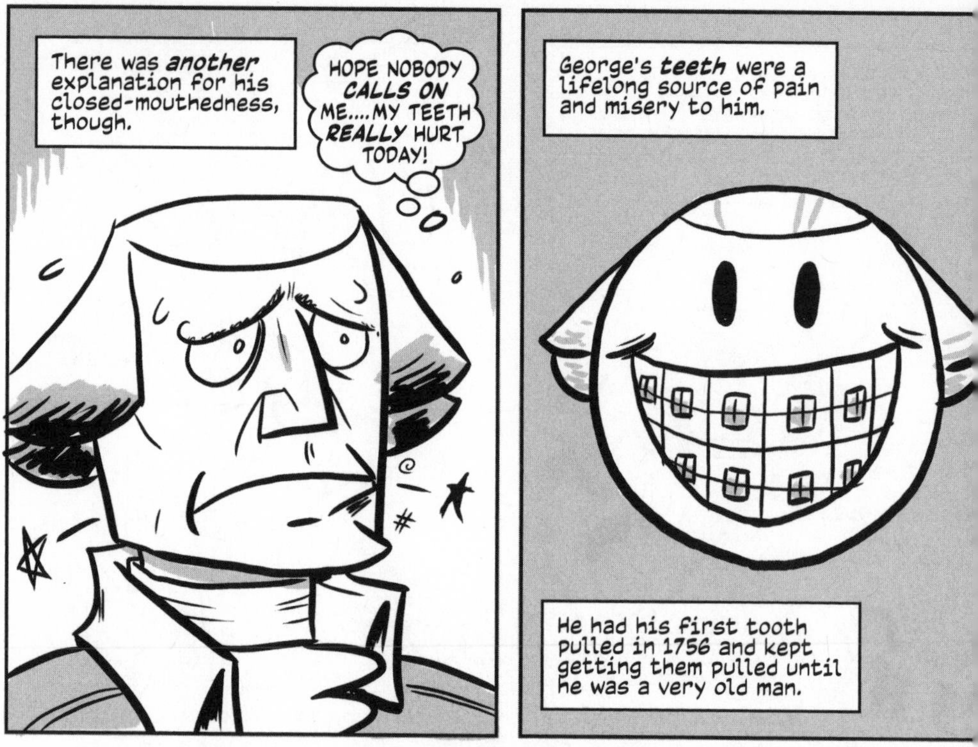
There was *another* explanation for his closed-mouthedness, though.
HOPE NOBODY *CALLS ON* ME....MY TEETH *REALLY* HURT TODAY!
George's *teeth* were a lifelong source of pain and misery to him.
He had his first tooth pulled in 1756 and kept getting them pulled until he was a very old man.

He told fellow Continental Congressman ***John Adams*** his teeth had gone bad from him cracking too many ***walnuts*** with them when he was a kid.

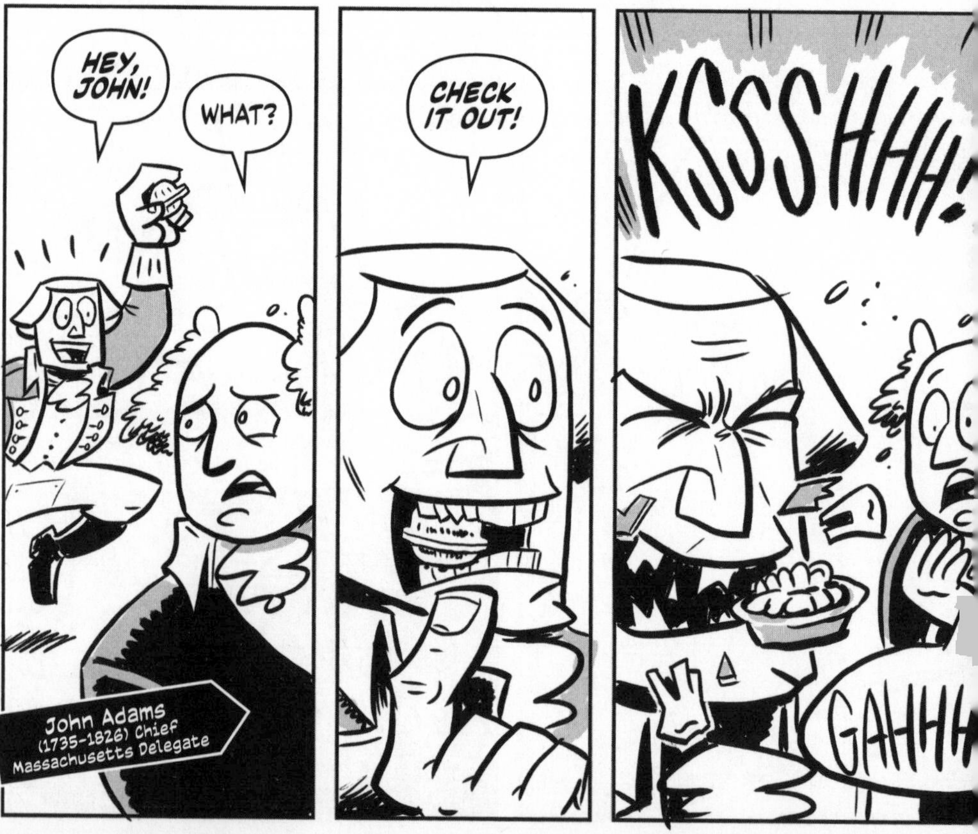
HEY, JOHN!
WHAT?
John Adams
(1735–1826) Chief Massachusetts Delegate
CHECK IT OUT!
KSSSHHH!
GAHHH

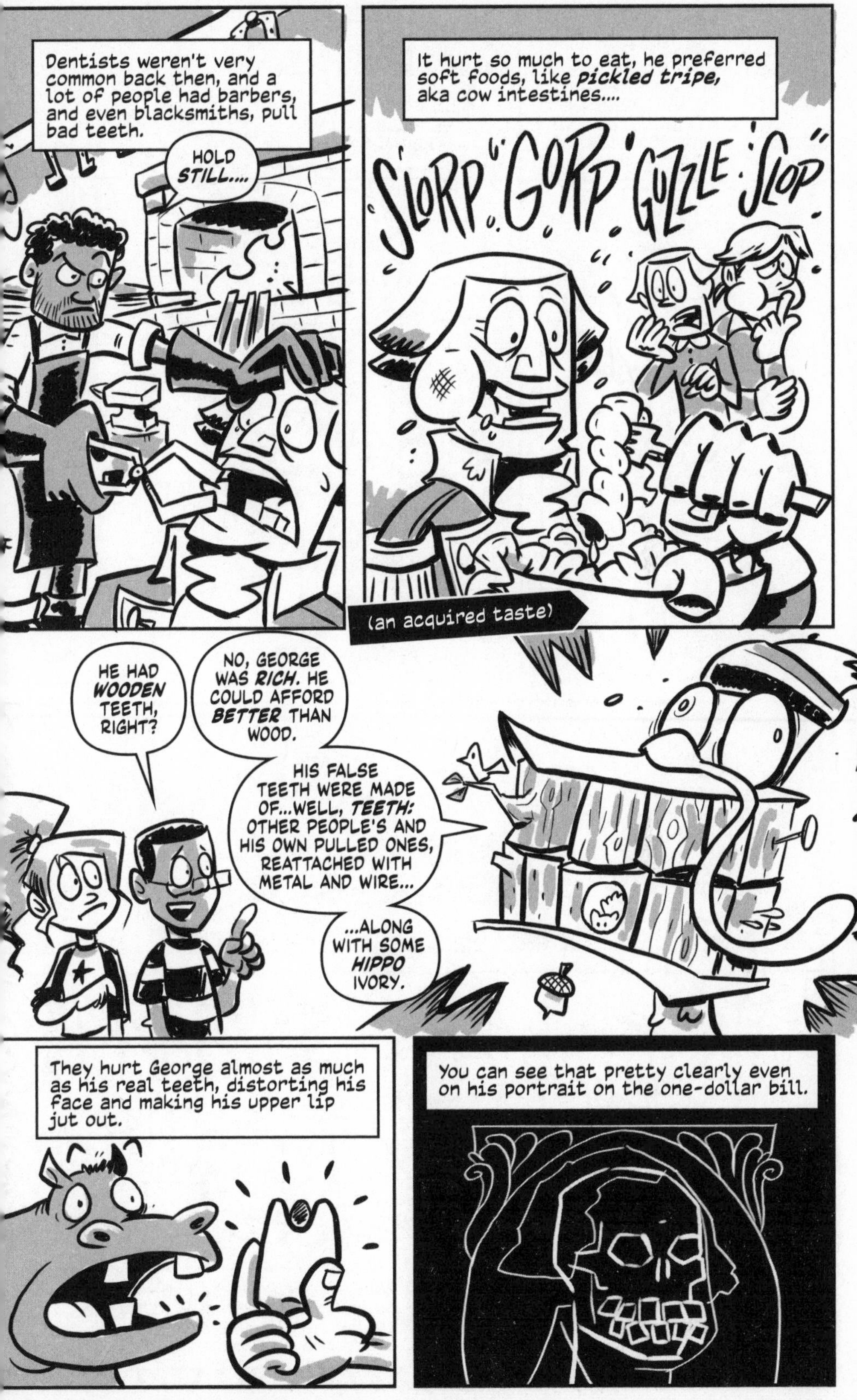

Dentists weren't very common back then, and a lot of people had barbers, and even blacksmiths, pull bad teeth.
HOLD STILL....
It hurt so much to eat, he preferred soft foods, like pickled tripe, aka cow intestines....
SLORP GORP GUZZLE SLOP
(an acquired taste)
HE HAD WOODEN TEETH, RIGHT?
NO, GEORGE WAS RICH. HE COULD AFFORD BETTER THAN WOOD.
HIS FALSE TEETH WERE MADE OF...WELL, TEETH: OTHER PEOPLE'S AND HIS OWN PULLED ONES, REATTACHED WITH METAL AND WIRE...
...ALONG WITH SOME HIPPO IVORY.
They hurt George almost as much as his real teeth, distorting his face and making his upper lip jut out.
You can see that pretty clearly even on his portrait on the one-dollar bill.

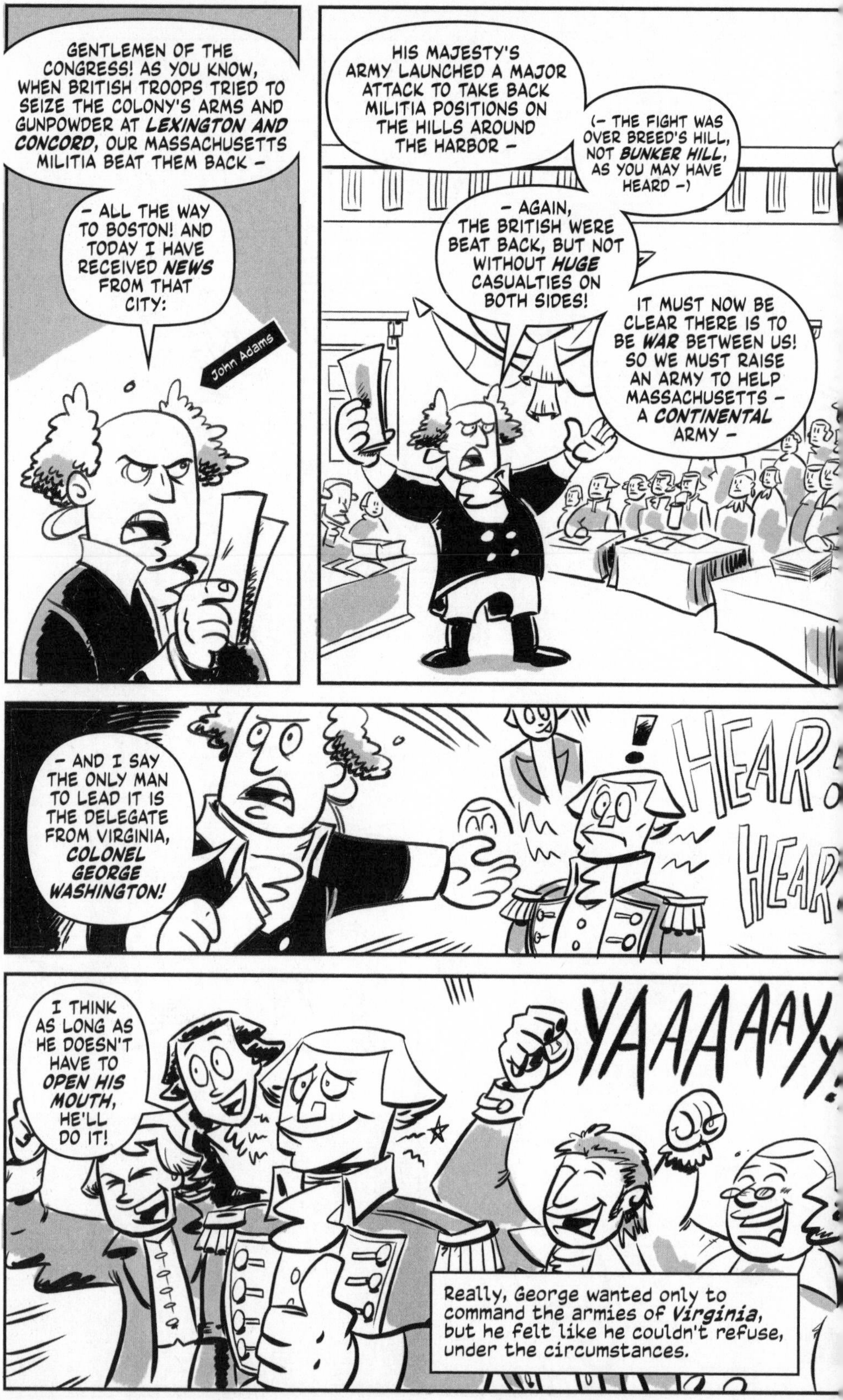
GENTLEMEN OF THE CONGRESS! AS YOU KNOW, WHEN BRITISH TROOPS TRIED TO SEIZE THE COLONY'S ARMS AND GUNPOWDER AT *LEXINGTON AND CONCORD*, OUR MASSACHUSETTS MILITIA BEAT THEM BACK –
– ALL THE WAY TO BOSTON! AND TODAY I HAVE RECEIVED *NEWS* FROM THAT CITY:
John Adams
HIS MAJESTY'S ARMY LAUNCHED A MAJOR ATTACK TO TAKE BACK MILITIA POSITIONS ON THE HILLS AROUND THE HARBOR –
(– THE FIGHT WAS OVER BREED'S HILL, NOT *BUNKER HILL*, AS YOU MAY HAVE HEARD –)
– AGAIN, THE BRITISH WERE BEAT BACK, BUT NOT WITHOUT *HUGE* CASUALTIES ON BOTH SIDES!
IT MUST NOW BE CLEAR THERE IS TO BE *WAR* BETWEEN US! SO WE MUST RAISE AN ARMY TO HELP MASSACHUSETTS – A *CONTINENTAL* ARMY –
– AND I SAY THE ONLY MAN TO LEAD IT IS THE DELEGATE FROM VIRGINIA, ***COLONEL GEORGE WASHINGTON!***
HEAR
HEAR
I THINK AS LONG AS HE DOESN'T HAVE TO *OPEN HIS MOUTH*, HE'LL DO IT!
YAAAAAY
Really, George wanted only to command the armies of *Virginia*, but he felt like he couldn't refuse, under the circumstances.

With the rebels holding the hills surrounding Boston Harbor, the British couldn't defend their position. When George and Will arrived for him to take command of the army, the enemy left the city.

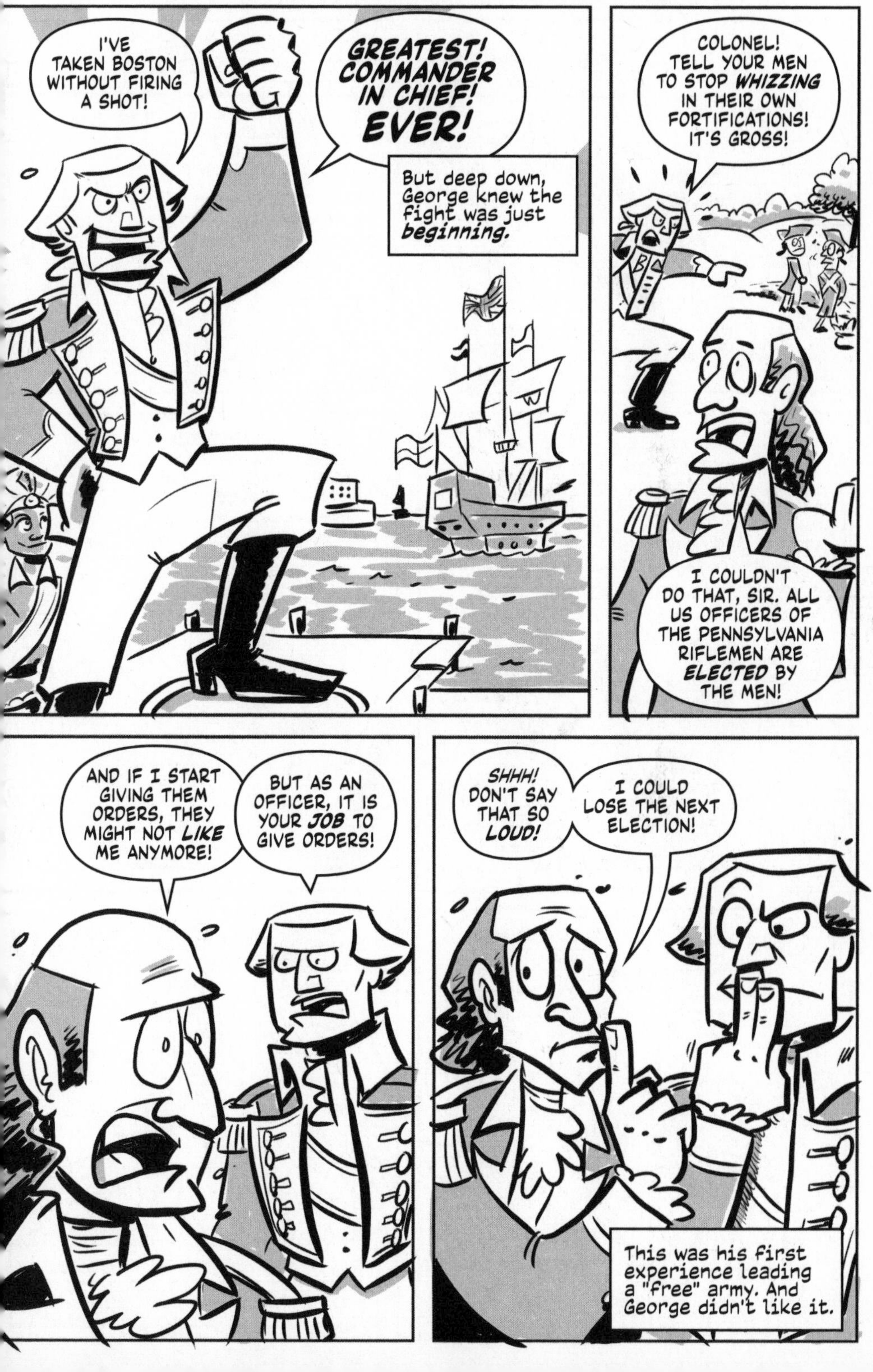
I'VE TAKEN BOSTON WITHOUT FIRING A SHOT!
GREATEST! COMMANDER IN CHIEF! EVER!
But deep down, George knew the fight was just beginning.
COLONEL! TELL YOUR MEN TO STOP WHIZZING IN THEIR OWN FORTIFICATIONS! IT'S GROSS!
I COULDN'T DO THAT, SIR. ALL US OFFICERS OF THE PENNSYLVANIA RIFLEMEN ARE ELECTED BY THE MEN!
AND IF I START GIVING THEM ORDERS, THEY MIGHT NOT LIKE ME ANYMORE!
BUT AS AN OFFICER, IT IS YOUR JOB TO GIVE ORDERS!
SHHH! DON'T SAY THAT SO LOUD!
I COULD LOSE THE NEXT ELECTION!
This was his first experience leading a "free" army. And George didn't like it.

The Continental Army was made up of militiamen from ***thirteen*** separate colonies, each with their own special way of doing things.

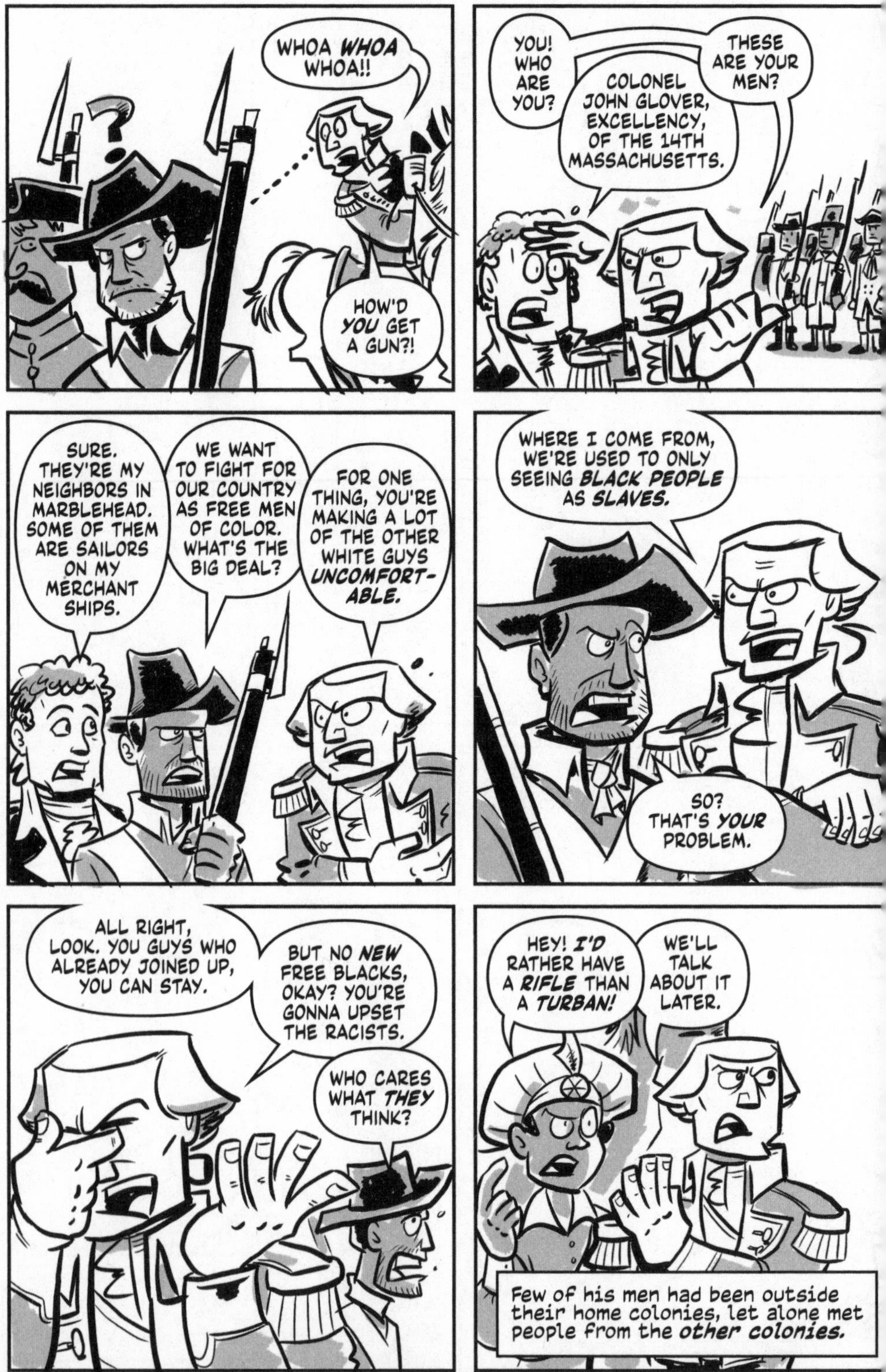

WHOA *WHOA* WHOA!!
HOW'D *YOU* GET A GUN?!
YOU! WHO ARE YOU?
COLONEL JOHN GLOVER, EXCELLENCY, OF THE 14TH MASSACHUSETTS.
THESE ARE YOUR MEN?
SURE. THEY'RE MY NEIGHBORS IN MARBLEHEAD. SOME OF THEM ARE SAILORS ON MY MERCHANT SHIPS.
WE WANT TO FIGHT FOR OUR COUNTRY AS FREE MEN OF COLOR. WHAT'S THE BIG DEAL?
FOR ONE THING, YOU'RE MAKING A LOT OF THE OTHER WHITE GUYS *UNCOMFORTABLE.*
WHERE I COME FROM, WE'RE USED TO ONLY SEEING *BLACK PEOPLE* AS *SLAVES.*
SO? THAT'S *YOUR* PROBLEM.
ALL RIGHT, LOOK. YOU GUYS WHO ALREADY JOINED UP, YOU CAN STAY.
BUT NO *NEW* FREE BLACKS, OKAY? YOU'RE GONNA UPSET THE RACISTS.
WHO CARES WHAT *THEY* THINK?
HEY! *I'D* RATHER HAVE A *RIFLE* THAN A *TURBAN!*
WE'LL TALK ABOUT IT LATER.
Few of his men had been outside their home colonies, let alone met people from the ***other colonies.***

These colonial militias had been raised to defend against attacks by Native Americans and put down slave rebellions. They weren't used to European-style military ***discipline,*** much less fighting alongside black soldiers.

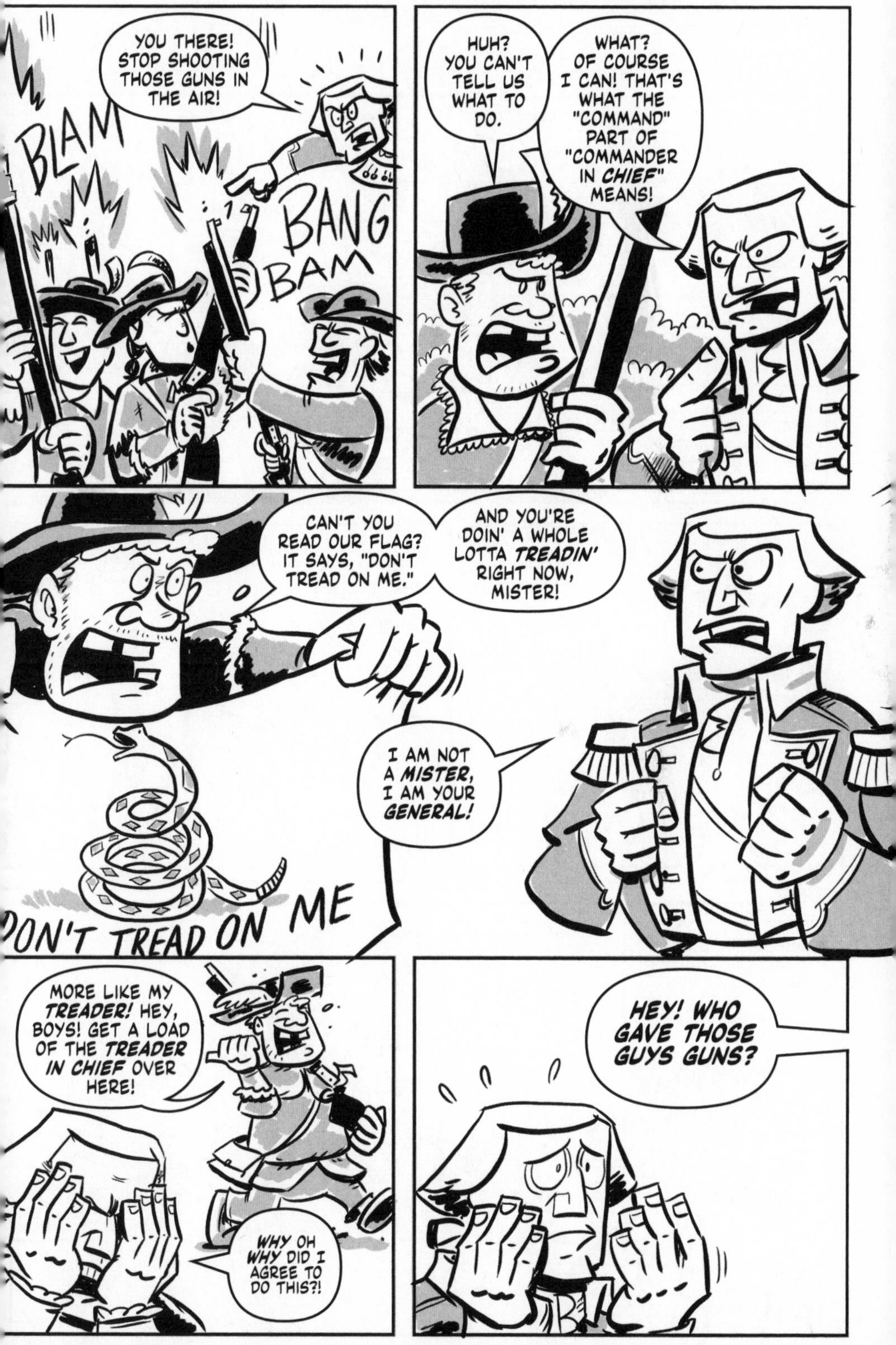
YOU THERE! STOP SHOOTING THOSE GUNS IN THE AIR!
BLAM
BANG
BAM
HUH? YOU CAN'T TELL US WHAT TO DO.
WHAT? OF COURSE I CAN! THAT'S WHAT THE "COMMAND" PART OF "COMMANDER IN CHIEF" MEANS!
CAN'T YOU READ OUR FLAG? IT SAYS, "DON'T TREAD ON ME."
AND YOU'RE DOIN' A WHOLE LOTTA TREADIN' RIGHT NOW, MISTER!
I AM NOT A MISTER, I AM YOUR GENERAL!
DON'T TREAD ON ME
MORE LIKE MY TREADER! HEY, BOYS! GET A LOAD OF THE TREADER IN CHIEF OVER HERE!
WHY OH WHY DID I AGREE TO DO THIS?!
HEY! WHO GAVE THOSE GUYS GUNS?

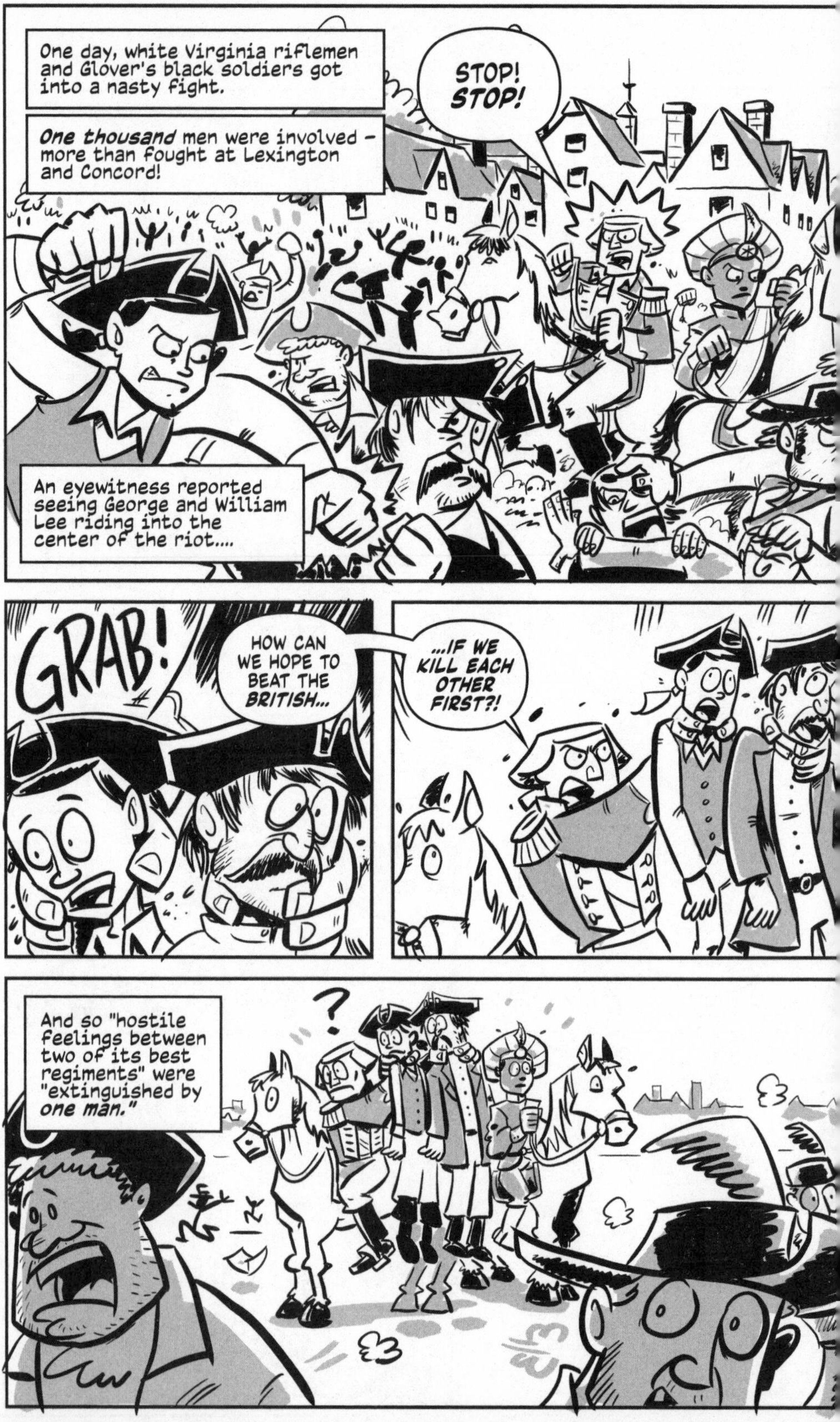

One day, white Virginia riflemen and Glover's black soldiers got into a nasty fight.
One thousand men were involved - more than fought at Lexington and Concord!
STOP! STOP!
An eyewitness reported seeing George and William Lee riding into the center of the riot....
GRAB!
HOW CAN WE HOPE TO BEAT THE BRITISH...
...IF WE KILL EACH OTHER FIRST?!
And so "hostile feelings between two of its best regiments" were "extinguished by one man."

The next obvious place for a British attack was *New York City*, right smack-dab in the middle of the colonies.

George relocated most of his troops there and began building forts around Manhattan and Brooklyn.

WHAT DID YOU GET FROM CONGRESS?

HMMM... ADAMS AND THEM HAVE DECIDED THAT REJOINING THE BRITISH EMPIRE IS NO LONGER AN OPTION.

THE MEN ARE TO BE GATHERED AND AT THE HEAD OF EACH BRIGADE SHOULD BE READ THIS... *DECLARATION.*

WE HOLD THESE TRUTHS TO BE SELF-EVIDENT, THAT ALL MEN ARE CREATED EQUAL...

HUZZAH! HUZZAH! HUZZAH!

In CONGRESS July 4
A DECLARATION
UNITED STATES OF AME

THERE'S NO GOING BACK NOW, BOYS!

WE'RE TO BE *INDEPENDENT* OF KING GEORGIE FOREVER!

HEY! THERE'S THAT STATUE TO OLE GEORGE III ON THE *BOWLING GREEN!*

July 9, 1776

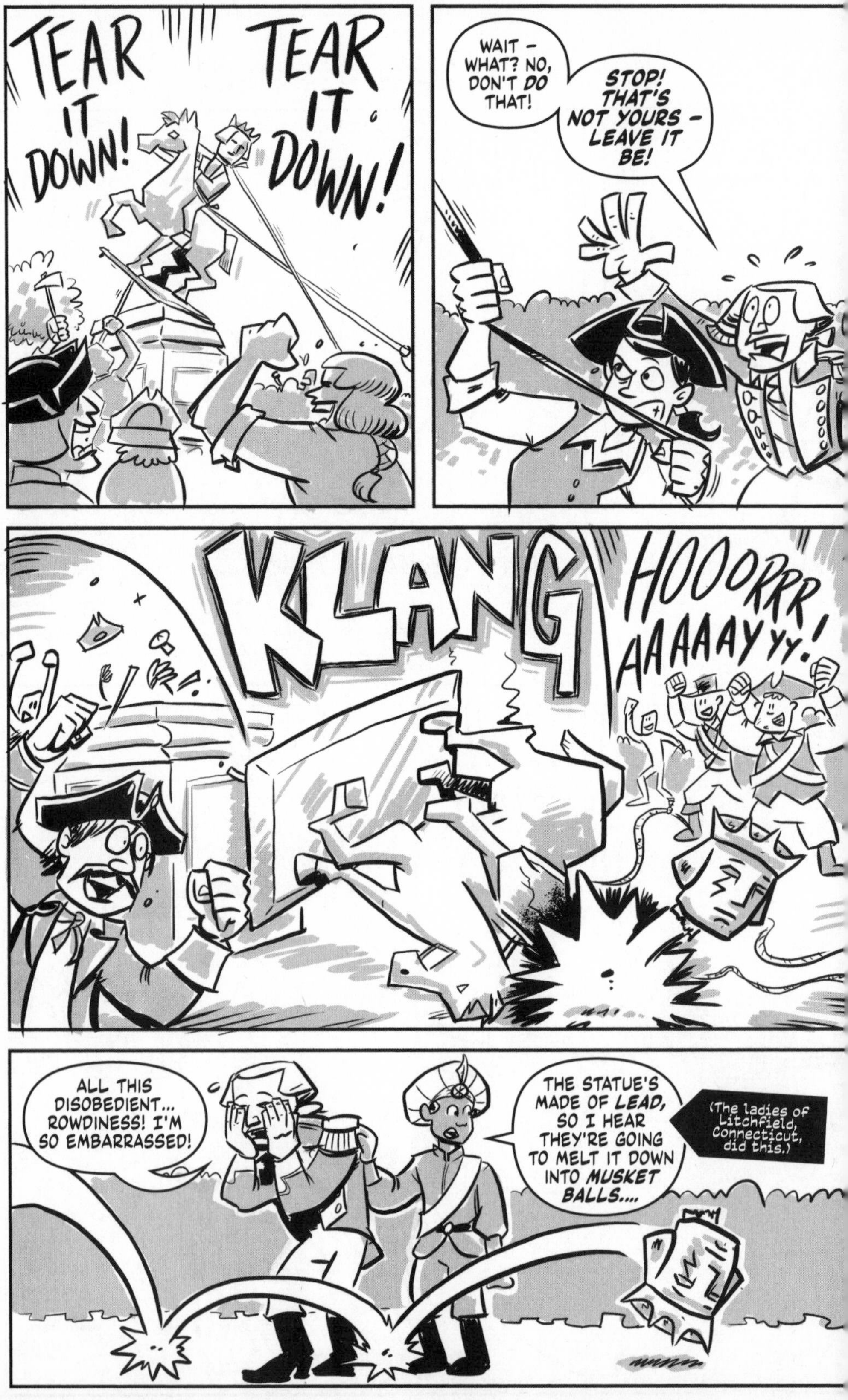
TEAR IT DOWN!
TEAR IT DOWN!
WAIT – WHAT? NO, DON'T *DO* THAT!
STOP! THAT'S NOT YOURS – LEAVE IT BE!
KLANG
HOOORRR AAAAAYYY!
ALL THIS DISOBEDIENT... ROWDINESS! I'M SO EMBARRASSED!
THE STATUE'S MADE OF *LEAD*, SO I HEAR THEY'RE GOING TO MELT IT DOWN INTO *MUSKET BALLS*....
(The ladies of Litchfield, Connecticut, did this.)

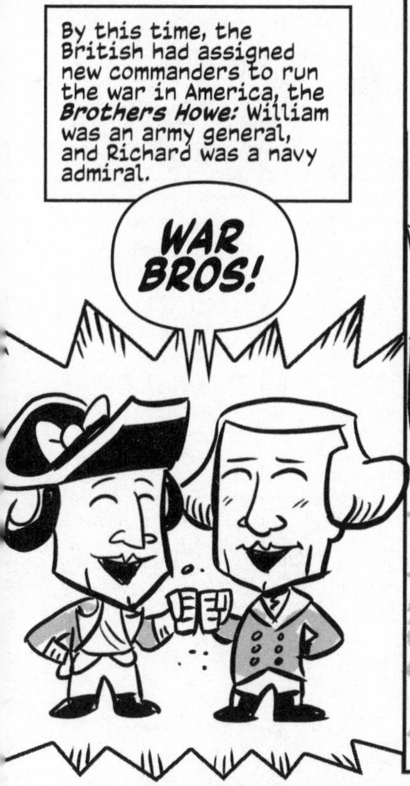
By this time, the British had assigned new commanders to run the war in America, the ***Brothers Howe:*** William was an army general, and Richard was a navy admiral.
WAR BROS!

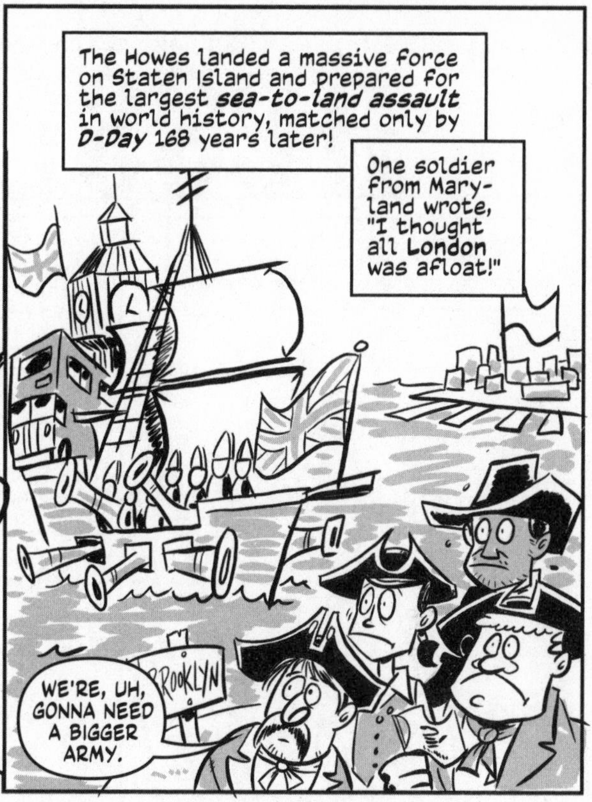
The Howes landed a massive force on Staten Island and prepared for the largest ***sea-to-land assault*** in world history, matched only by ***D-Day*** 168 years later!
One soldier from Maryland wrote, "I thought all **London** was afloat!"
BROOKLYN
WE'RE, UH, GONNA NEED A BIGGER ARMY.

George hoped to draw the British into attacking a heavily guarded position like Bunker (uh, ***Breed's***) Hill, but it became more and more obvious the city was too big, and too spread out across too many islands, to defend against such a large force.

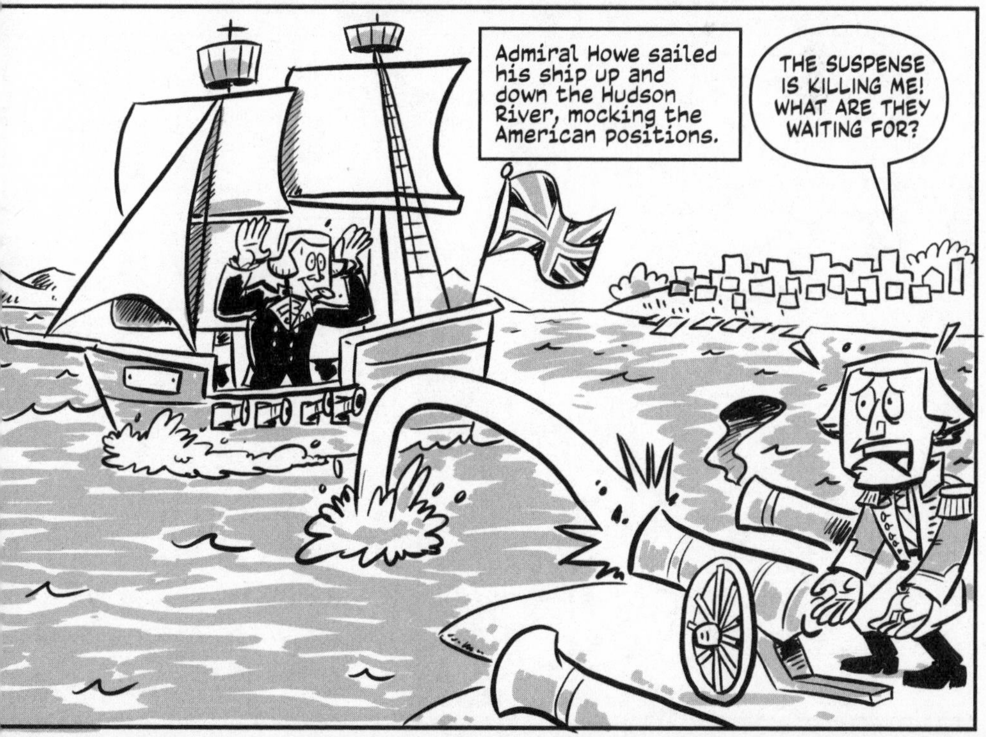
Admiral Howe sailed his ship up and down the Hudson River, mocking the American positions.
THE SUSPENSE IS KILLING ME! WHAT ARE THEY WAITING FOR?

On August 15 George found out, when two convoys arrived on Staten Island full of...

HESSIANS

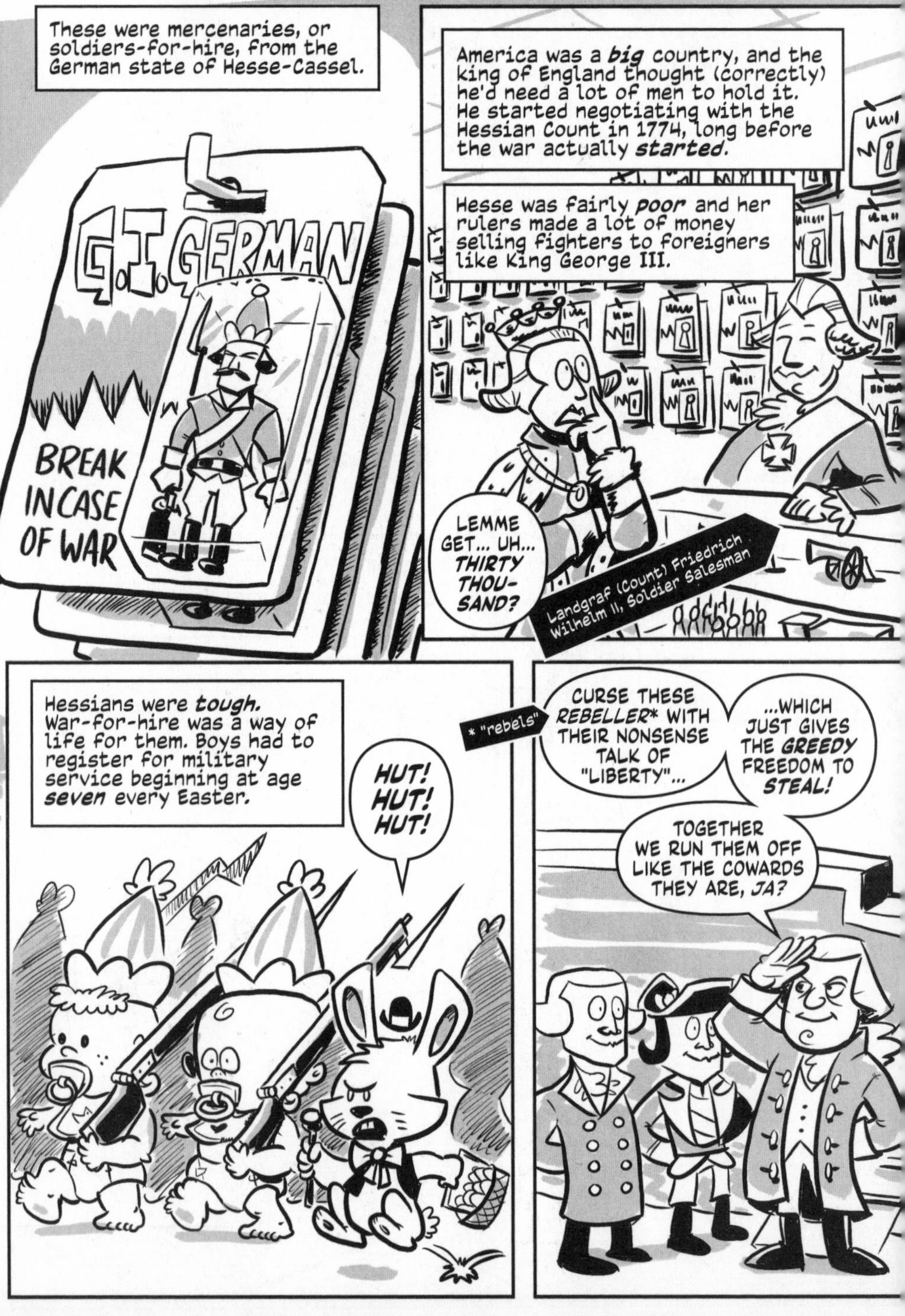
These were mercenaries, or soldiers-for-hire, from the German state of Hesse-Cassel.
G.I. GERMAN
BREAK IN CASE OF WAR
America was a *big* country, and the king of England thought (correctly) he'd need a lot of men to hold it. He started negotiating with the Hessian Count in 1774, long before the war actually *started*.
Hesse was fairly *poor* and her rulers made a lot of money selling fighters to foreigners like King George III.
LEMME GET... UH... *THIRTY THOU-SAND?*
Landgraf (Count) Friedrich Wilhelm II, Soldier Salesman
Hessians were *tough.* War-for-hire was a way of life for them. Boys had to register for military service beginning at age *seven* every Easter.
HUT! HUT! HUT!
CURSE THESE *REBELLER** WITH THEIR NONSENSE TALK OF "LIBERTY"...
* "rebels"
...WHICH JUST GIVES THE *GREEDY* FREEDOM TO *STEAL!*
TOGETHER WE RUN THEM OFF LIKE THE COWARDS THEY ARE, *JA?*

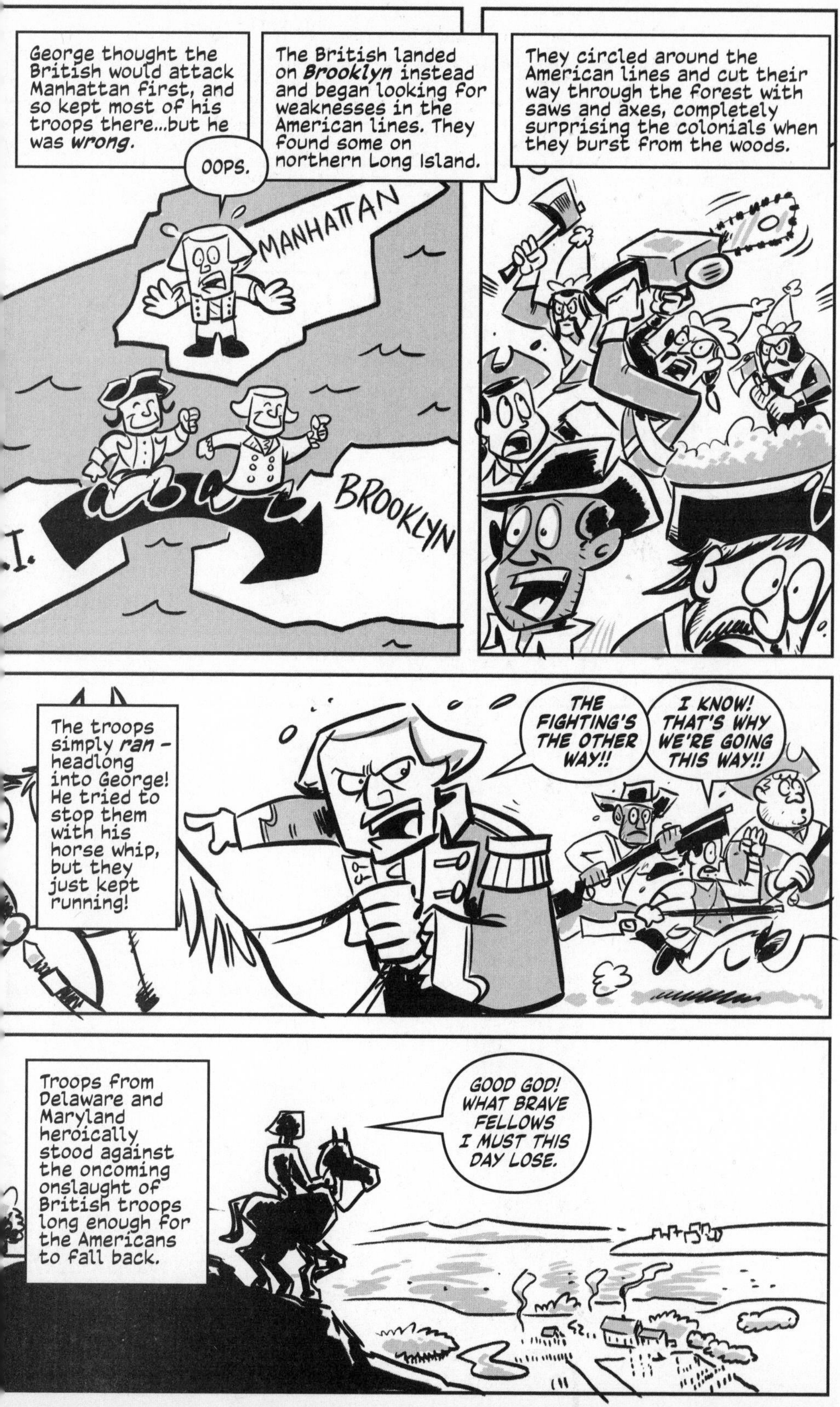

George thought the British would attack Manhattan first, and so kept most of his troops there...but he was *wrong*.
OOPS.
MANHATTAN
BROOKLYN
The British landed on *Brooklyn* instead and began looking for weaknesses in the American lines. They found some on northern Long Island.
They circled around the American lines and cut their way through the forest with saws and axes, completely surprising the colonials when they burst from the woods.
The troops simply *ran* – headlong into George! He tried to stop them with his horse whip, but they just kept running!
THE FIGHTING'S THE OTHER WAY!!
I KNOW! THAT'S WHY WE'RE GOING THIS WAY!!
Troops from Delaware and Maryland heroically stood against the oncoming onslaught of British troops long enough for the Americans to fall back.
GOOD GOD! WHAT BRAVE FELLOWS I MUST THIS DAY LOSE.

Part of the Empire's strategy was to terrorize the Americans and crush their will to resist.

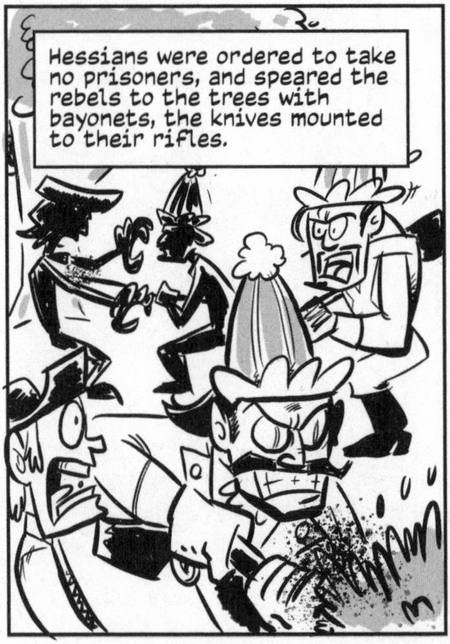
Hessians were ordered to take no prisoners, and speared the rebels to the trees with bayonets, the knives mounted to their rifles.

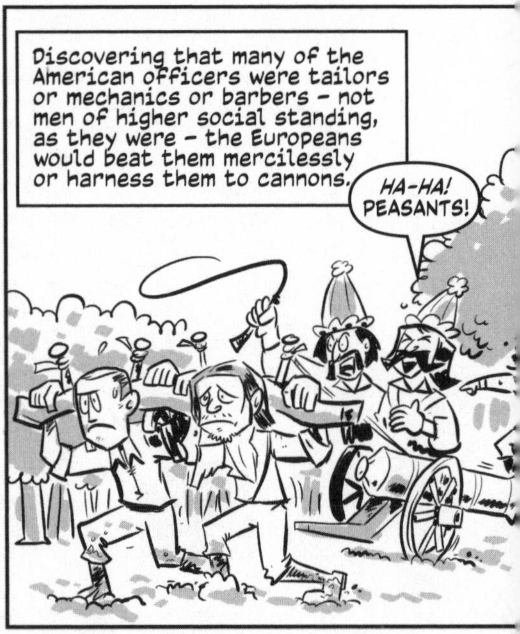
Discovering that many of the American officers were tailors or mechanics or barbers – not men of higher social standing, as they were – the Europeans would beat them mercilessly or harness them to cannons.
HA-HA! PEASANTS!

George and the nearly ten thousand American troops left rushed to the East River. Admiral Howe was ready to cut him off and trap them.

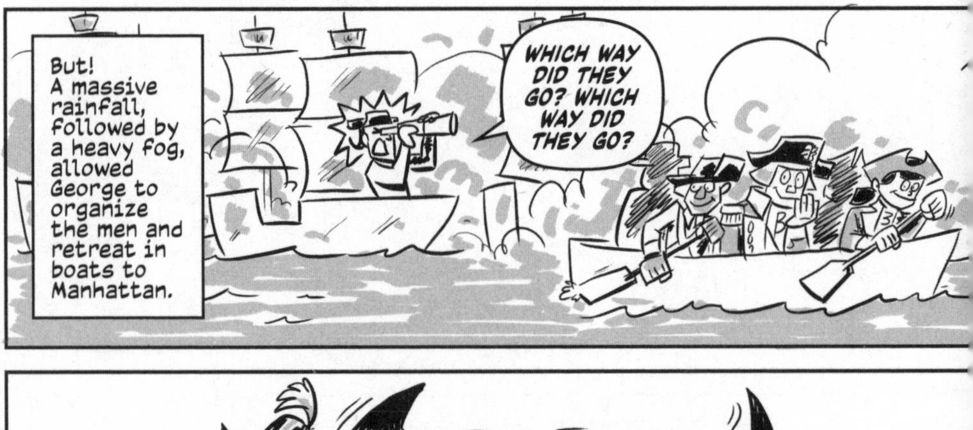
But! A massive rainfall, followed by a heavy fog, allowed George to organize the men and retreat in boats to Manhattan.
WHICH WAY DID THEY GO? WHICH WAY DID THEY GO?

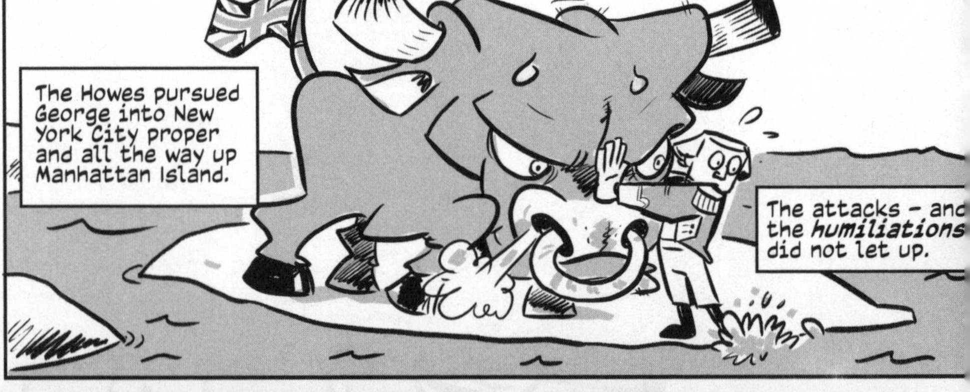
The Howes pursued George into New York City proper and all the way up Manhattan Island.
The attacks – and the *humiliations* did not let up.

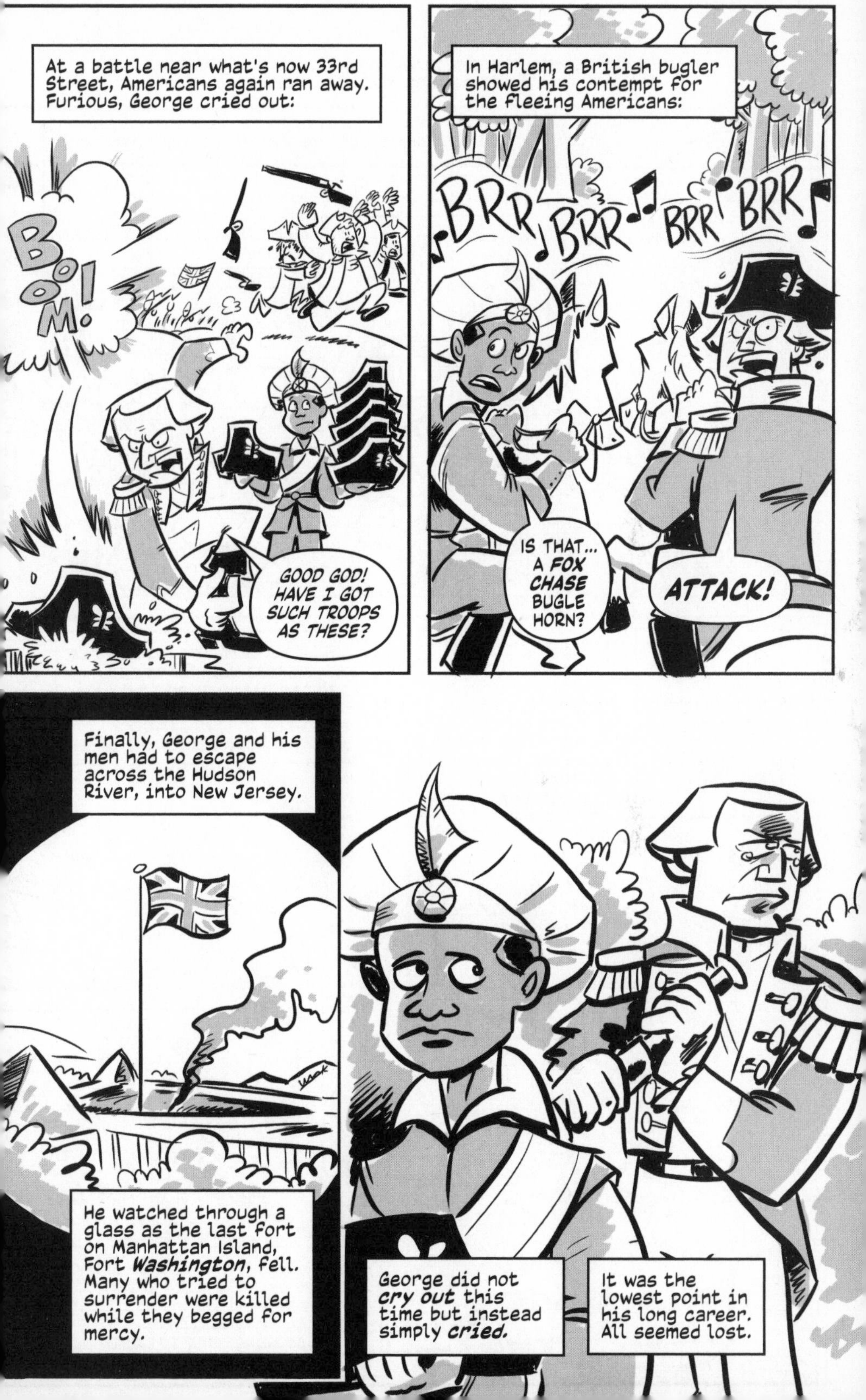
At a battle near what's now 33rd Street, Americans again ran away. Furious, George cried out:
BOOM!
GOOD GOD! HAVE I GOT SUCH TROOPS AS THESE?
In Harlem, a British bugler showed his contempt for the fleeing Americans:
BRR BRR BRR BRR
IS THAT... A FOX CHASE BUGLE HORN?
ATTACK!
Finally, George and his men had to escape across the Hudson River, into New Jersey.
He watched through a glass as the last fort on Manhattan Island, Fort Washington, fell. Many who tried to surrender were killed while they begged for mercy.
George did not cry out this time but instead simply cried.
It was the lowest point in his long career. All seemed lost.

But he summoned the inner strength to not give up.
And that meant retreating. More and more retreating...

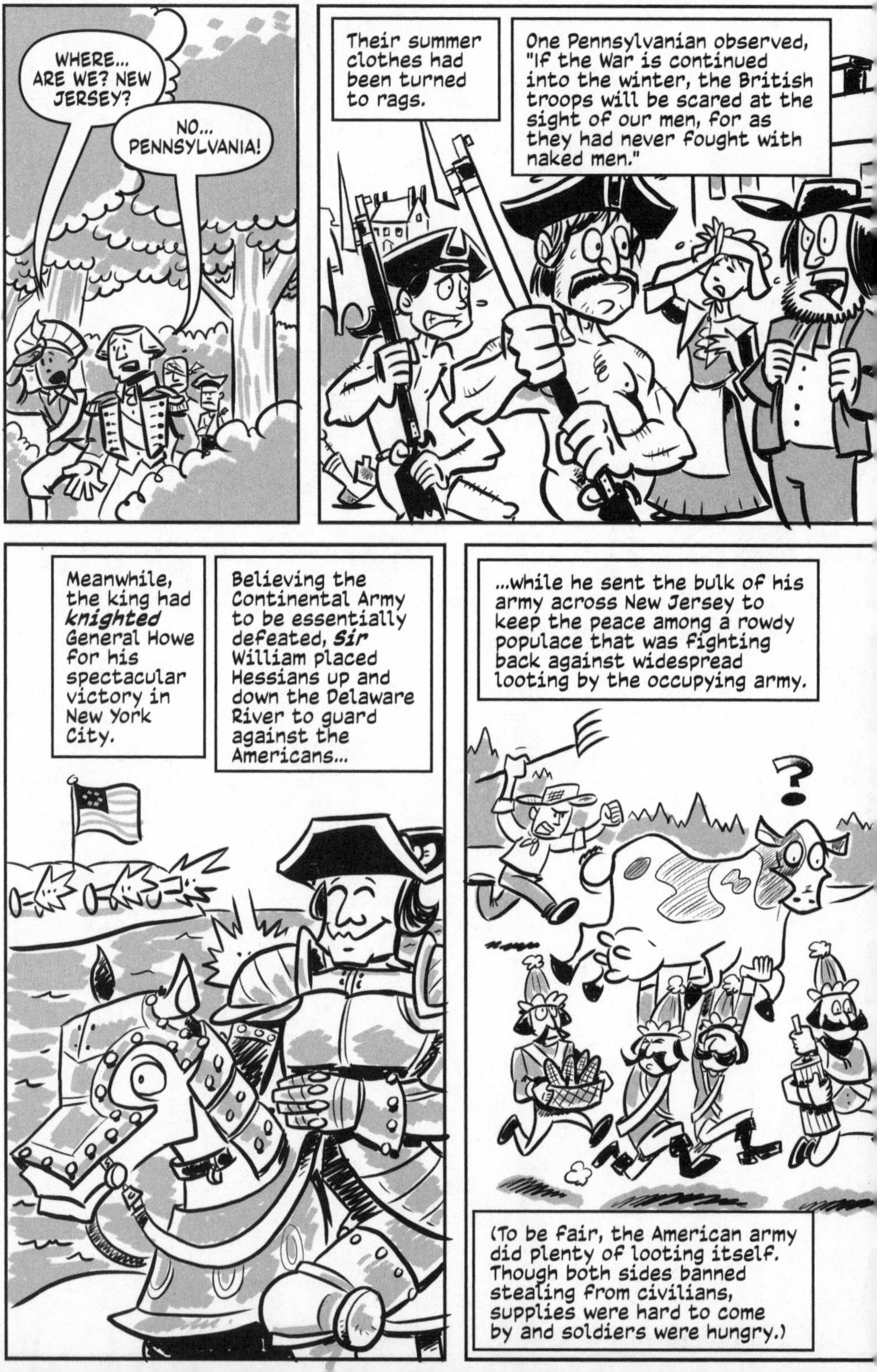

WHERE... ARE WE? NEW JERSEY?
NO... PENNSYLVANIA!
Their summer clothes had been turned to rags.
One Pennsylvanian observed, "If the War is continued into the winter, the British troops will be scared at the sight of our men, for as they had never fought with naked men."
Meanwhile, the king had ***knighted*** General Howe for his spectacular victory in New York City.
Believing the Continental Army to be essentially defeated, ***Sir*** William placed Hessians up and down the Delaware River to guard against the Americans...
...while he sent the bulk of his army across New Jersey to keep the peace among a rowdy populace that was fighting back against widespread looting by the occupying army.
?
(To be fair, the American army did plenty of looting itself. Though both sides banned stealing from civilians, supplies were hard to come by and soldiers were hungry.)

This was *the* problem the British would have over and over during the war: America is really, really, really *big.*

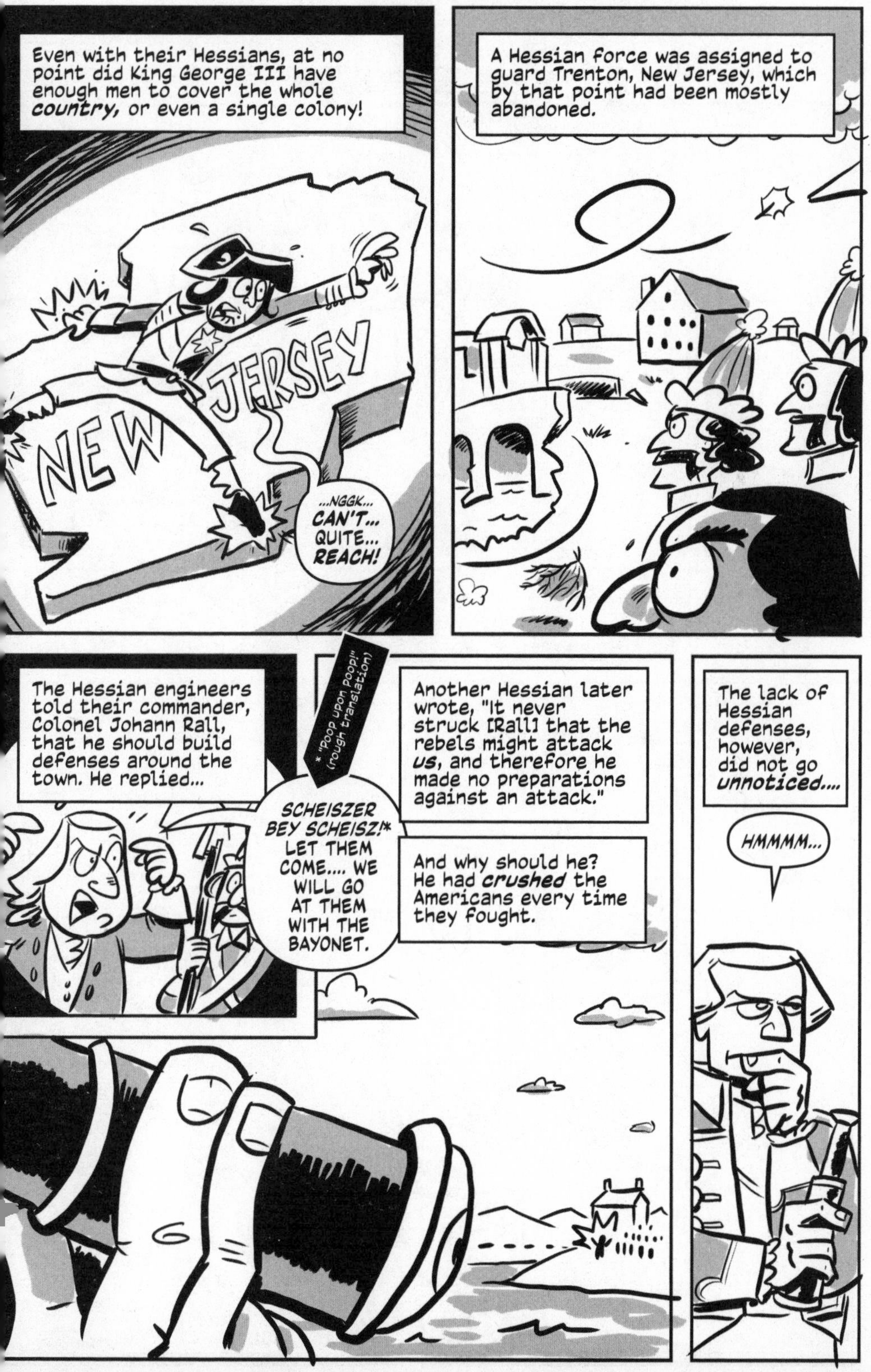
Even with their Hessians, at no point did King George III have enough men to cover the whole *country,* or even a single colony!
NEW JERSEY
...NGGK... CAN'T... QUITE... REACH!
A Hessian force was assigned to guard Trenton, New Jersey, which by that point had been mostly abandoned.
The Hessian engineers told their commander, Colonel Johann Rall, that he should build defenses around the town. He replied...
SCHEISZER BEY SCHEISZ!* LET THEM COME.... WE WILL GO AT THEM WITH THE BAYONET.
* "Poop upon poop!" (rough translation)
Another Hessian later wrote, "It never struck [Rall] that the rebels might attack *us*, and therefore he made no preparations against an attack."
And why should he? He had *crushed* the Americans every time they fought.
The lack of Hessian defenses, however, did not go *unnoticed....*
HMMMM...

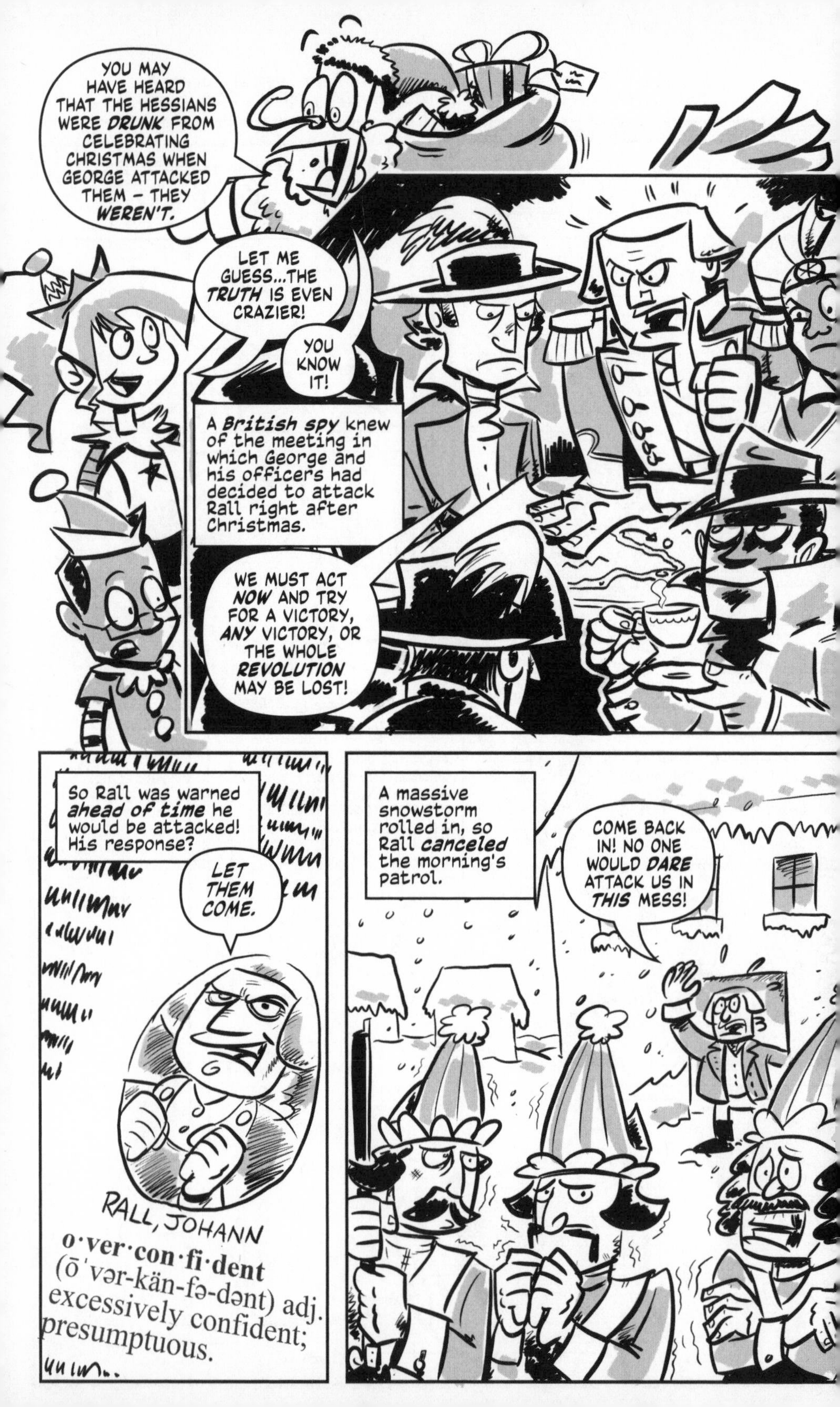

YOU MAY HAVE HEARD THAT THE HESSIANS WERE *DRUNK* FROM CELEBRATING CHRISTMAS WHEN GEORGE ATTACKED THEM – THEY *WEREN'T.*
LET ME GUESS...THE *TRUTH* IS EVEN CRAZIER!
YOU KNOW IT!
A *British spy* knew of the meeting in which George and his officers had decided to attack Rall right after Christmas.
WE MUST ACT *NOW* AND TRY FOR A VICTORY, *ANY* VICTORY, OR THE WHOLE *REVOLUTION* MAY BE LOST!
So Rall was warned *ahead of time* he would be attacked! His response?
LET THEM COME.
RALL, JOHANN
o·ver·con·fi·dent (ō´vər-kän-fə-dənt) adj. excessively confident; presumptuous.
A massive snowstorm rolled in, so Rall *canceled* the morning's patrol.
COME BACK IN! NO ONE WOULD *DARE* ATTACK US IN *THIS* MESS!

Washington's troops crossed the Delaware River in flat longboats, everyone having to ***stand*** to get as many people as possible on board.

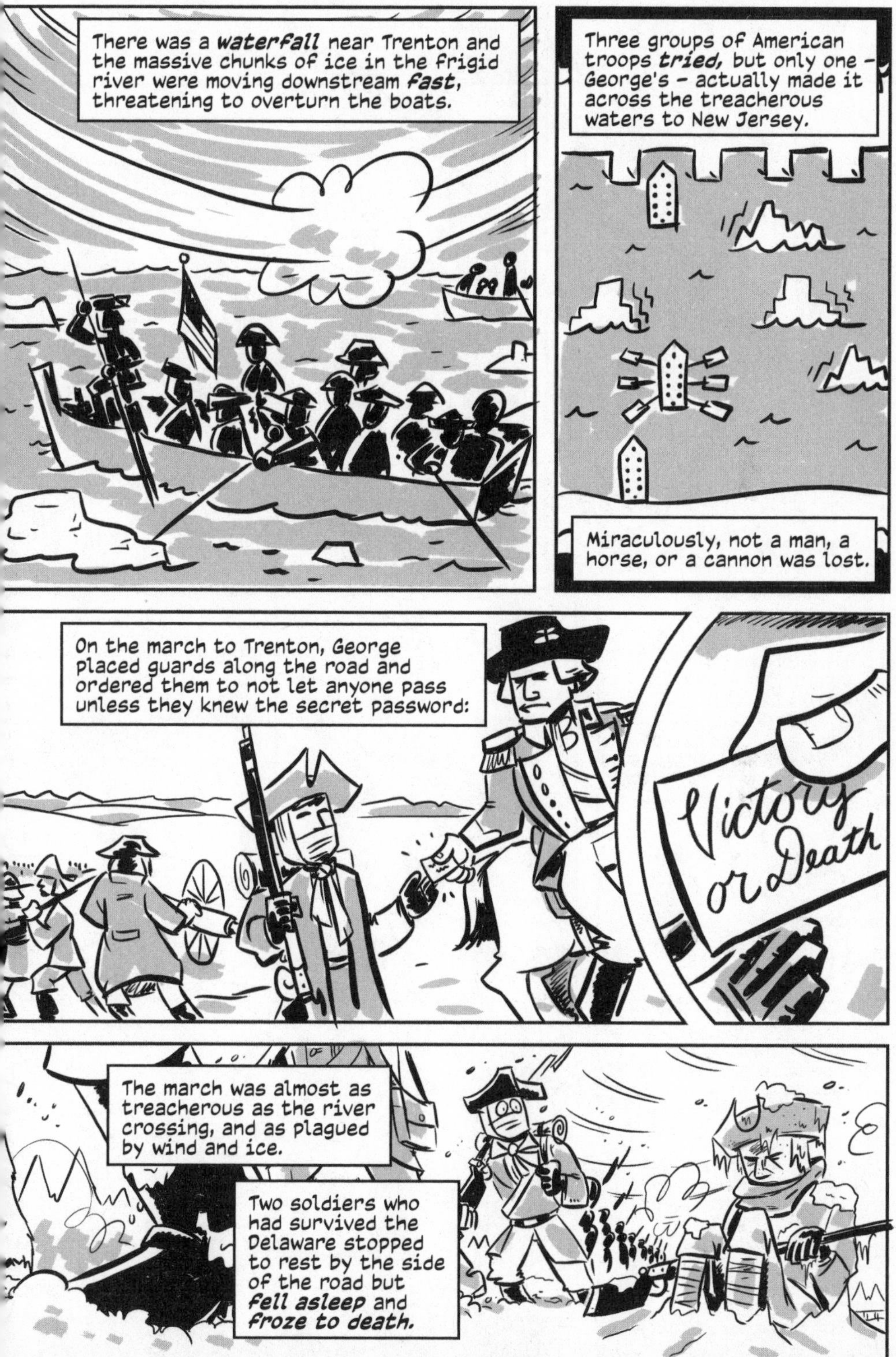
There was a waterfall near Trenton and the massive chunks of ice in the frigid river were moving downstream fast, threatening to overturn the boats.
Three groups of American troops tried, but only one - George's - actually made it across the treacherous waters to New Jersey.
Miraculously, not a man, a horse, or a cannon was lost.
On the march to Trenton, George placed guards along the road and ordered them to not let anyone pass unless they knew the secret password:
Victory or Death
The march was almost as treacherous as the river crossing, and as plagued by wind and ice.
Two soldiers who had survived the Delaware stopped to rest by the side of the road but fell asleep and froze to death.

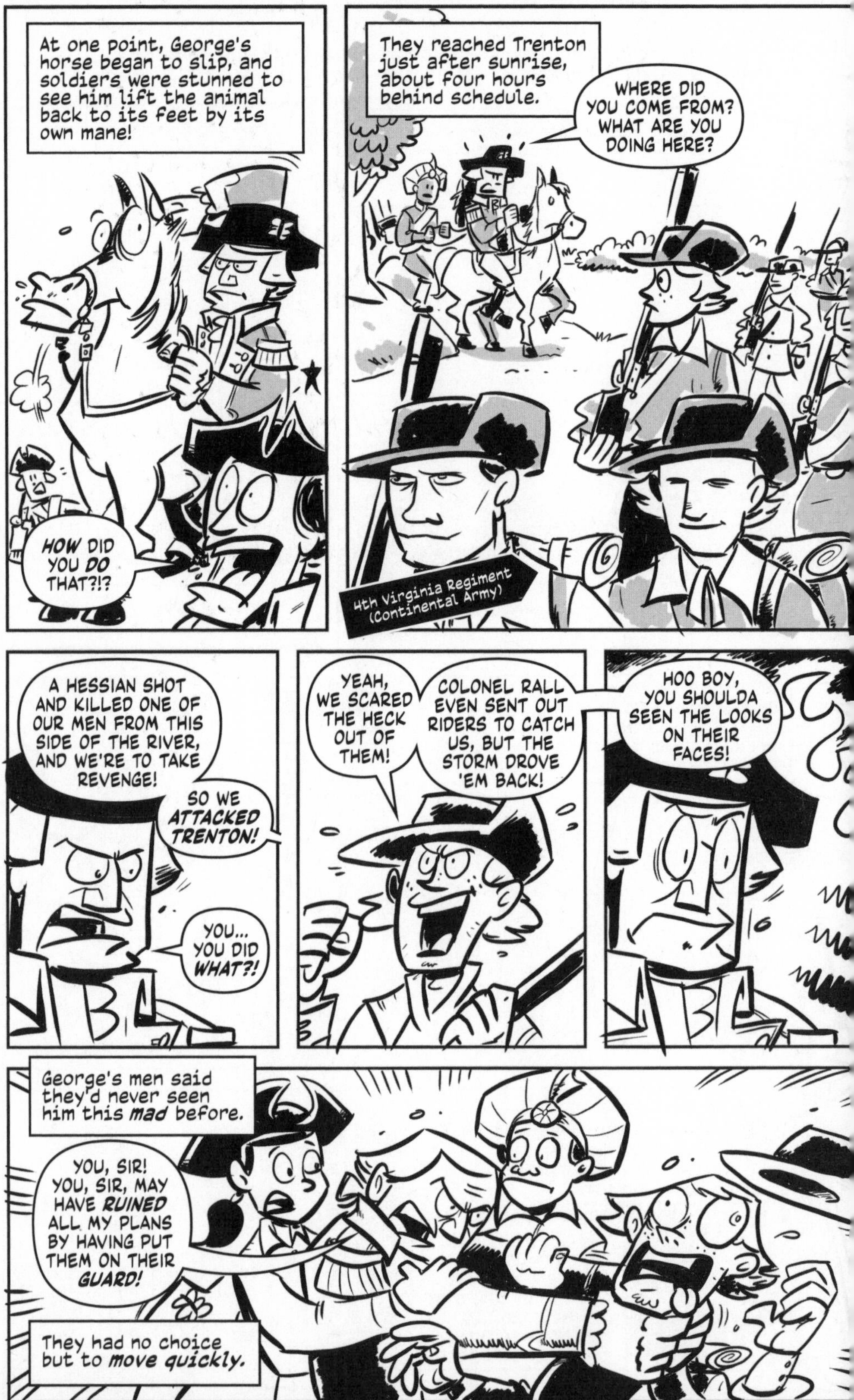
At one point, George's horse began to slip, and soldiers were stunned to see him lift the animal back to its feet by its own mane!
HOW DID YOU DO THAT?!?
They reached Trenton just after sunrise, about four hours behind schedule.
WHERE DID YOU COME FROM? WHAT ARE YOU DOING HERE?
4th Virginia Regiment (Continental Army)
A HESSIAN SHOT AND KILLED ONE OF OUR MEN FROM THIS SIDE OF THE RIVER, AND WE'RE TO TAKE REVENGE!
SO WE ATTACKED TRENTON!
YOU... YOU DID WHAT?!
YEAH, WE SCARED THE HECK OUT OF THEM!
COLONEL RALL EVEN SENT OUT RIDERS TO CATCH US, BUT THE STORM DROVE 'EM BACK!
HOO BOY, YOU SHOULDA SEEN THE LOOKS ON THEIR FACES!
George's men said they'd never seen him this mad before.
YOU, SIR! YOU, SIR, MAY HAVE RUINED ALL MY PLANS BY HAVING PUT THEM ON THEIR GUARD!
They had no choice but to move quickly.

THE BATTLE OF TRENTON

December 26, 1776:
Continentals vs. Hessians

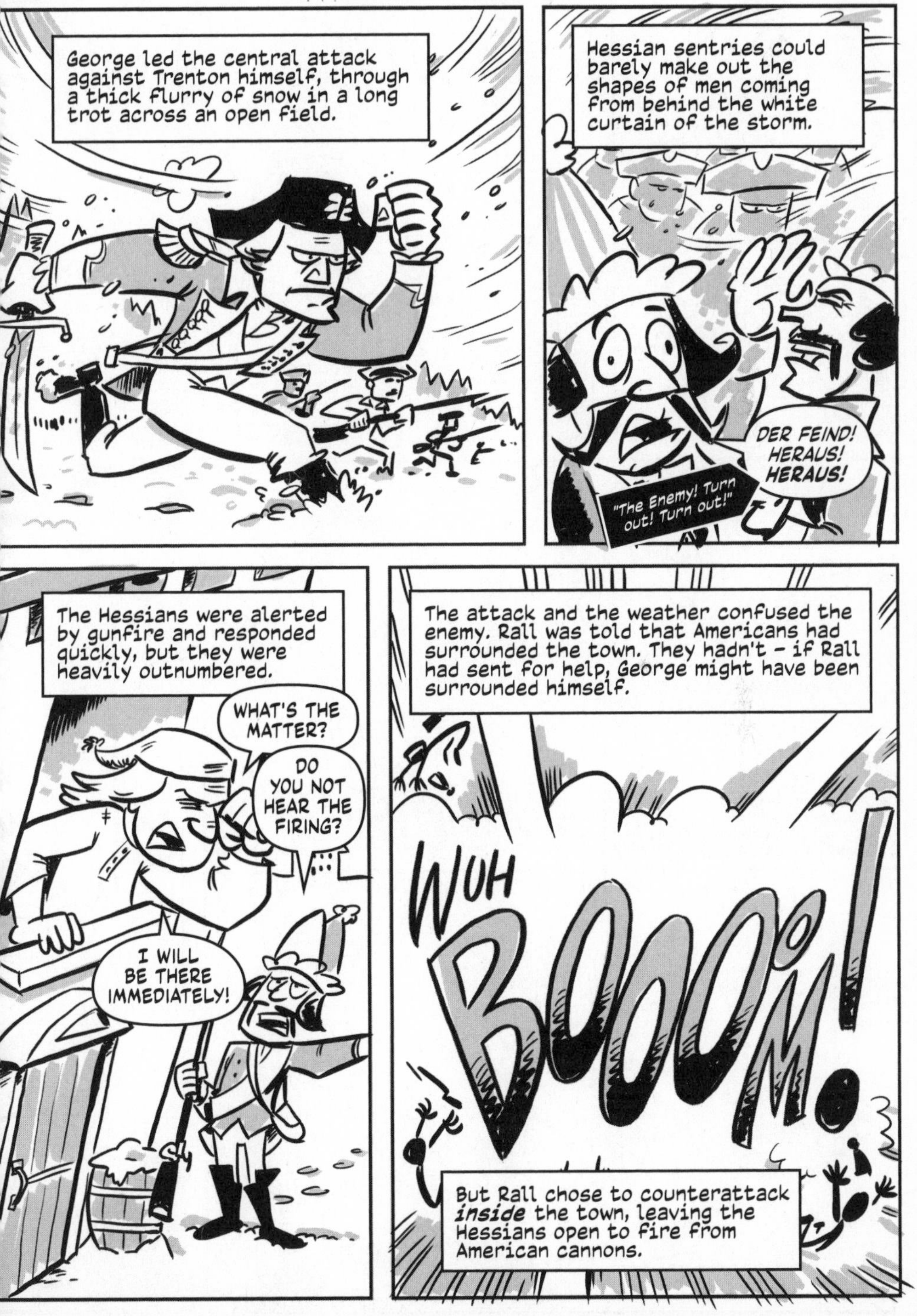
George led the central attack against Trenton himself, through a thick flurry of snow in a long trot across an open field.
Hessian sentries could barely make out the shapes of men coming from behind the white curtain of the storm.
DER FEIND! HERAUS! HERAUS!
"The Enemy! Turn out! Turn out!"
The Hessians were alerted by gunfire and responded quickly, but they were heavily outnumbered.
WHAT'S THE MATTER?
DO YOU NOT HEAR THE FIRING?
I WILL BE THERE IMMEDIATELY!
The attack and the weather confused the enemy. Rall was told that Americans had surrounded the town. They hadn't - if Rall had sent for help, George might have been surrounded himself.
WUH BOOOOM!
But Rall chose to counterattack *inside* the town, leaving the Hessians open to fire from American cannons.

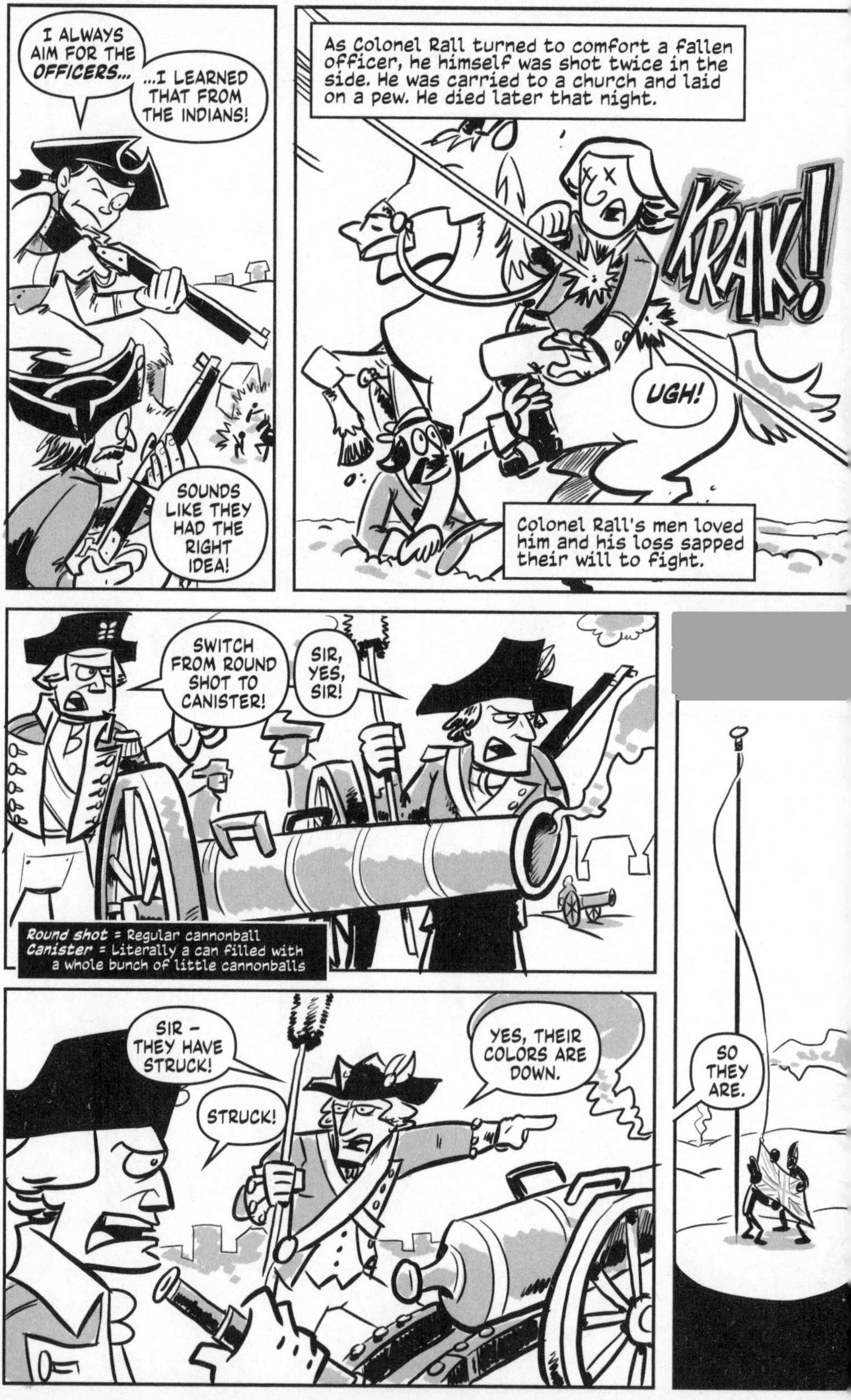

I ALWAYS AIM FOR THE *OFFICERS...*
...I LEARNED THAT FROM THE INDIANS!
SOUNDS LIKE THEY HAD THE RIGHT IDEA!
As Colonel Rall turned to comfort a fallen officer, he himself was shot twice in the side. He was carried to a church and laid on a pew. He died later that night.
KRAK!
UGH!
Colonel Rall's men loved him and his loss sapped their will to fight.
SWITCH FROM ROUND SHOT TO CANISTER!
SIR, YES, SIR!
Round shot = Regular cannonball
Canister = Literally a can filled with a whole bunch of little cannonballs
SIR – THEY HAVE STRUCK!
STRUCK!
YES, THEIR COLORS ARE DOWN.
SO THEY ARE.

All the Hessians surrendered. The Americans didn't lose a single man in the fight.

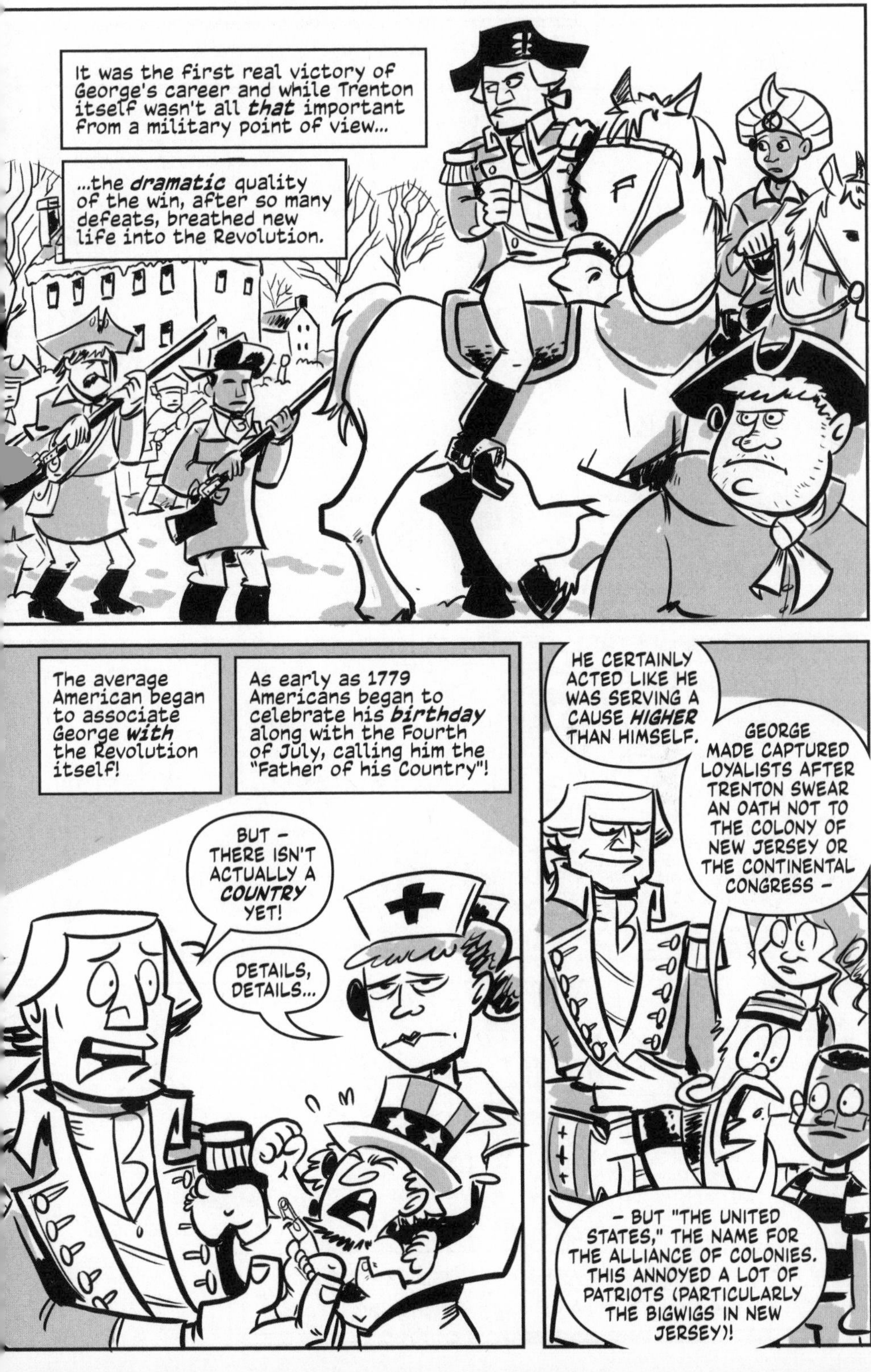
It was the first real victory of George's career and while Trenton itself wasn't all *that* important from a military point of view...
...the *dramatic* quality of the win, after so many defeats, breathed new life into the Revolution.
The average American began to associate George *with* the Revolution itself!
As early as 1779 Americans began to celebrate his *birthday* along with the Fourth of July, calling him the "Father of his Country"!
BUT – THERE ISN'T ACTUALLY A *COUNTRY* YET!
DETAILS, DETAILS...
HE CERTAINLY ACTED LIKE HE WAS SERVING A CAUSE *HIGHER* THAN HIMSELF.
GEORGE MADE CAPTURED LOYALISTS AFTER TRENTON SWEAR AN OATH NOT TO THE COLONY OF NEW JERSEY OR THE CONTINENTAL CONGRESS –
– BUT "THE UNITED STATES," THE NAME FOR THE ALLIANCE OF COLONIES. THIS ANNOYED A LOT OF PATRIOTS (PARTICULARLY THE BIGWIGS IN NEW JERSEY)!

In those days, wars typically took ***winter breaks*** because the weather made it too hard to fight (that's partly why George's attack on Trenton was so unusual).

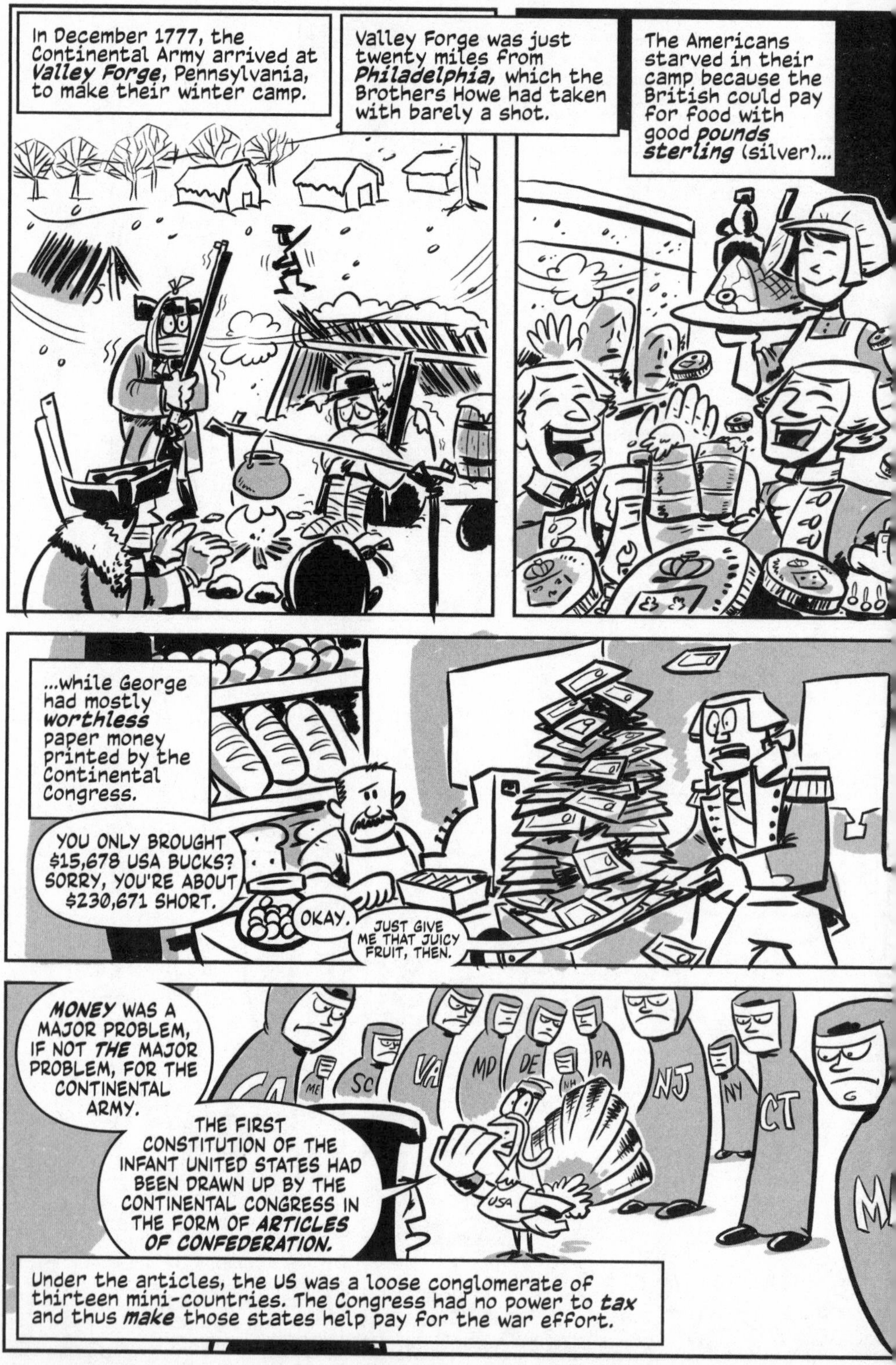
In December 1777, the Continental Army arrived at Valley Forge, Pennsylvania, to make their winter camp.
Valley Forge was just twenty miles from Philadelphia, which the Brothers Howe had taken with barely a shot.
The Americans starved in their camp because the British could pay for food with good pounds sterling (silver)...
...while George had mostly worthless paper money printed by the Continental Congress.
YOU ONLY BROUGHT $15,678 USA BUCKS? SORRY, YOU'RE ABOUT $230,671 SHORT.
OKAY.
JUST GIVE ME THAT JUICY FRUIT, THEN.
MONEY WAS A MAJOR PROBLEM, IF NOT THE MAJOR PROBLEM, FOR THE CONTINENTAL ARMY.
THE FIRST CONSTITUTION OF THE INFANT UNITED STATES HAD BEEN DRAWN UP BY THE CONTINENTAL CONGRESS IN THE FORM OF ARTICLES OF CONFEDERATION.
ME
SC
VA
MD
DE
NH
PA
NJ
NY
CT
USA
Under the articles, the US was a loose conglomerate of thirteen mini-countries. The Congress had no power to tax and thus make those states help pay for the war effort.

But hardship can ***strengthen*** the bonds between people who experience it ***together***. That's just what happened at Valley Forge!

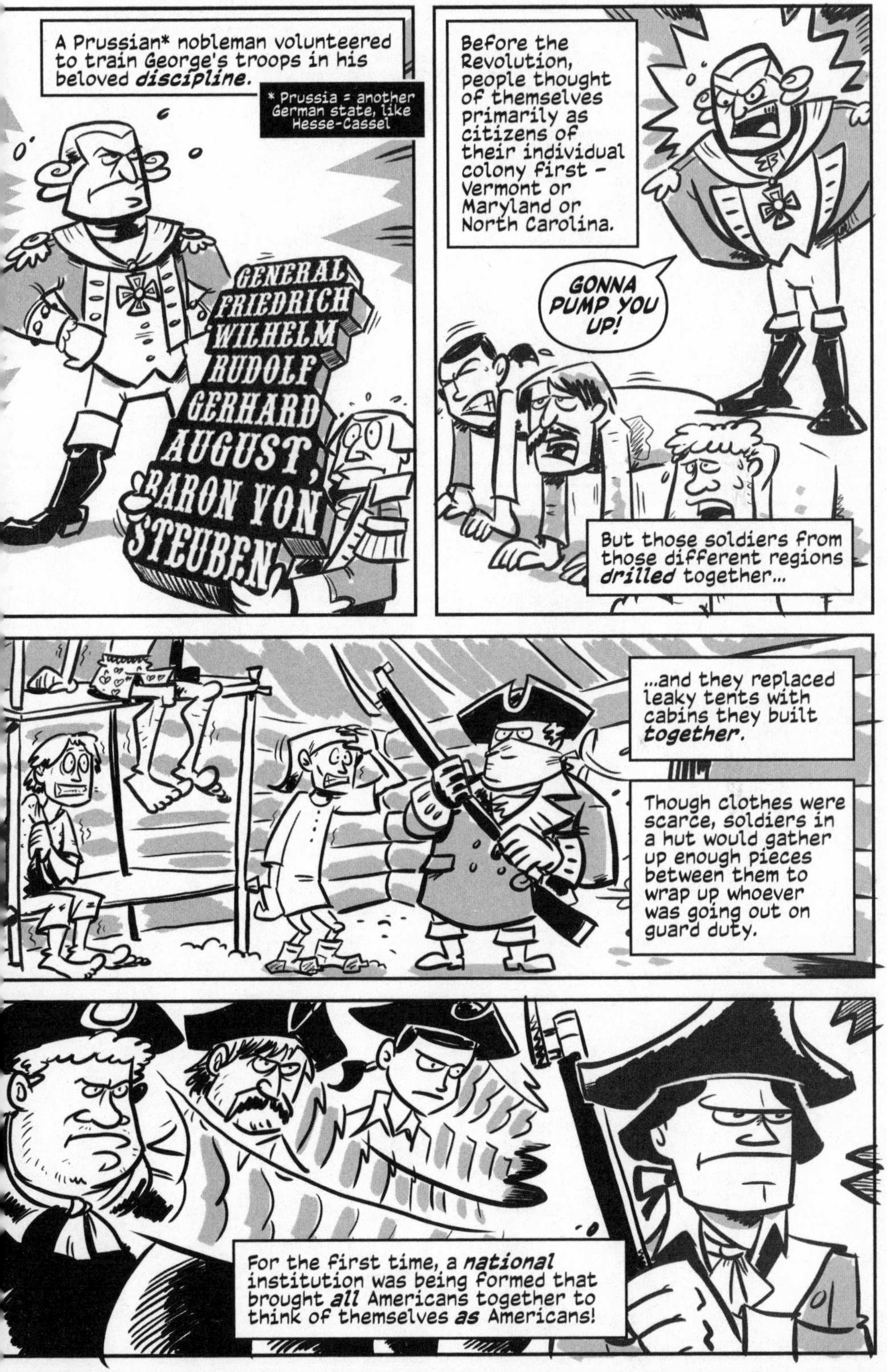
A Prussian* nobleman volunteered to train George's troops in his beloved *discipline*.
* Prussia = another German state, like Hesse-Cassel
GENERAL FRIEDRICH WILHELM RUDOLF GERHARD AUGUST, BARON VON STEUBEN
Before the Revolution, people thought of themselves primarily as citizens of their individual colony first – Vermont or Maryland or North Carolina.
GONNA PUMP YOU UP!
But those soldiers from those different regions *drilled* together...
...and they replaced leaky tents with cabins they built *together*.
Though clothes were scarce, soldiers in a hut would gather up enough pieces between them to wrap up whoever was going out on guard duty.
For the first time, a *national* institution was being formed that brought *all* Americans together to think of themselves *as* Americans!

Valley Forge ended up being a happy time for George, too, because Martha came up from Mount Vernon to spend the winter with him.

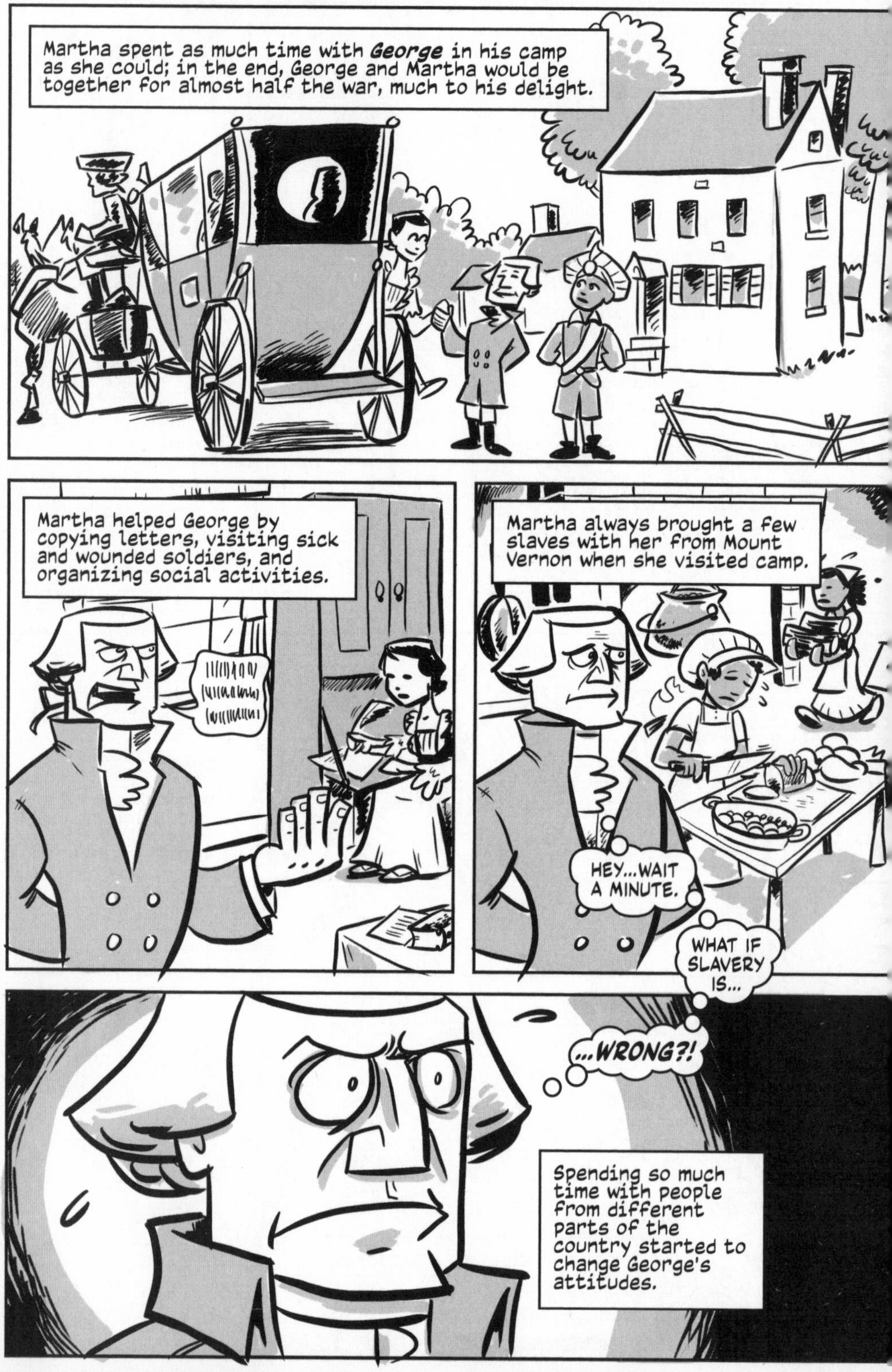
Martha spent as much time with *George* in his camp as she could; in the end, George and Martha would be together for almost half the war, much to his delight.
Martha helped George by copying letters, visiting sick and wounded soldiers, and organizing social activities.
Martha always brought a few slaves with her from Mount Vernon when she visited camp.
HEY...WAIT A MINUTE.
WHAT IF SLAVERY IS...
...WRONG?!
Spending so much time with people from different parts of the country started to change George's attitudes.

George had been born into a world where ***slaveholding*** was the norm.
He had owned human beings since he was ***eleven years old.***

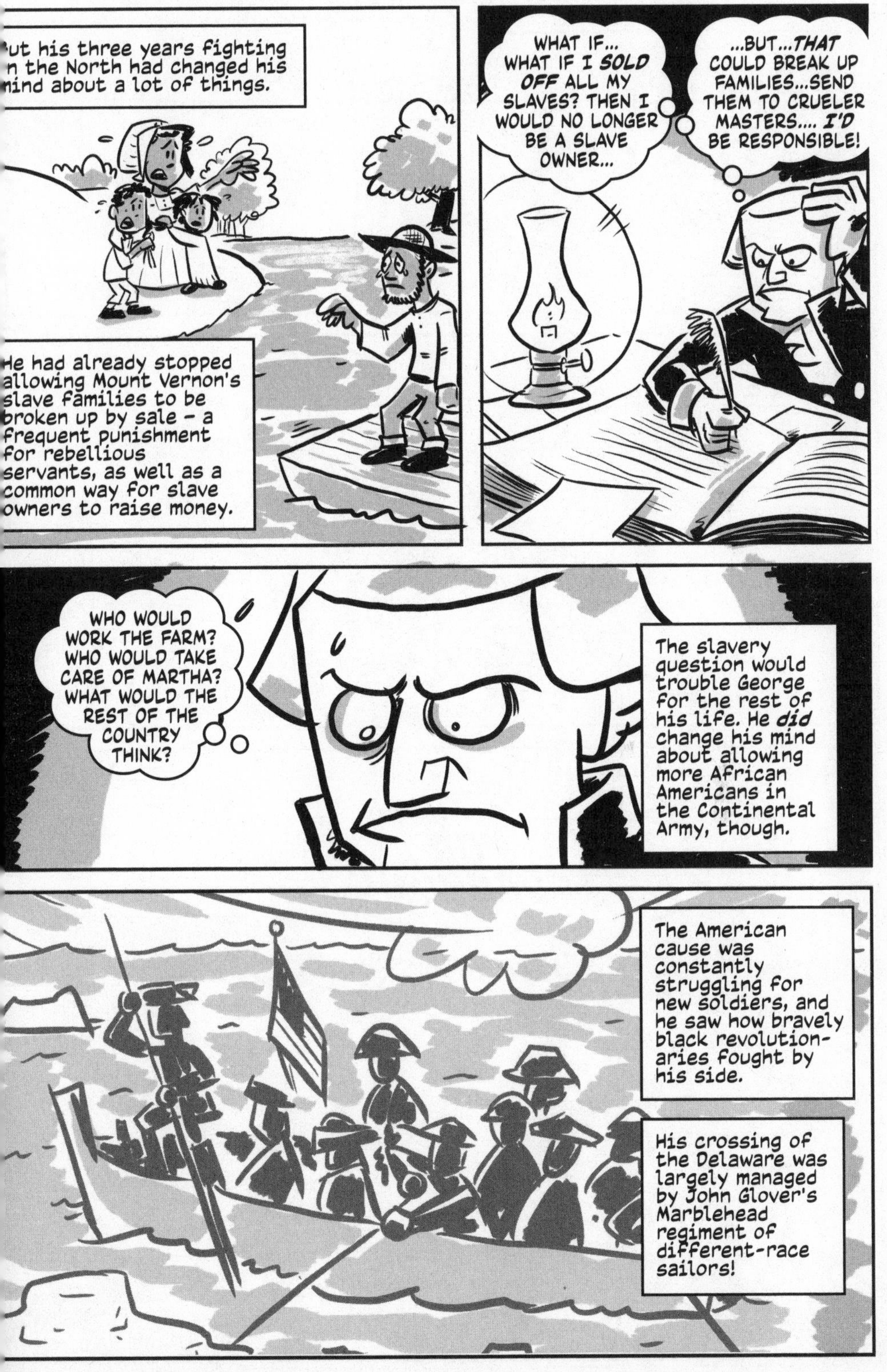

ut his three years fighting
n the North had changed his
mind about a lot of things.
He had already stopped
allowing Mount Vernon's
slave families to be
broken up by sale - a
frequent punishment
for rebellious
servants, as well as a
common way for slave
owners to raise money.
WHAT IF... WHAT IF I SOLD OFF ALL MY SLAVES? THEN I WOULD NO LONGER BE A SLAVE OWNER...
...BUT...THAT COULD BREAK UP FAMILIES...SEND THEM TO CRUELER MASTERS.... I'D BE RESPONSIBLE!
WHO WOULD WORK THE FARM? WHO WOULD TAKE CARE OF MARTHA? WHAT WOULD THE REST OF THE COUNTRY THINK?
The slavery question would trouble George for the rest of his life. He did change his mind about allowing more African Americans in the Continental Army, though.
The American cause was constantly struggling for new soldiers, and he saw how bravely black revolutionaries fought by his side.
His crossing of the Delaware was largely managed by John Glover's Marblehead regiment of different-race sailors!

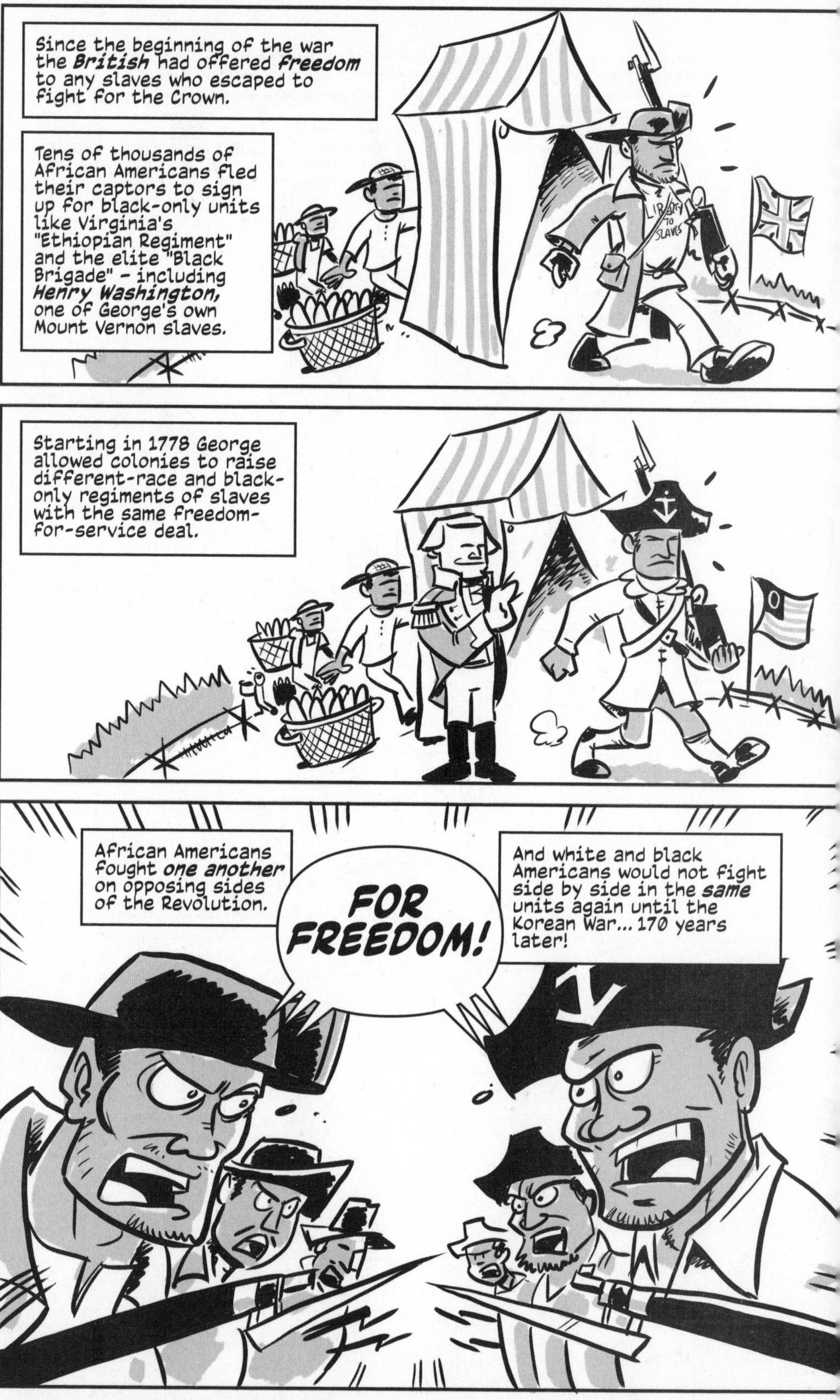
Since the beginning of the war the ***British*** had offered ***freedom*** to any slaves who escaped to fight for the Crown.
Tens of thousands of African Americans fled their captors to sign up for black-only units like Virginia's "Ethiopian Regiment" and the elite "Black Brigade" – including ***Henry Washington,*** one of George's own Mount Vernon slaves.
LIBERTY TO SLAVES
Starting in 1778 George allowed colonies to raise different-race and black-only regiments of slaves with the same freedom-for-service deal.
African Americans fought ***one another*** on opposing sides of the Revolution.
FOR FREEDOM!
And white and black Americans would not fight side by side in the ***same*** units again until the Korean War... 170 years later!

More help was on the way. After a major American victory, the French king, Louis XVI, agreed to join the war on the colonies' side. The American Revolution was now a ***world war!***

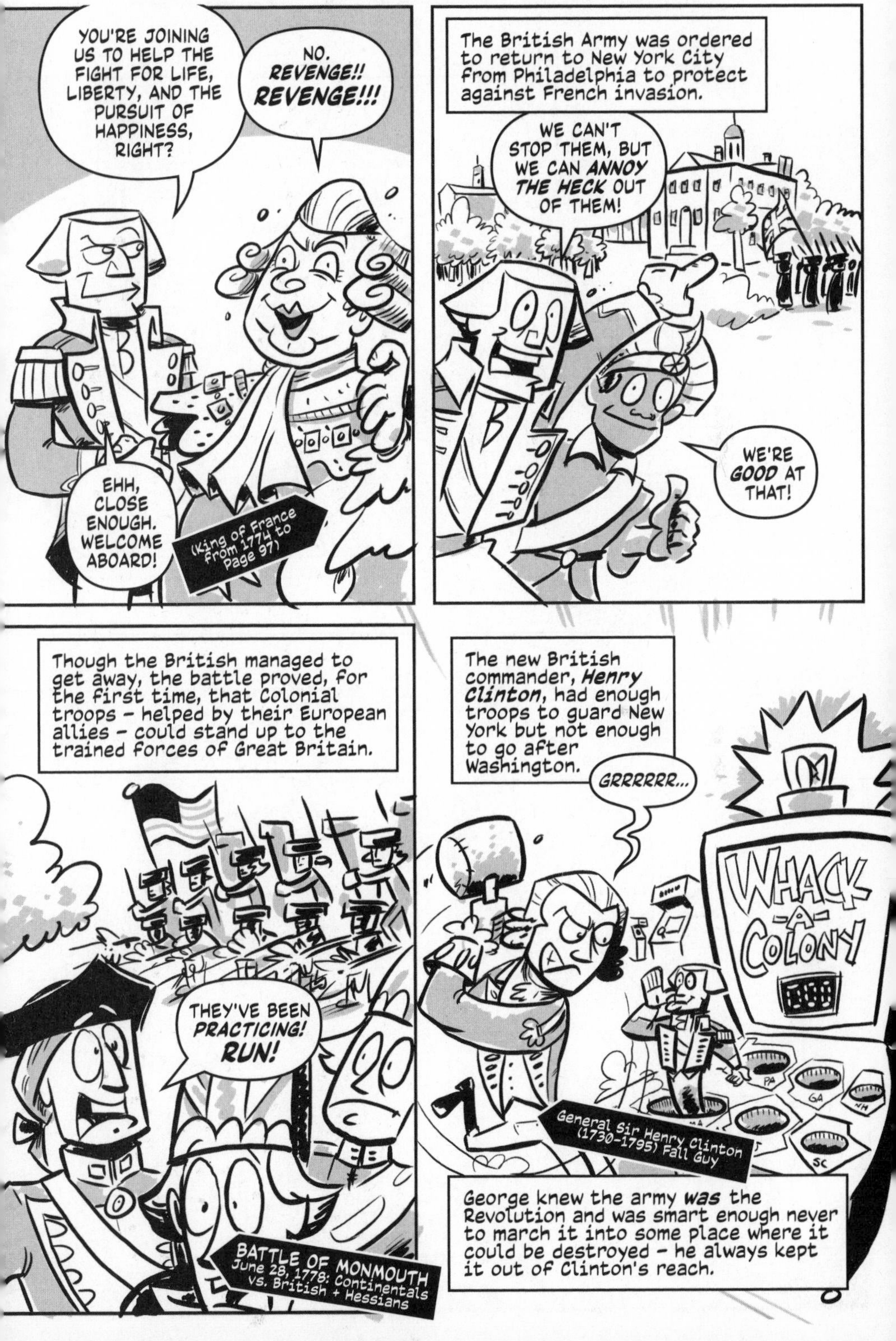
YOU'RE JOINING US TO HELP THE FIGHT FOR LIFE, LIBERTY, AND THE PURSUIT OF HAPPINESS, RIGHT?
NO. REVENGE!! REVENGE!!!
EHH, CLOSE ENOUGH. WELCOME ABOARD!
(King of France from 1774 to Page 97)
The British Army was ordered to return to New York City from Philadelphia to protect against French invasion.
WE CAN'T STOP THEM, BUT WE CAN ANNOY THE HECK OUT OF THEM!
WE'RE GOOD AT THAT!
Though the British managed to get away, the battle proved, for the first time, that Colonial troops – helped by their European allies – could stand up to the trained forces of Great Britain.
THEY'VE BEEN PRACTICING! RUN!
BATTLE OF MONMOUTH
June 28, 1778: Continentals vs. British + Hessians
The new British commander, Henry Clinton, had enough troops to guard New York but not enough to go after Washington.
GRRRRRR...
WHACK-A-COLONY
PA
GA
NH
SC
General Sir Henry Clinton (1730–1795) Fall Guy
George knew the army was the Revolution and was smart enough never to march it into some place where it could be destroyed – he always kept it out of Clinton's reach.

Instead, Clinton decided to send a third of his army ***south.*** The South was believed to be more loyal to the Crown than the rest of the country, so they thought it would be easier to conquer.

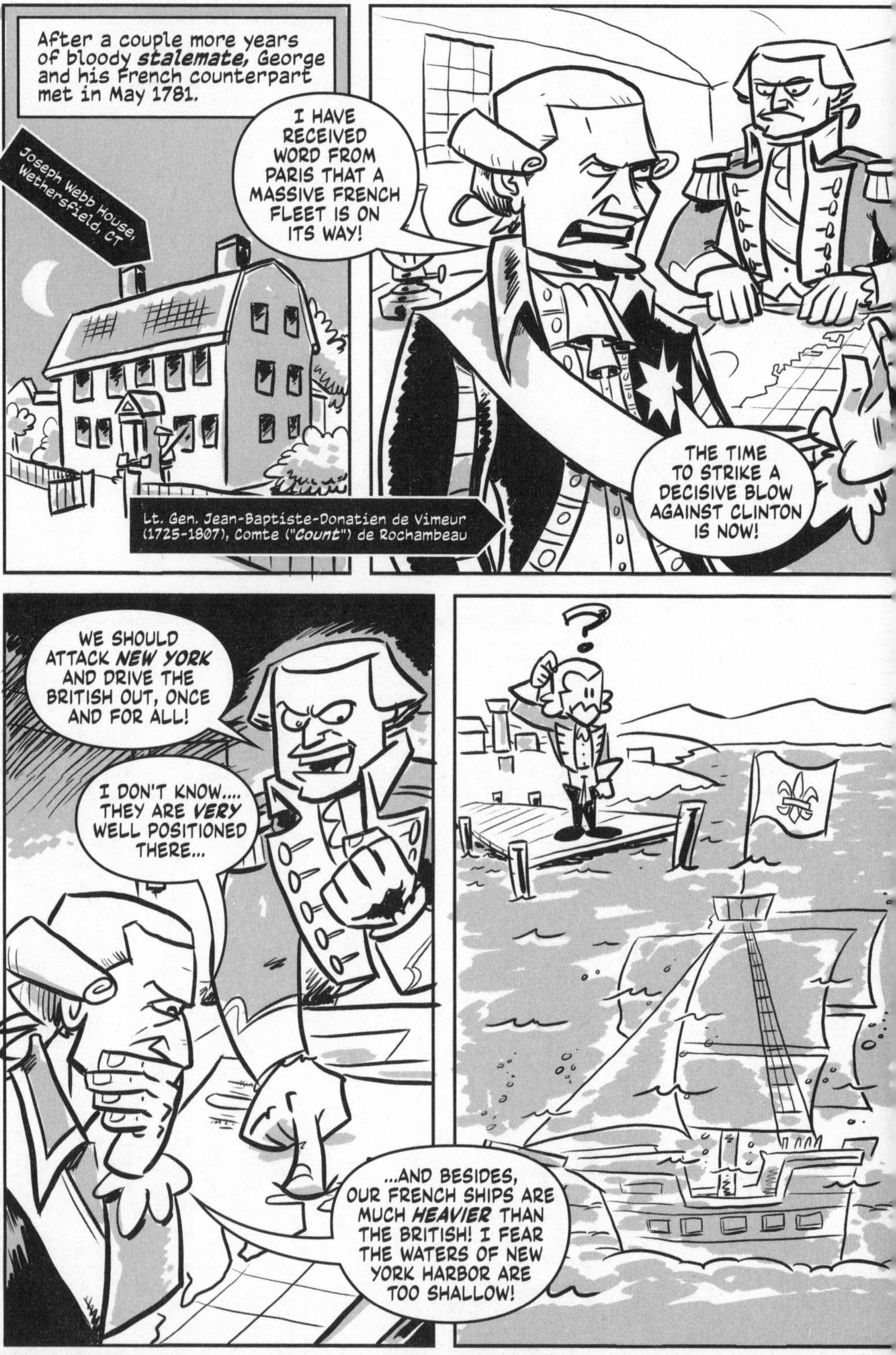
After a couple more years of bloody ***stalemate,*** George and his French counterpart met in May 1781.
Joseph Webb House, Wethersfield, CT
I HAVE RECEIVED WORD FROM PARIS THAT A MASSIVE FRENCH FLEET IS ON ITS WAY!
Lt. Gen. Jean-Baptiste-Donatien de Vimeur (1725-1807), Comte ("*Count*") de Rochambeau
THE TIME TO STRIKE A DECISIVE BLOW AGAINST CLINTON IS NOW!
WE SHOULD ATTACK ***NEW YORK*** AND DRIVE THE BRITISH OUT, ONCE AND FOR ALL!
I DON'T KNOW.... THEY ARE ***VERY*** WELL POSITIONED THERE...
...AND BESIDES, OUR FRENCH SHIPS ARE MUCH ***HEAVIER*** THAN THE BRITISH! I FEAR THE WATERS OF NEW YORK HARBOR ARE TOO SHALLOW!
?

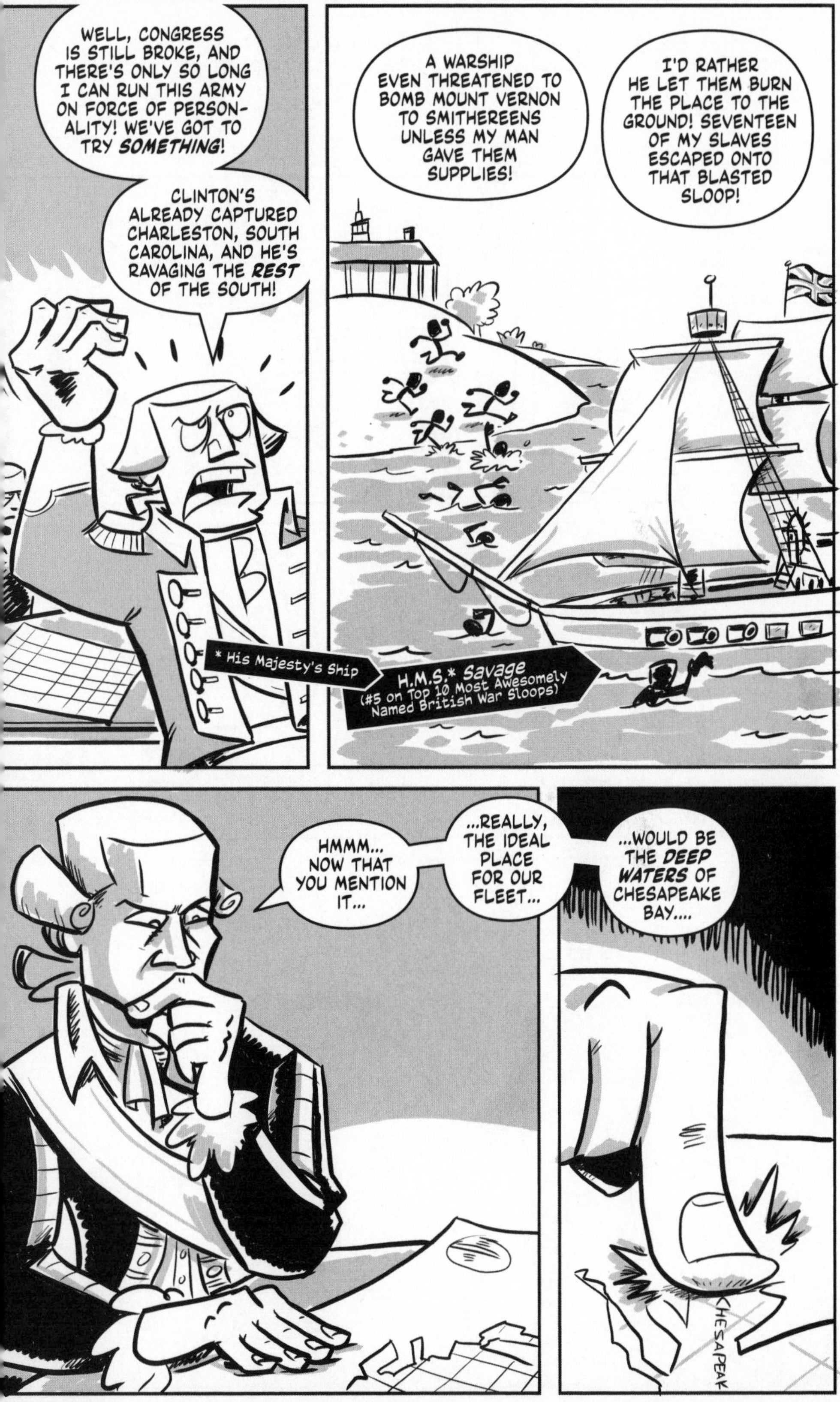
WELL, CONGRESS IS STILL BROKE, AND THERE'S ONLY SO LONG I CAN RUN THIS ARMY ON FORCE OF PERSON-ALITY! WE'VE GOT TO TRY SOMETHING!
CLINTON'S ALREADY CAPTURED CHARLESTON, SOUTH CAROLINA, AND HE'S RAVAGING THE REST OF THE SOUTH!
A WARSHIP EVEN THREATENED TO BOMB MOUNT VERNON TO SMITHEREENS UNLESS MY MAN GAVE THEM SUPPLIES!
I'D RATHER HE LET THEM BURN THE PLACE TO THE GROUND! SEVENTEEN OF MY SLAVES ESCAPED ONTO THAT BLASTED SLOOP!
* His Majesty's Ship
H.M.S.* Savage
(#5 on Top 10 Most Awesomely Named British War Sloops)
HMMM... NOW THAT YOU MENTION IT...
...REALLY, THE IDEAL PLACE FOR OUR FLEET...
...WOULD BE THE DEEP WATERS OF CHESAPEAKE BAY....
CHESAPEAK

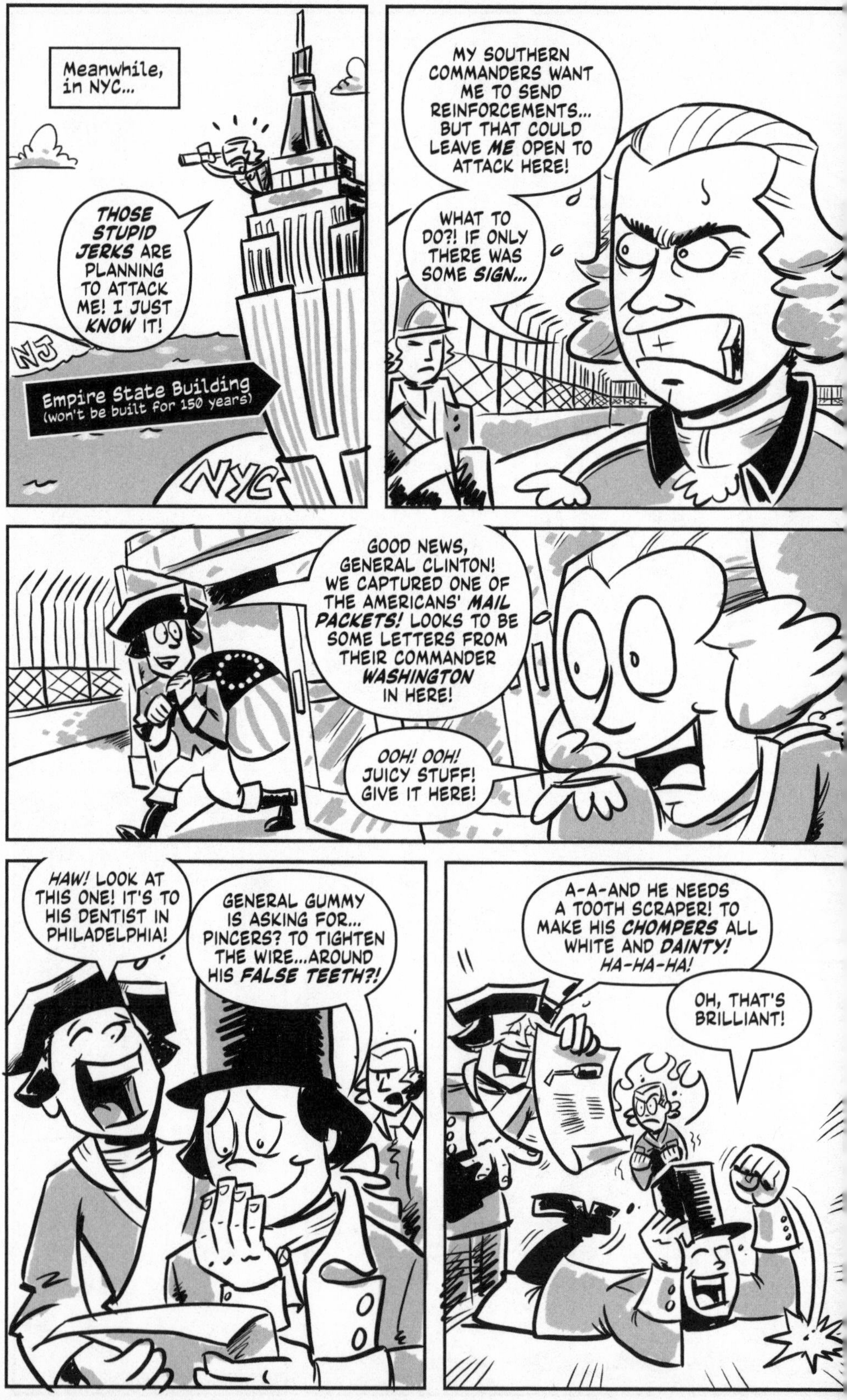
Meanwhile, in NYC...
THOSE STUPID JERKS ARE PLANNING TO ATTACK ME! I JUST KNOW IT!
NJ
Empire State Building (won't be built for 150 years)
NYC
MY SOUTHERN COMMANDERS WANT ME TO SEND REINFORCEMENTS... BUT THAT COULD LEAVE ME OPEN TO ATTACK HERE!
WHAT TO DO?! IF ONLY THERE WAS SOME SIGN...
GOOD NEWS, GENERAL CLINTON! WE CAPTURED ONE OF THE AMERICANS' MAIL PACKETS! LOOKS TO BE SOME LETTERS FROM THEIR COMMANDER WASHINGTON IN HERE!
OOH! OOH! JUICY STUFF! GIVE IT HERE!
HAW! LOOK AT THIS ONE! IT'S TO HIS DENTIST IN PHILADELPHIA!
GENERAL GUMMY IS ASKING FOR... PINCERS? TO TIGHTEN THE WIRE...AROUND HIS FALSE TEETH?!
A-A-AND HE NEEDS A TOOTH SCRAPER! TO MAKE HIS CHOMPERS ALL WHITE AND DAINTY! HA-HA-HA!
OH, THAT'S BRILLIANT!

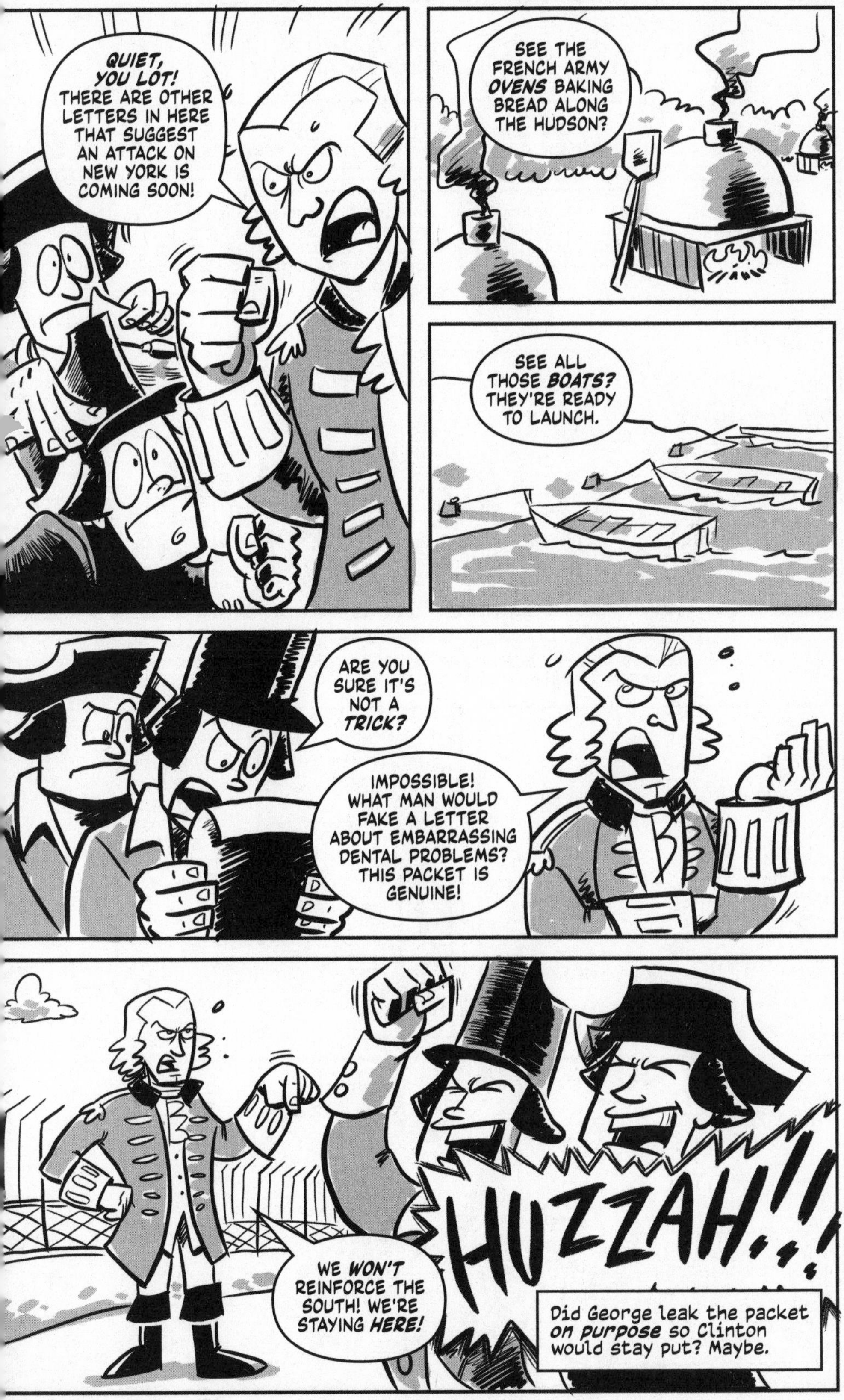
QUIET, YOU LOT! THERE ARE OTHER LETTERS IN HERE THAT SUGGEST AN ATTACK ON NEW YORK IS COMING SOON!
SEE THE FRENCH ARMY OVENS BAKING BREAD ALONG THE HUDSON?
SEE ALL THOSE BOATS? THEY'RE READY TO LAUNCH.
ARE YOU SURE IT'S NOT A TRICK?
IMPOSSIBLE! WHAT MAN WOULD FAKE A LETTER ABOUT EMBARRASSING DENTAL PROBLEMS? THIS PACKET IS GENUINE!
WE WON'T REINFORCE THE SOUTH! WE'RE STAYING HERE!
HUZZAH!!!
Did George leak the packet on purpose so Clinton would stay put? Maybe.

SIEGE of YORKTOWN

September 28 - October 19, 1781:
Continentals + French vs. British + Hessians.

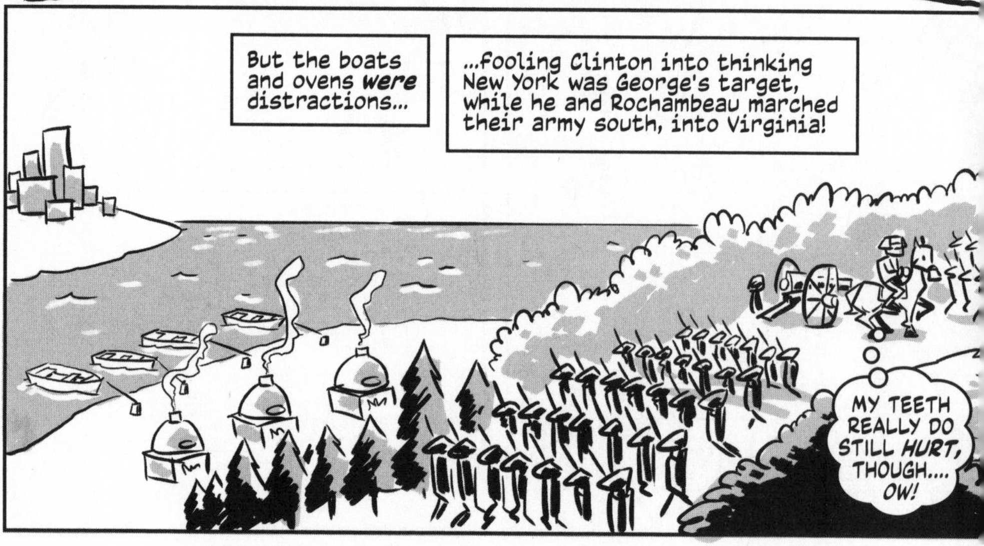
But the boats and ovens *were* distractions...
...fooling Clinton into thinking New York was George's target, while he and Rochambeau marched their army south, into Virginia!
MY TEETH REALLY DO STILL *HURT,* THOUGH.... *OW!*

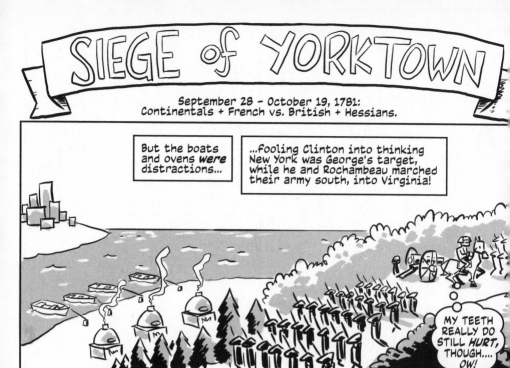

In the end, it was the admiral of the French Navy who decided to head to the Chesapeake Bay in Virginia, to prevent the southern British Army from escaping or being resupplied.

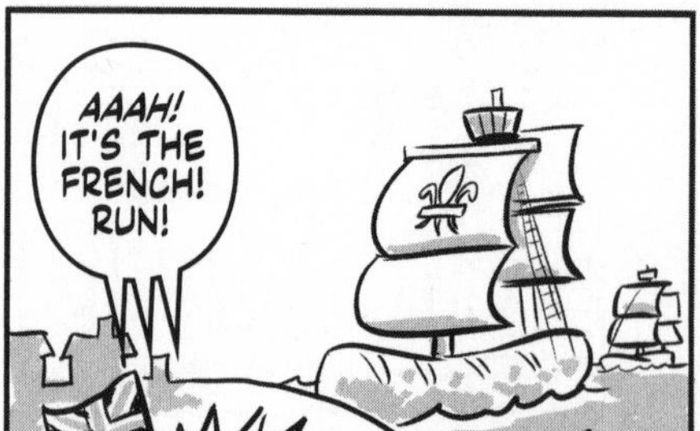
AAAH! IT'S THE FRENCH! RUN!

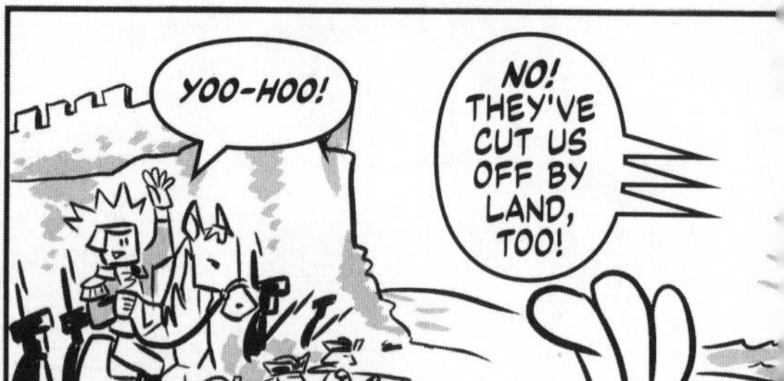
YOO-HOO!
NO! THEY'VE CUT US OFF BY LAND, TOO!

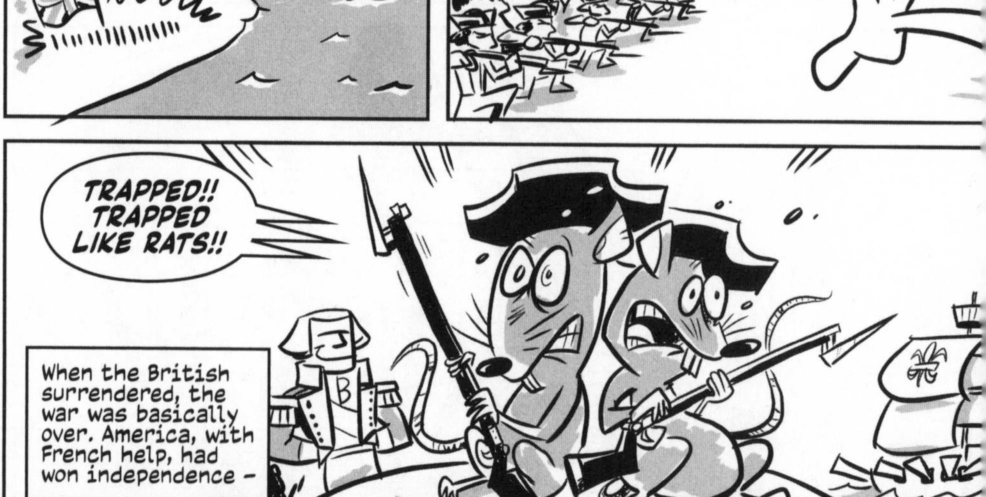
TRAPPED!! TRAPPED LIKE RATS!!
When the British surrendered, the war was basically over. America, with French help, had won independence -

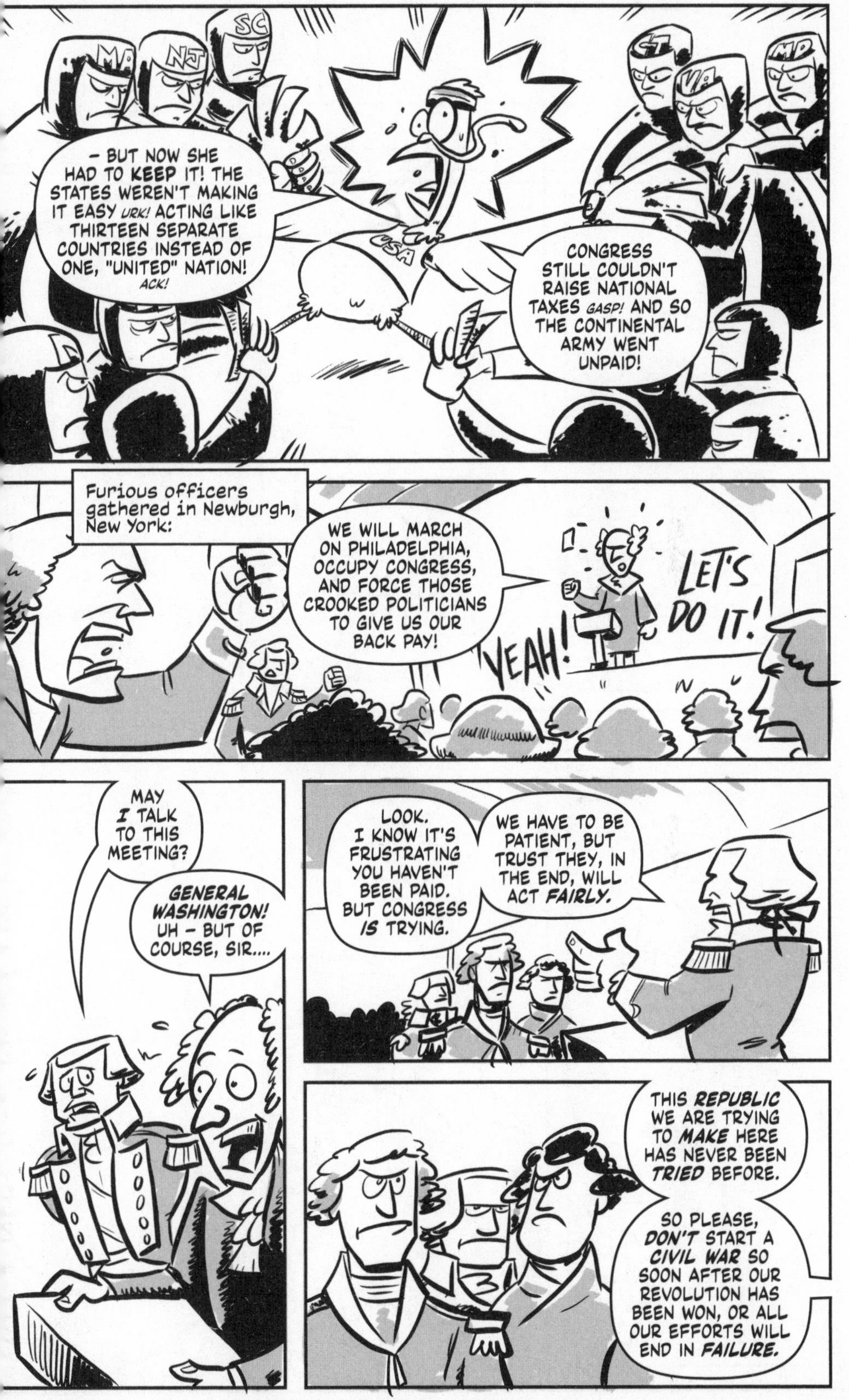

MA
NJ
SC
CT
VA
MD
– BUT NOW SHE HAD TO KEEP IT! THE STATES WEREN'T MAKING IT EASY URK! ACTING LIKE THIRTEEN SEPARATE COUNTRIES INSTEAD OF ONE, "UNITED" NATION! ACK!
USA
CONGRESS STILL COULDN'T RAISE NATIONAL TAXES GASP! AND SO THE CONTINENTAL ARMY WENT UNPAID!
Furious officers gathered in Newburgh, New York:
WE WILL MARCH ON PHILADELPHIA, OCCUPY CONGRESS, AND FORCE THOSE CROOKED POLITICIANS TO GIVE US OUR BACK PAY!
YEAH!
LET'S DO IT!
MAY I TALK TO THIS MEETING?
GENERAL WASHINGTON! UH – BUT OF COURSE, SIR....
LOOK. I KNOW IT'S FRUSTRATING YOU HAVEN'T BEEN PAID. BUT CONGRESS IS TRYING.
WE HAVE TO BE PATIENT, BUT TRUST THEY, IN THE END, WILL ACT FAIRLY.
THIS REPUBLIC WE ARE TRYING TO MAKE HERE HAS NEVER BEEN TRIED BEFORE.
SO PLEASE, DON'T START A CIVIL WAR SO SOON AFTER OUR REVOLUTION HAS BEEN WON, OR ALL OUR EFFORTS WILL END IN FAILURE.

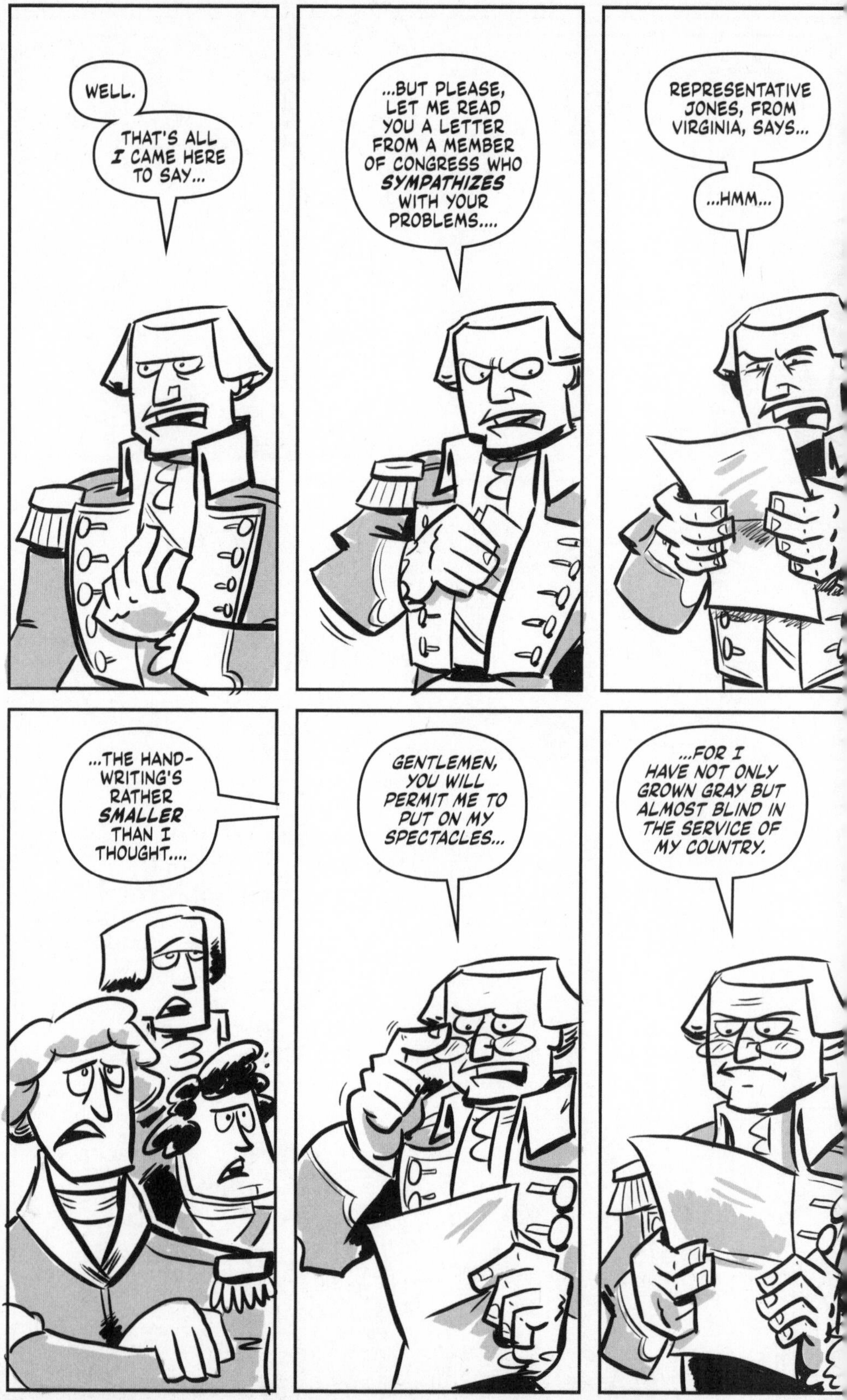
WELL.
THAT'S ALL *I* CAME HERE TO SAY...
...BUT PLEASE, LET ME READ YOU A LETTER FROM A MEMBER OF CONGRESS WHO **SYMPATHIZES** WITH YOUR PROBLEMS....
REPRESENTATIVE JONES, FROM VIRGINIA, SAYS...
...HMM...
...THE HAND-WRITING'S RATHER **SMALLER** THAN I THOUGHT....
GENTLEMEN, YOU WILL PERMIT ME TO PUT ON MY SPECTACLES...
...FOR I HAVE NOT ONLY GROWN GRAY BUT ALMOST BLIND IN THE SERVICE OF MY COUNTRY.

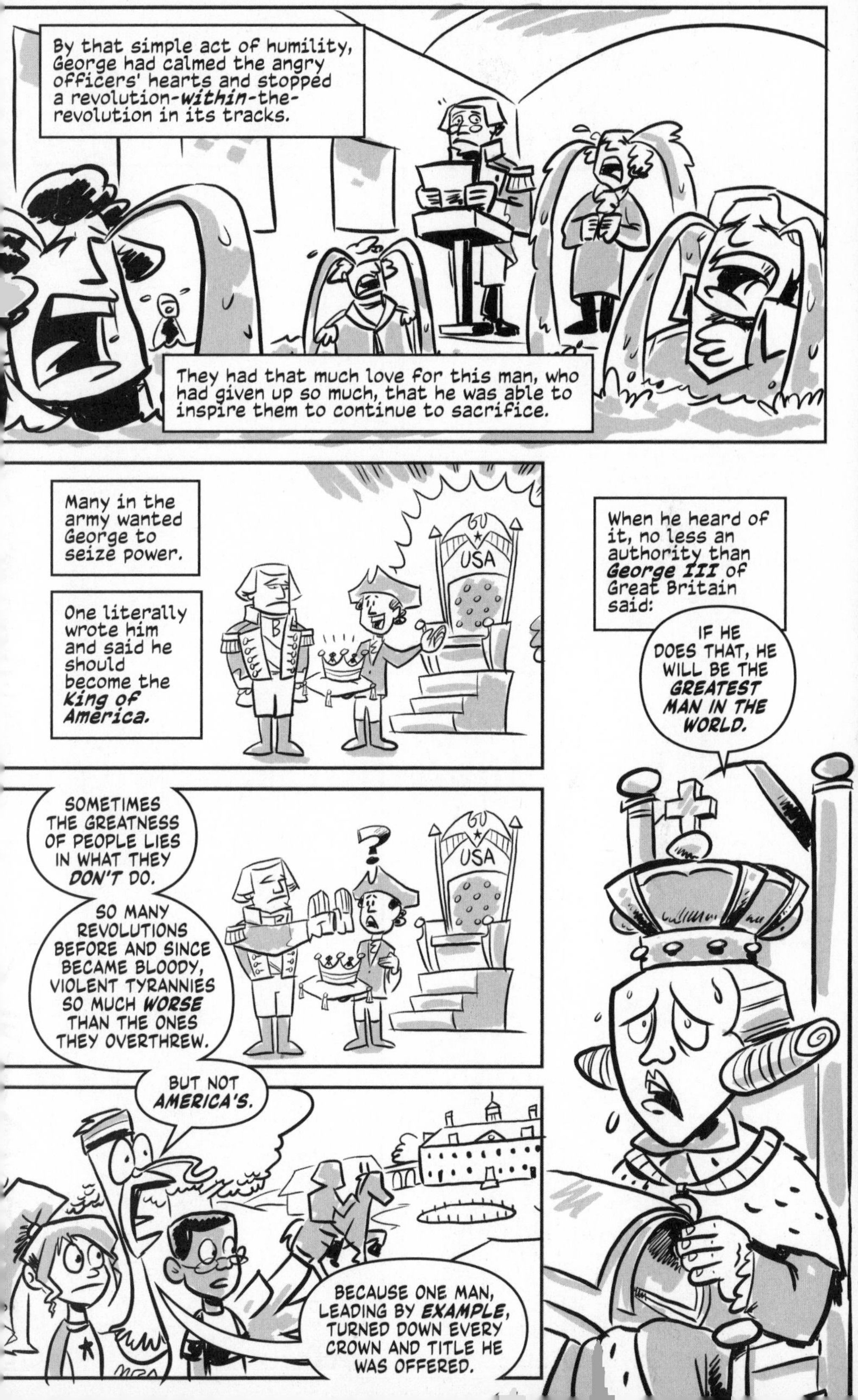

By that simple act of humility, George had calmed the angry officers' hearts and stopped a revolution-*within*-the-revolution in its tracks.
They had that much love for this man, who had given up so much, that he was able to inspire them to continue to sacrifice.
Many in the army wanted George to seize power.
One literally wrote him and said he should become the *King of America.*
USA
When he heard of it, no less an authority than *George III* of Great Britain said:
IF HE DOES THAT, HE WILL BE THE *GREATEST MAN IN THE WORLD.*
SOMETIMES THE GREATNESS OF PEOPLE LIES IN WHAT THEY *DON'T* DO.
SO MANY REVOLUTIONS BEFORE AND SINCE BECAME BLOODY, VIOLENT TYRANNIES SO MUCH *WORSE* THAN THE ONES THEY OVERTHREW.
BUT NOT *AMERICA'S.*
BECAUSE ONE MAN, LEADING BY *EXAMPLE*, TURNED DOWN EVERY CROWN AND TITLE HE WAS OFFERED.

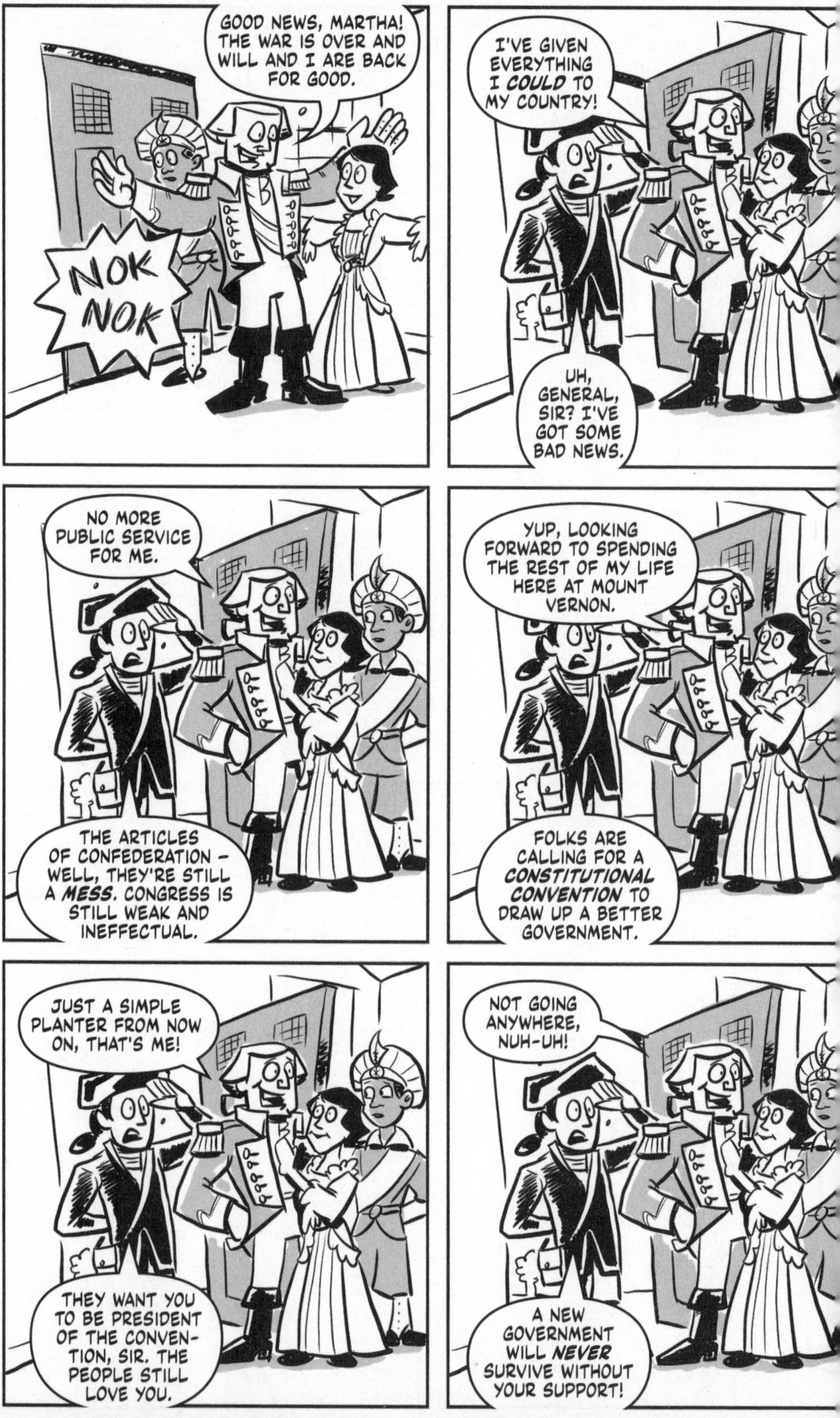
GOOD NEWS, MARTHA! THE WAR IS OVER AND WILL AND I ARE BACK FOR GOOD.
NOK NOK
I'VE GIVEN EVERYTHING I *COULD* TO MY COUNTRY!
UH, GENERAL, SIR? I'VE GOT SOME BAD NEWS.
NO MORE PUBLIC SERVICE FOR ME.
THE ARTICLES OF CONFEDERATION – WELL, THEY'RE STILL A *MESS*. CONGRESS IS STILL WEAK AND INEFFECTUAL.
YUP, LOOKING FORWARD TO SPENDING THE REST OF MY LIFE HERE AT MOUNT VERNON.
FOLKS ARE CALLING FOR A ***CONSTITUTIONAL CONVENTION*** TO DRAW UP A BETTER GOVERNMENT.
JUST A SIMPLE PLANTER FROM NOW ON, THAT'S ME!
THEY WANT YOU TO BE PRESIDENT OF THE CONVEN-TION, SIR. THE PEOPLE STILL LOVE YOU.
NOT GOING ANYWHERE, NUH-UH!
A NEW GOVERNMENT WILL ***NEVER*** SURVIVE WITHOUT YOUR SUPPORT!

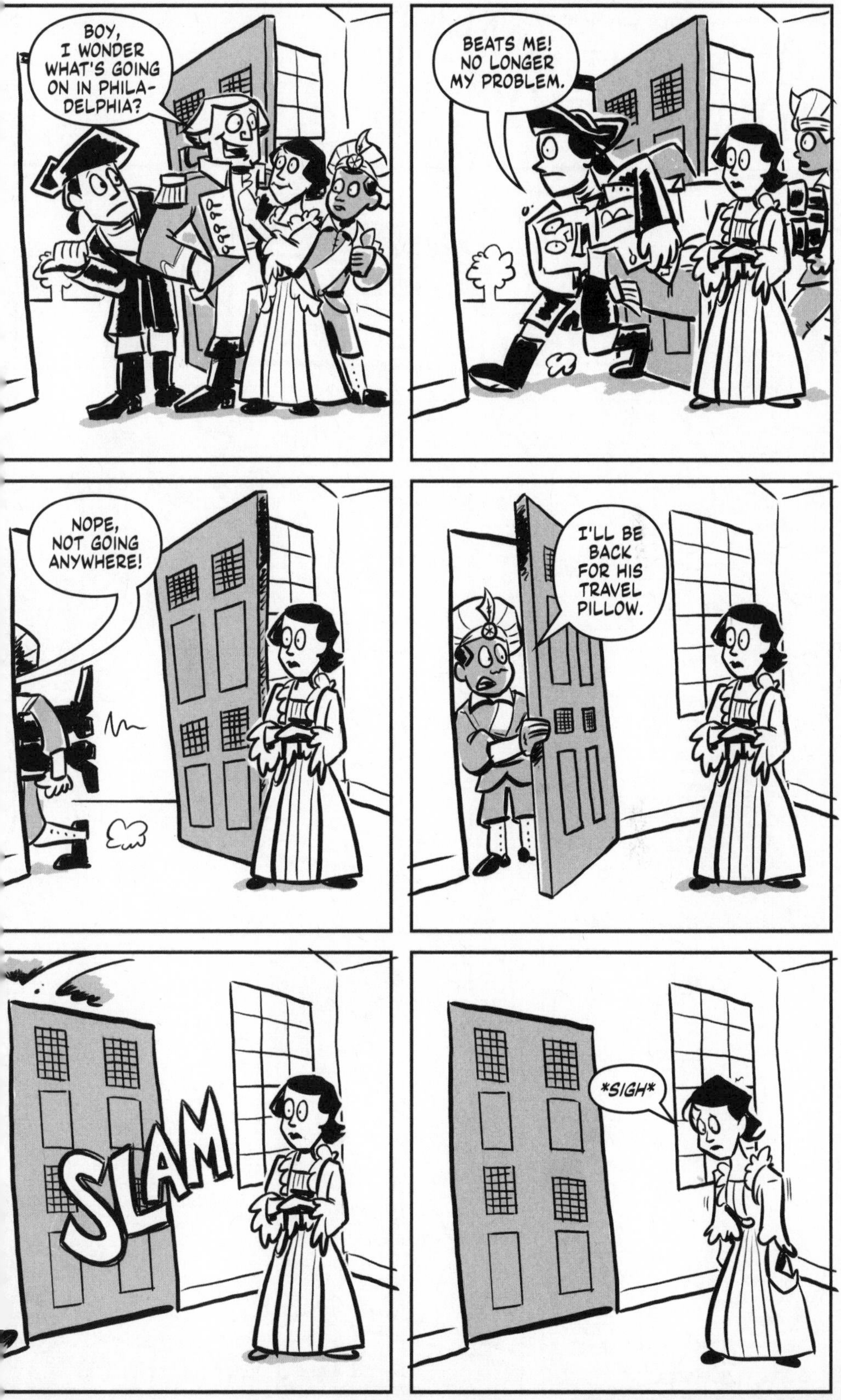
BOY, I WONDER WHAT'S GOING ON IN PHILA-DELPHIA?
BEATS ME! NO LONGER MY PROBLEM.
NOPE, NOT GOING ANYWHERE!
I'LL BE BACK FOR HIS TRAVEL PILLOW.
SLAM
SIGH

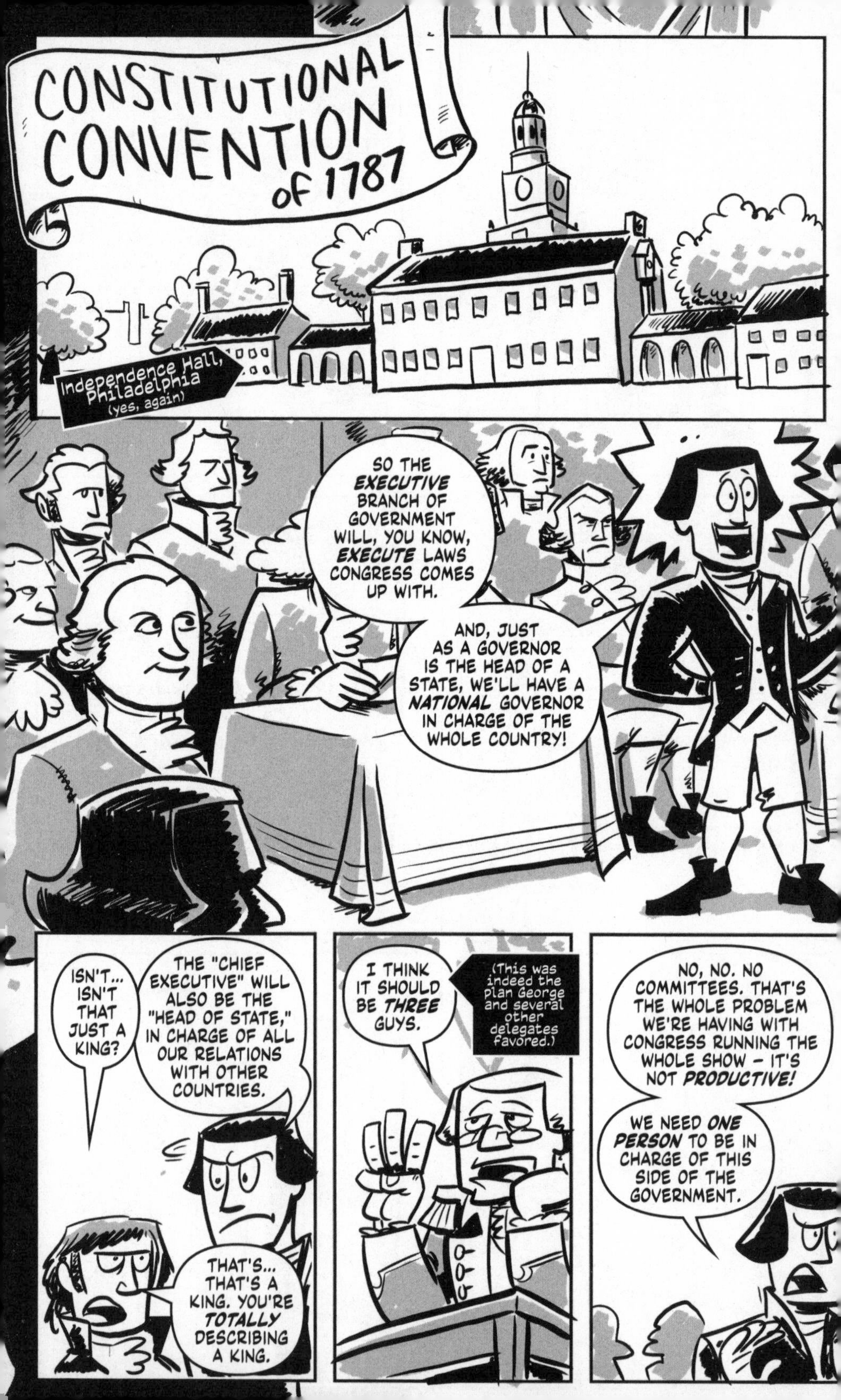

CONSTITUTIONAL CONVENTION of 1787
Independence Hall, Philadelphia (yes, again)
SO THE EXECUTIVE BRANCH OF GOVERNMENT WILL, YOU KNOW, EXECUTE LAWS CONGRESS COMES UP WITH.
AND, JUST AS A GOVERNOR IS THE HEAD OF A STATE, WE'LL HAVE A NATIONAL GOVERNOR IN CHARGE OF THE WHOLE COUNTRY!
ISN'T... ISN'T THAT JUST A KING?
THE "CHIEF EXECUTIVE" WILL ALSO BE THE "HEAD OF STATE," IN CHARGE OF ALL OUR RELATIONS WITH OTHER COUNTRIES.
THAT'S... THAT'S A KING. YOU'RE TOTALLY DESCRIBING A KING.
I THINK IT SHOULD BE THREE GUYS.
(This was indeed the plan George and several other delegates favored.)
NO, NO. NO COMMITTEES. THAT'S THE WHOLE PROBLEM WE'RE HAVING WITH CONGRESS RUNNING THE WHOLE SHOW – IT'S NOT PRODUCTIVE!
WE NEED ONE PERSON TO BE IN CHARGE OF THIS SIDE OF THE GOVERNMENT.

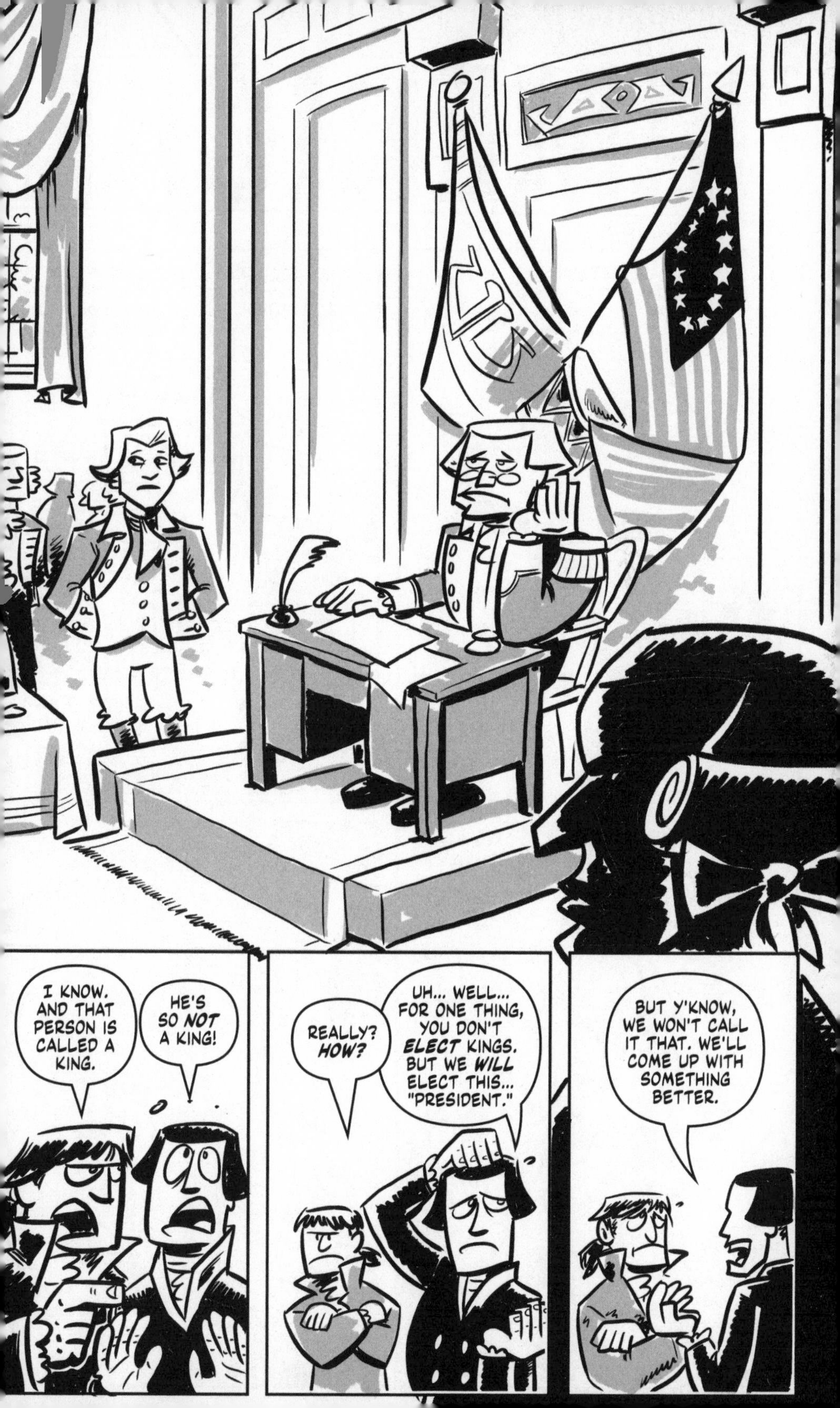
I KNOW. AND THAT PERSON IS CALLED A KING.
HE'S SO *NOT* A KING!
REALLY? *HOW?*
UH... WELL... FOR ONE THING, YOU DON'T *ELECT* KINGS. BUT WE *WILL* ELECT THIS... "PRESIDENT."
BUT Y'KNOW, WE WON'T CALL IT THAT. WE'LL COME UP WITH SOMETHING BETTER.

THE AMERICAN

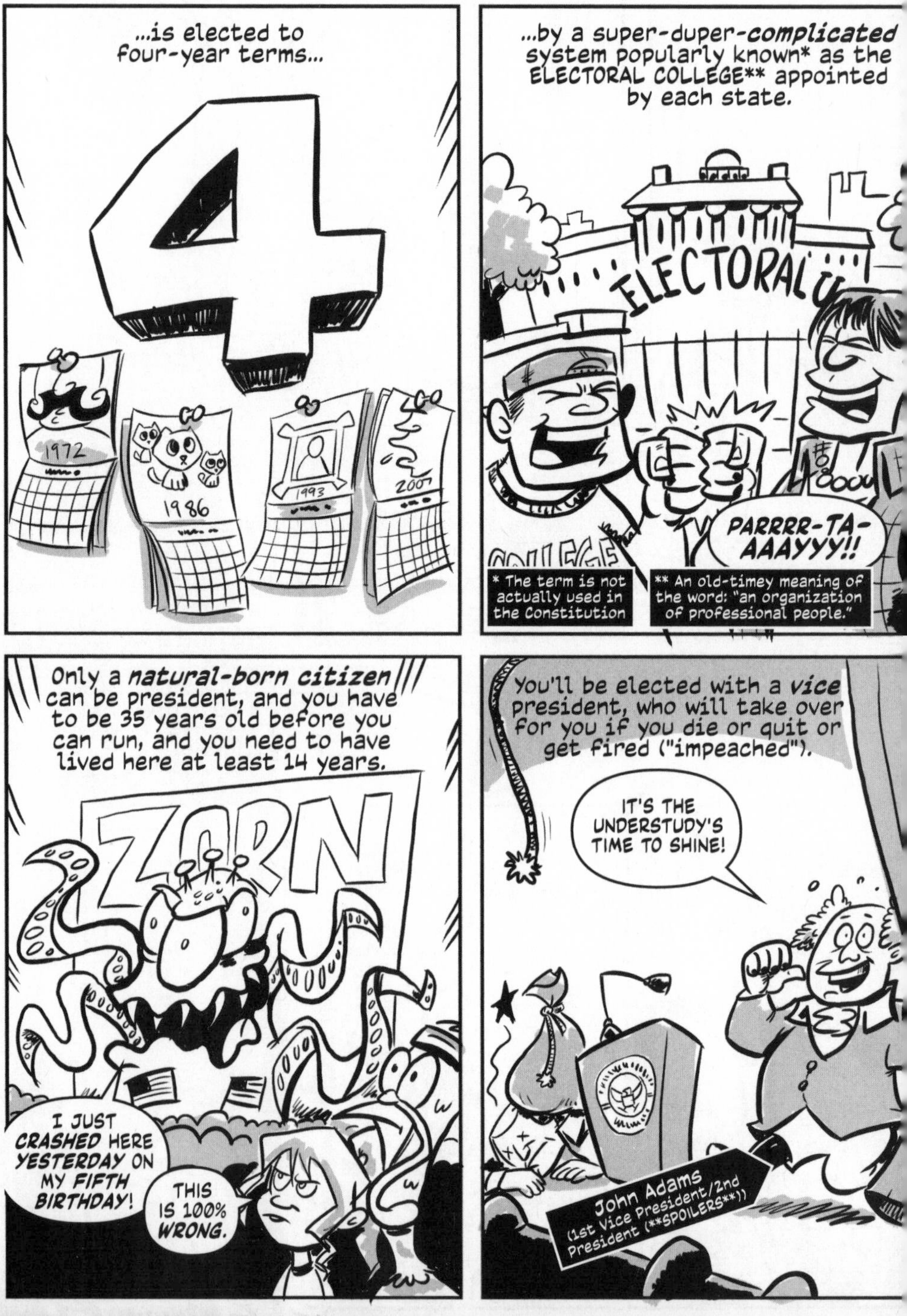

...is elected to four-year terms...
4
1972
1986
1993
2007
...by a super-duper-*complicated* system popularly known* as the ELECTORAL COLLEGE** appointed by each state.
ELECTORAL
PARRRR-TA-AAAYYY!!
* The term is not actually used in the Constitution
** An old-timey meaning of the word: "an organization of professional people."
Only a *natural-born citizen* can be president, and you have to be 35 years old before you can run, and you need to have lived here at least 14 years.
ZORN
I JUST *CRASHED* HERE *YESTERDAY* ON MY *FIFTH BIRTHDAY*!
THIS IS 100% *WRONG*.
You'll be elected with a *vice* president, who will take over for you if you die or quit or get fired ("impeached").
IT'S THE UNDERSTUDY'S TIME TO SHINE!
John Adams (1st Vice President/2nd President (**SPOILERS**))

PRESIDENT...

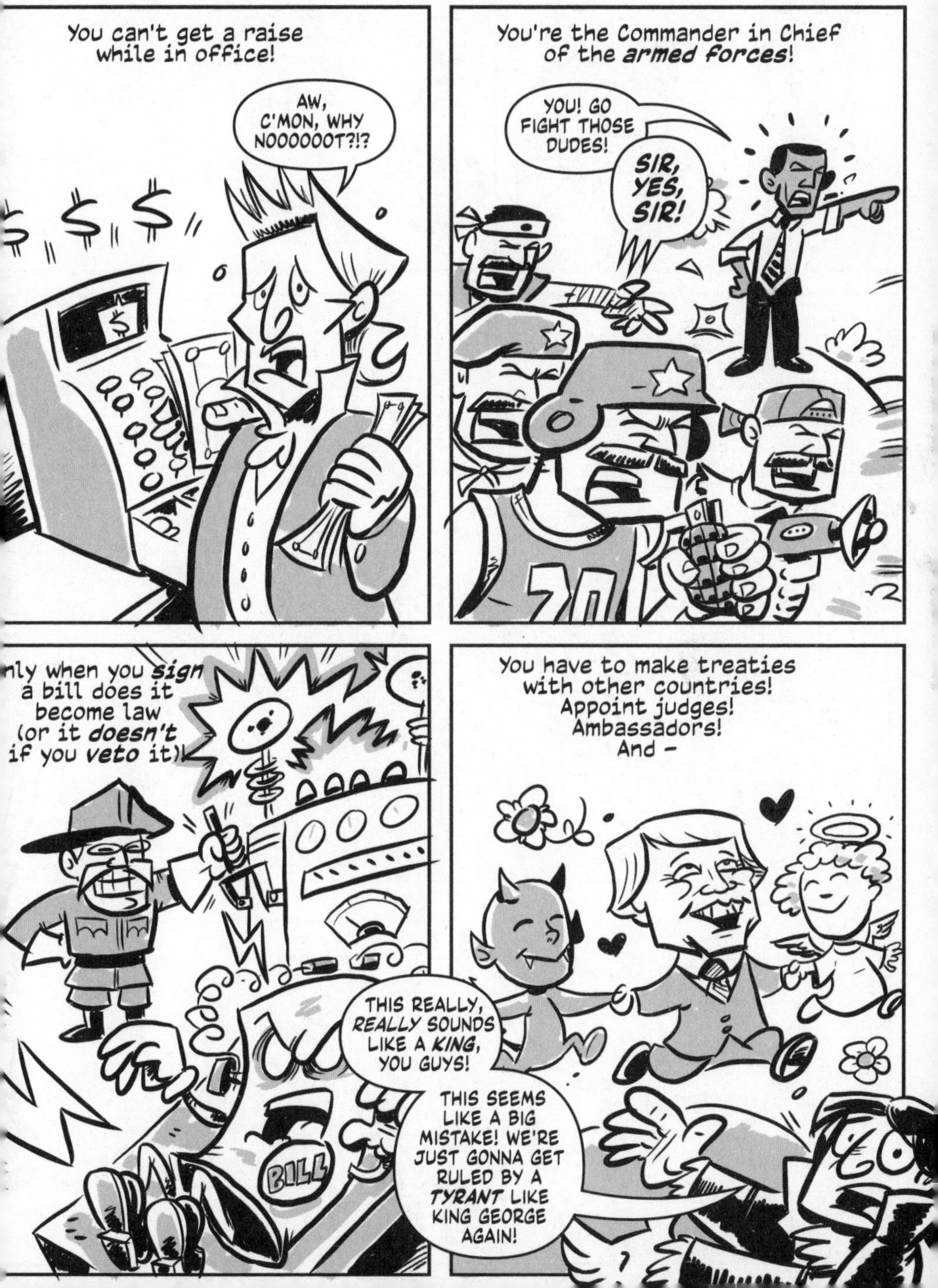

You can't get a raise while in office!
AW, C'MON, WHY NOOOOOOT?!?
You're the Commander in Chief of the *armed forces*!
YOU! GO FIGHT THOSE DUDES!
SIR, YES, SIR!
nly when you *sign* a bill does it become law (or it *doesn't* if you *veto* it)!
BILL
You have to make treaties with other countries! Appoint judges! Ambassadors! And –
THIS REALLY, *REALLY* SOUNDS LIKE A *KING*, YOU GUYS!
THIS SEEMS LIKE A BIG MISTAKE! WE'RE JUST GONNA GET RULED BY A *TYRANT* LIKE KING GEORGE AGAIN!

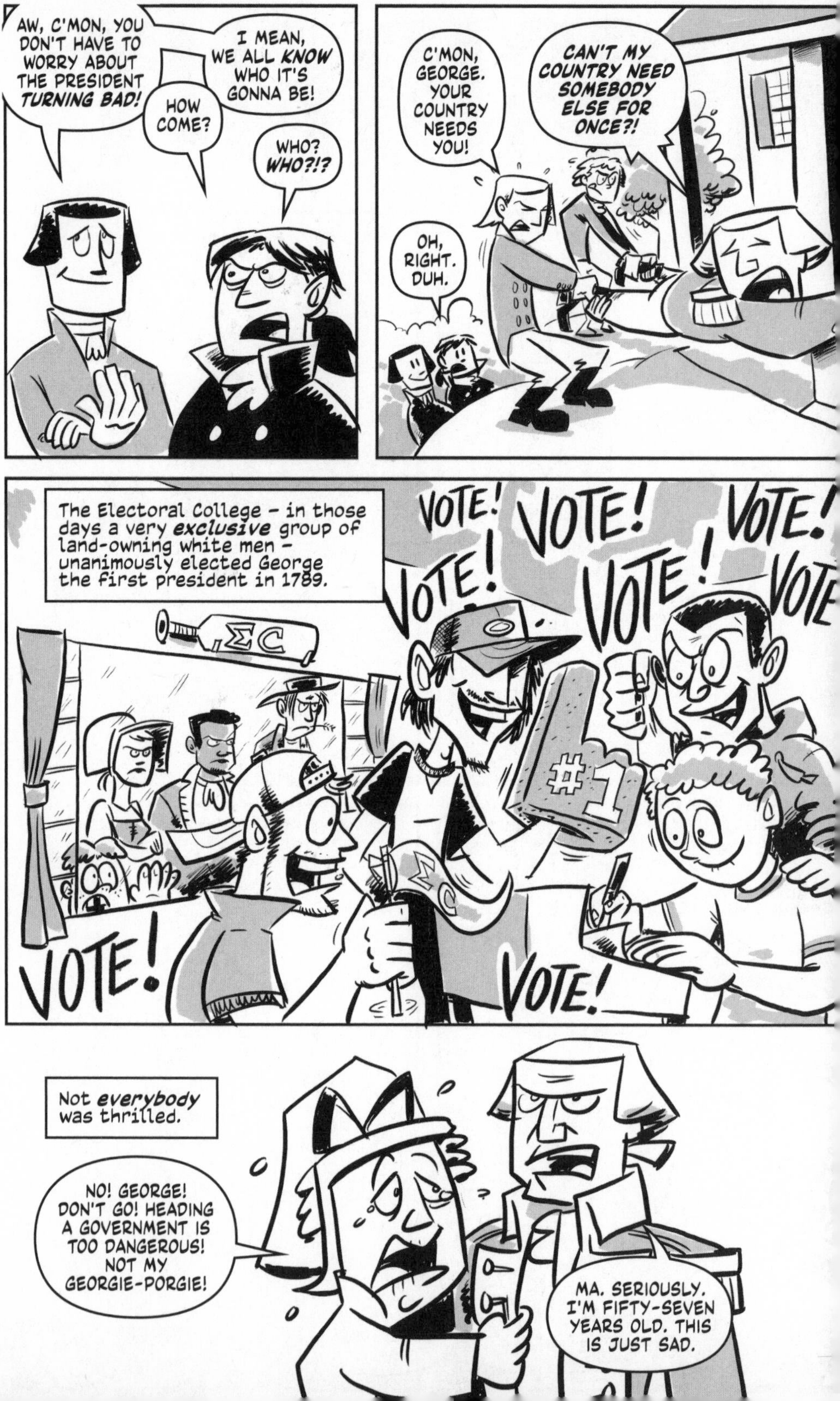
AW, C'MON, YOU DON'T HAVE TO WORRY ABOUT THE PRESIDENT *TURNING BAD!*
HOW COME?
I MEAN, WE ALL *KNOW* WHO IT'S GONNA BE!
WHO? *WHO?!?*
C'MON, GEORGE. YOUR COUNTRY NEEDS YOU!
CAN'T MY COUNTRY NEED SOMEBODY ELSE FOR ONCE?!
OH, RIGHT. DUH.
The Electoral College - in those days a very *exclusive* group of land-owning white men - unanimously elected George the first president in 1789.
VOTE! VOTE! VOTE! VOTE! VOTE! VOTE!
ΣC
#1
VOTE! VOTE!
Not *everybody* was thrilled.
NO! GEORGE! DON'T GO! HEADING A GOVERNMENT IS TOO DANGEROUS! NOT MY GEORGIE-PORGIE!
MA. SERIOUSLY. I'M FIFTY-SEVEN YEARS OLD. THIS IS JUST SAD.

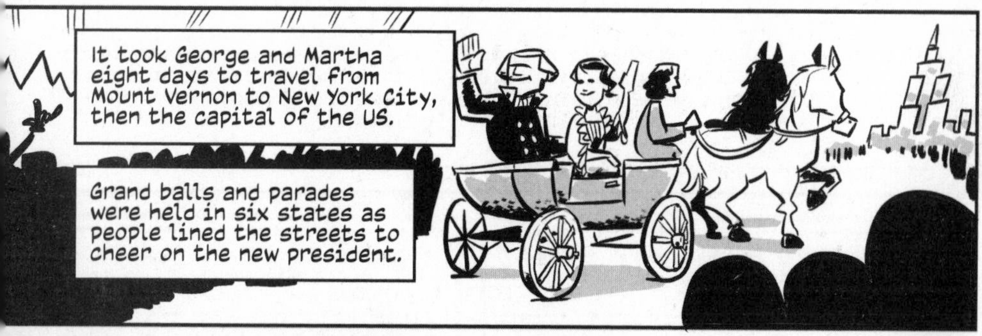
It took George and Martha eight days to travel from Mount Vernon to New York City, then the capital of the US.
Grand balls and parades were held in six states as people lined the streets to cheer on the new president.

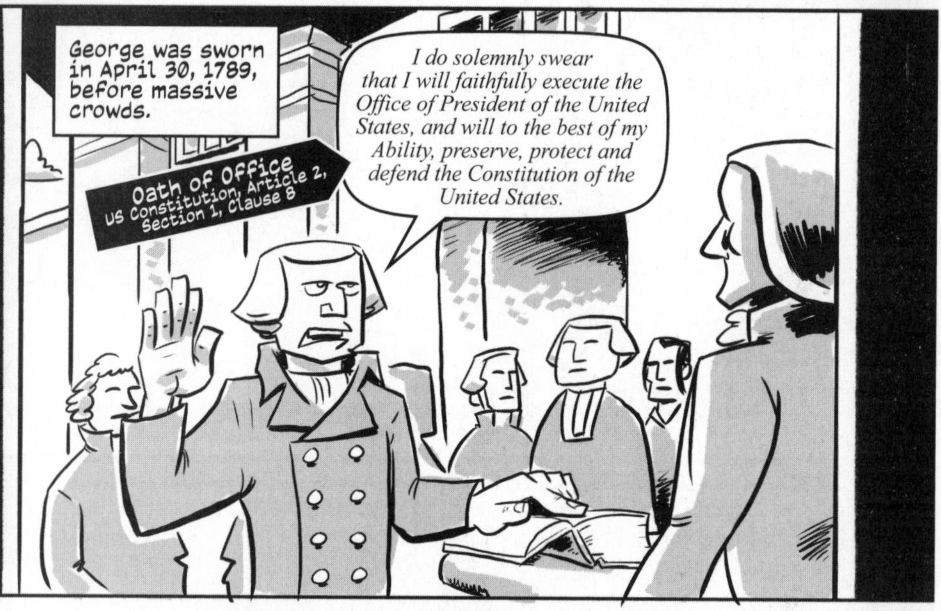
George was sworn in April 30, 1789, before massive crowds.
I do solemnly swear that I will faithfully execute the Office of President of the United States, and will to the best of my Ability, preserve, protect and defend the Constitution of the United States.
Oath of Office
US Constitution, Article 2, Section 1, Clause 8

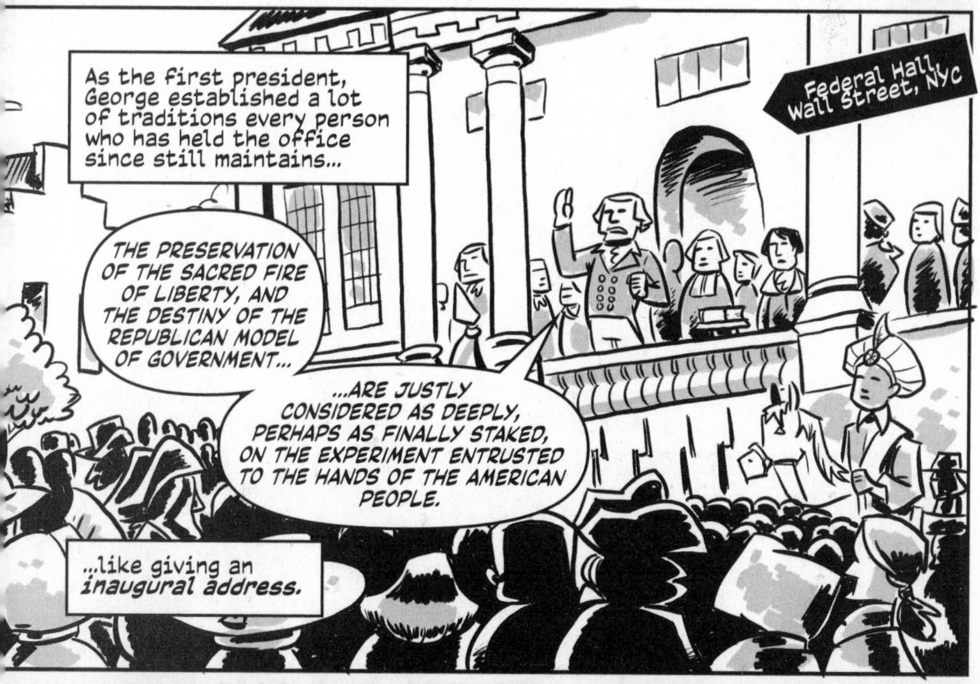
As the first president, George established a lot of traditions every person who has held the office since still maintains...
Federal Hall, Wall Street, NYC
THE PRESERVATION OF THE SACRED FIRE OF LIBERTY, AND THE DESTINY OF THE REPUBLICAN MODEL OF GOVERNMENT...
...ARE JUSTLY CONSIDERED AS DEEPLY, PERHAPS AS FINALLY STAKED, ON THE EXPERIMENT ENTRUSTED TO THE HANDS OF THE AMERICAN PEOPLE.
...like giving an *inaugural address.*

The president doesn't have to run the Executive Branch by himself. The Constitution also suggests the president set up "executive departments," the secretaries of which form his main team of advisers.

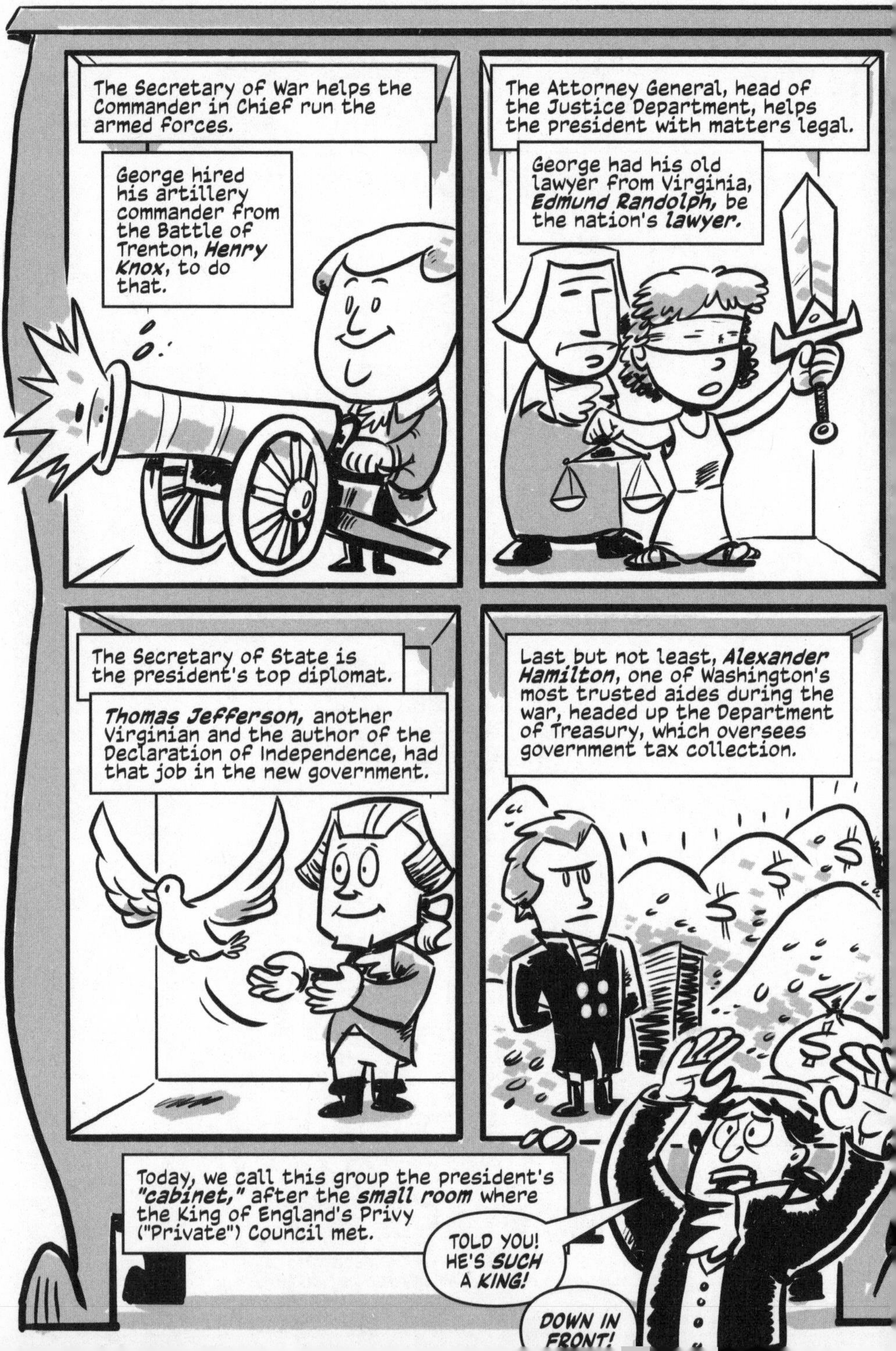
The Secretary of War helps the Commander in Chief run the armed forces.
George hired his artillery commander from the Battle of Trenton, ***Henry Knox***, to do that.
The Attorney General, head of the Justice Department, helps the president with matters legal.
George had his old lawyer from Virginia, ***Edmund Randolph,*** be the nation's ***lawyer.***
The Secretary of State is the president's top diplomat.
Thomas Jefferson, another Virginian and the author of the Declaration of Independence, had that job in the new government.
Last but not least, ***Alexander Hamilton***, one of Washington's most trusted aides during the war, headed up the Department of Treasury, which oversees government tax collection.
Today, we call this group the president's ***"cabinet,"*** after the ***small room*** where the King of England's Privy ("Private") Council met.
TOLD YOU! HE'S ***SUCH*** A ***KING!***
DOWN IN FRONT!

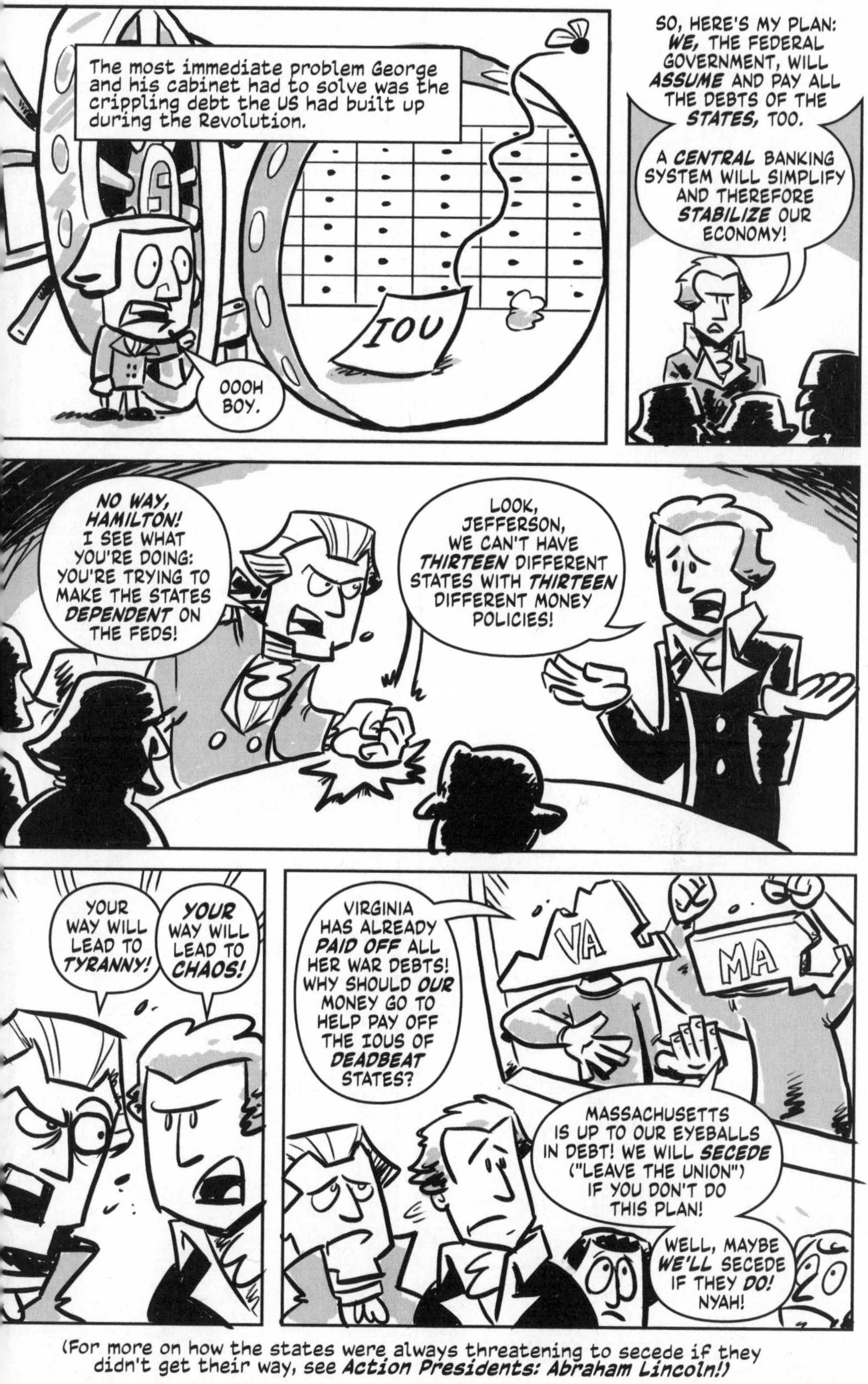

The most immediate problem George and his cabinet had to solve was the crippling debt the US had built up during the Revolution.
IOU
OOOH BOY.
SO, HERE'S MY PLAN: *WE,* THE FEDERAL GOVERNMENT, WILL *ASSUME* AND PAY ALL THE DEBTS OF THE *STATES,* TOO.
A *CENTRAL* BANKING SYSTEM WILL SIMPLIFY AND THEREFORE *STABILIZE* OUR ECONOMY!
NO WAY, HAMILTON! I SEE WHAT YOU'RE DOING: YOU'RE TRYING TO MAKE THE STATES *DEPENDENT* ON THE FEDS!
LOOK, JEFFERSON, WE CAN'T HAVE *THIRTEEN* DIFFERENT STATES WITH *THIRTEEN* DIFFERENT MONEY POLICIES!
YOUR WAY WILL LEAD TO *TYRANNY!*
YOUR WAY WILL LEAD TO *CHAOS!*
VIRGINIA HAS ALREADY *PAID OFF* ALL HER WAR DEBTS! WHY SHOULD *OUR* MONEY GO TO HELP PAY OFF THE IOUS OF *DEADBEAT* STATES?
VA
MA
MASSACHUSETTS IS UP TO OUR EYEBALLS IN DEBT! WE WILL *SECEDE* ("LEAVE THE UNION") IF YOU DON'T DO THIS PLAN!
WELL, MAYBE *WE'LL* SECEDE IF THEY *DO!* NYAH!

(For more on how the states were always threatening to secede if they didn't get their way, see ***Action Presidents: Abraham Lincoln!***)

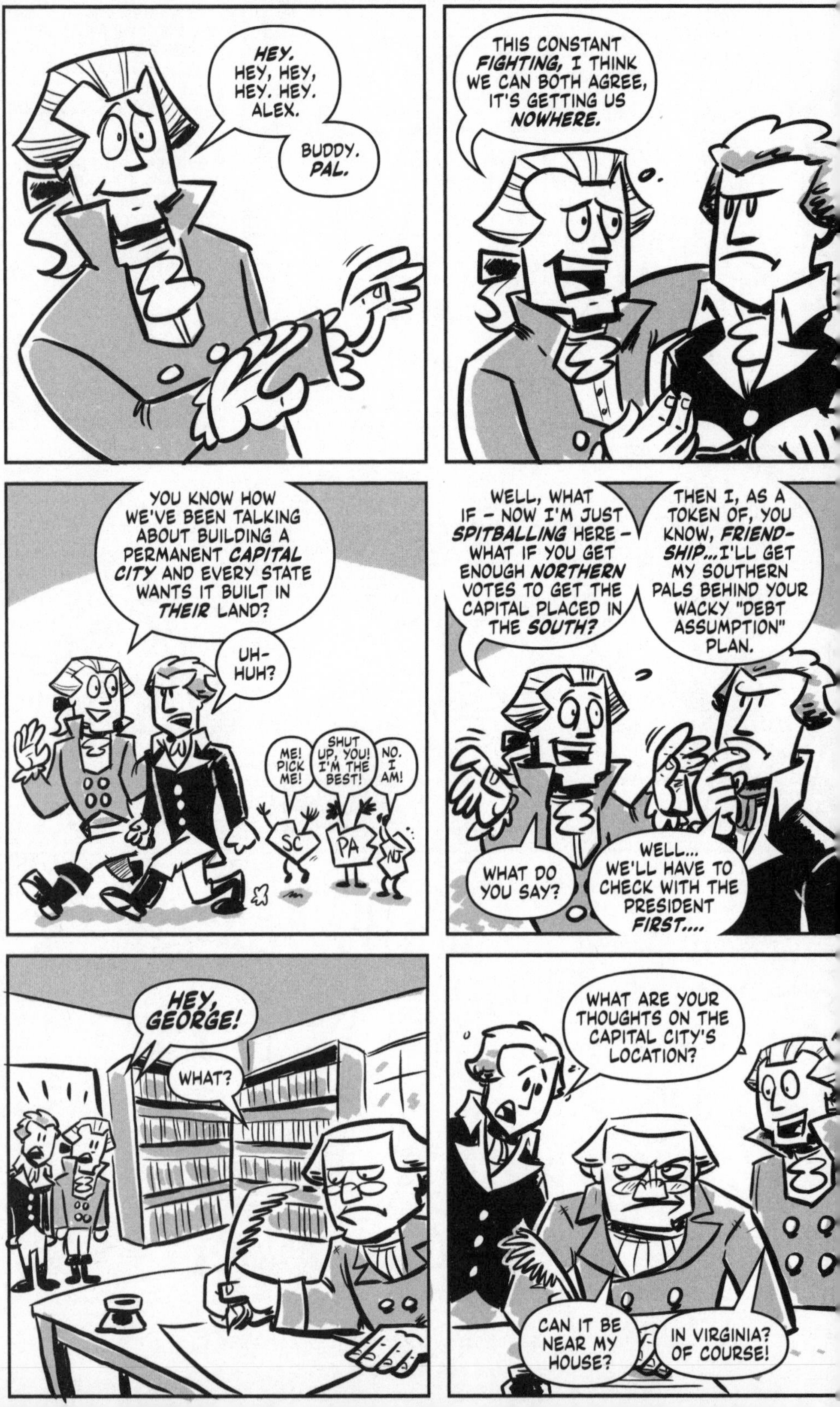
HEY. HEY, HEY, HEY. HEY. ALEX.
BUDDY. PAL.
THIS CONSTANT FIGHTING, I THINK WE CAN BOTH AGREE, IT'S GETTING US NOWHERE.
YOU KNOW HOW WE'VE BEEN TALKING ABOUT BUILDING A PERMANENT CAPITAL CITY AND EVERY STATE WANTS IT BUILT IN THEIR LAND?
UH-HUH?
ME! PICK ME!
SHUT UP, YOU! I'M THE BEST!
NO. I AM!
SC
PA
NJ
WELL, WHAT IF – NOW I'M JUST SPITBALLING HERE – WHAT IF YOU GET ENOUGH NORTHERN VOTES TO GET THE CAPITAL PLACED IN THE SOUTH?
THEN I, AS A TOKEN OF, YOU KNOW, FRIENDSHIP...I'LL GET MY SOUTHERN PALS BEHIND YOUR WACKY "DEBT ASSUMPTION" PLAN.
WHAT DO YOU SAY?
WELL... WE'LL HAVE TO CHECK WITH THE PRESIDENT FIRST....
HEY, GEORGE!
WHAT?
WHAT ARE YOUR THOUGHTS ON THE CAPITAL CITY'S LOCATION?
CAN IT BE NEAR MY HOUSE?
IN VIRGINIA? OF COURSE!

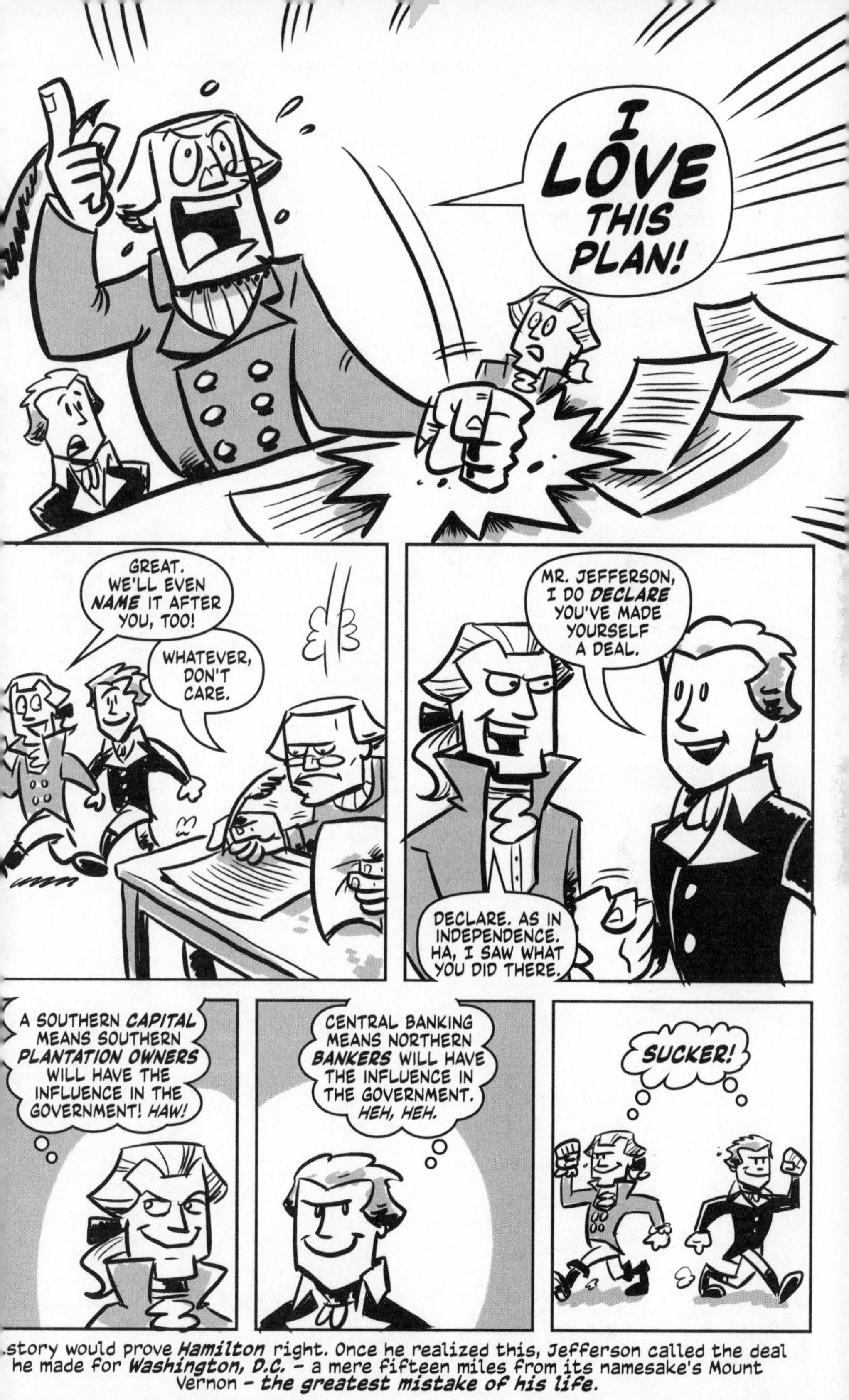
I LOVE THIS PLAN!
GREAT. WE'LL EVEN NAME IT AFTER YOU, TOO!
WHATEVER, DON'T CARE.
MR. JEFFERSON, I DO DECLARE YOU'VE MADE YOURSELF A DEAL.
DECLARE. AS IN INDEPENDENCE. HA, I SAW WHAT YOU DID THERE.
A SOUTHERN CAPITAL MEANS SOUTHERN PLANTATION OWNERS WILL HAVE THE INFLUENCE IN THE GOVERNMENT! HAW!
CENTRAL BANKING MEANS NORTHERN BANKERS WILL HAVE THE INFLUENCE IN THE GOVERNMENT. HEH, HEH.
SUCKER!

.story would prove ***Hamilton*** right. Once he realized this, Jefferson called the deal he made for ***Washington, D.C.*** – a mere fifteen miles from its namesake's Mount Vernon – ***the greatest mistake of his life***.

Now that Hamilton had all the ***states'*** debts too, he had to figure out a way to pay them ***off.***

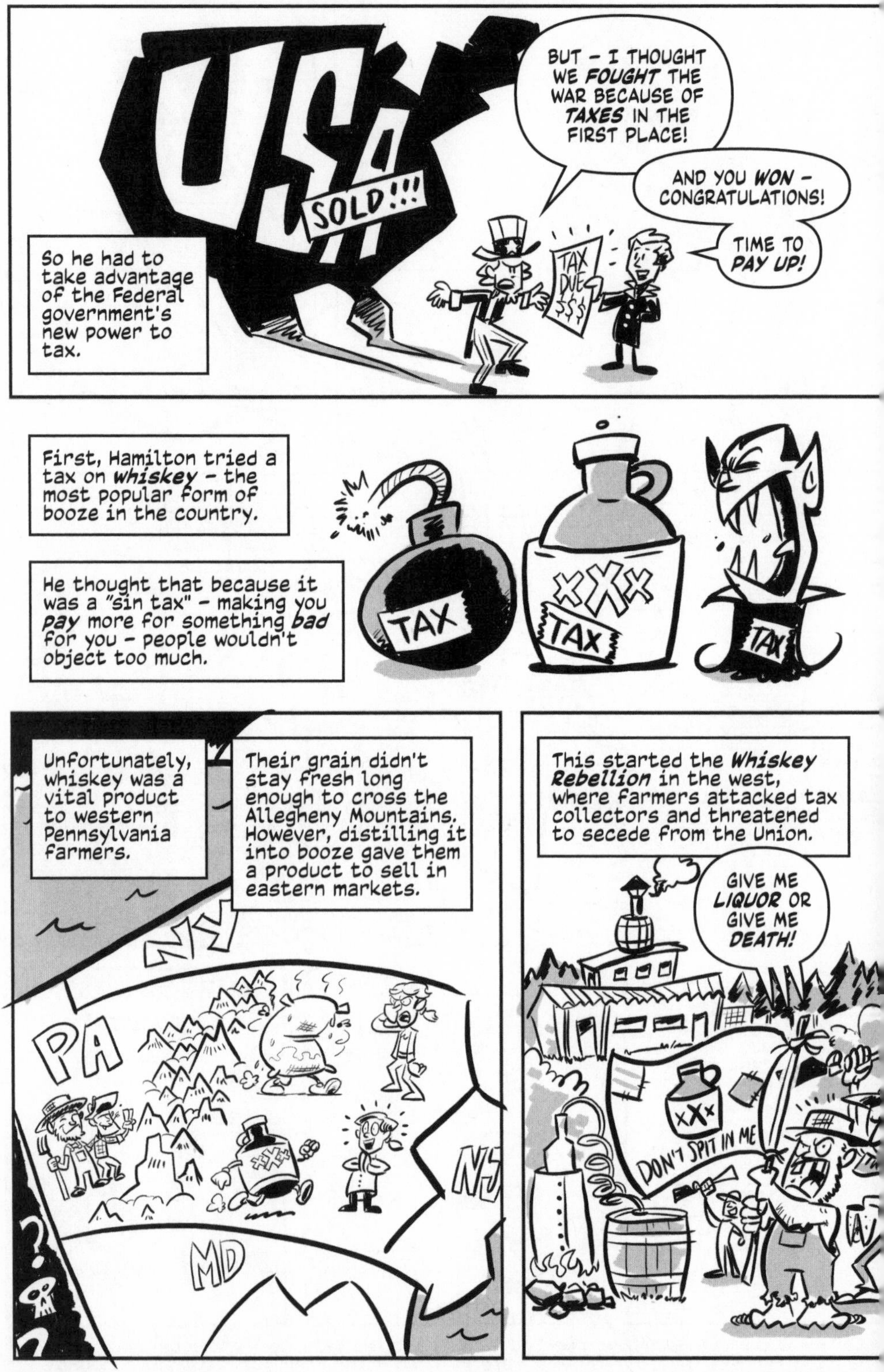
USA
SOLD!!!
So he had to take advantage of the Federal government's new power to tax.
BUT – I THOUGHT WE FOUGHT THE WAR BECAUSE OF TAXES IN THE FIRST PLACE!
AND YOU WON – CONGRATULATIONS!
TIME TO PAY UP!
TAX DUE $$$
First, Hamilton tried a tax on whiskey – the most popular form of booze in the country.
He thought that because it was a "sin tax" – making you pay more for something bad for you – people wouldn't object too much.
TAX
XXX
TAX
TAX
Unfortunately, whiskey was a vital product to western Pennsylvania farmers.
Their grain didn't stay fresh long enough to cross the Allegheny Mountains. However, distilling it into booze gave them a product to sell in eastern markets.
NY
PA
NJ
MD
This started the Whiskey Rebellion in the west, where farmers attacked tax collectors and threatened to secede from the Union.
GIVE ME LIQUOR OR GIVE ME DEATH!
XXX
DON'T SPIT IN ME

On top of all ***that***, like all the presidents ***after*** him, George also had to deal with problems coming in from the ***rest*** of the world too.

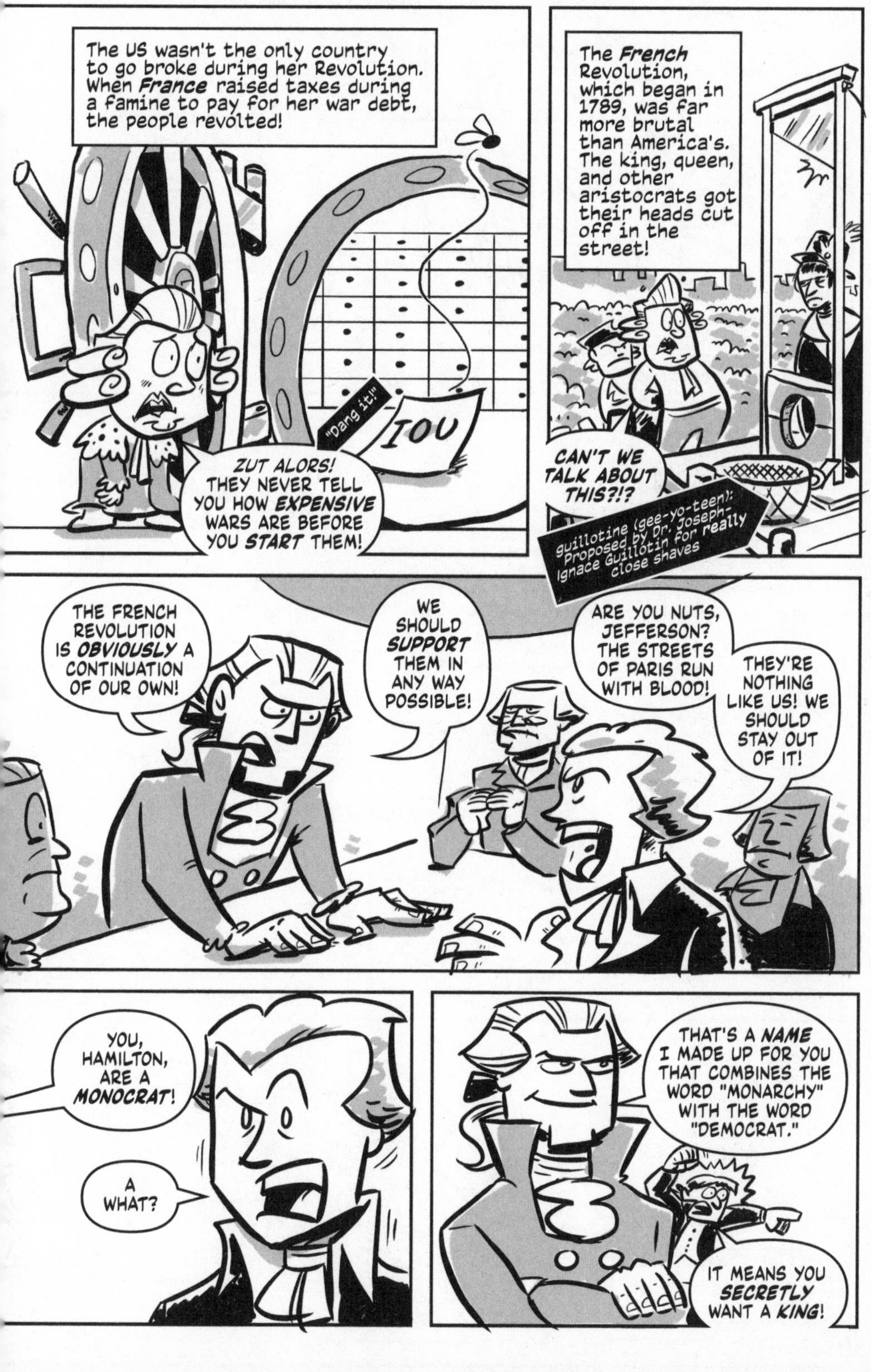
The US wasn't the only country to go broke during her Revolution. When France raised taxes during a famine to pay for her war debt, the people revolted!
"Dang it!"
IOU
ZUT ALORS! THEY NEVER TELL YOU HOW EXPENSIVE WARS ARE BEFORE YOU START THEM!
The French Revolution, which began in 1789, was far more brutal than America's. The king, queen, and other aristocrats got their heads cut off in the street!
CAN'T WE TALK ABOUT THIS?!?
guillotine (gee-yo-teen): Proposed by Dr. Joseph-Ignace Guillotin for really close shaves
THE FRENCH REVOLUTION IS OBVIOUSLY A CONTINUATION OF OUR OWN!
WE SHOULD SUPPORT THEM IN ANY WAY POSSIBLE!
ARE YOU NUTS, JEFFERSON? THE STREETS OF PARIS RUN WITH BLOOD!
THEY'RE NOTHING LIKE US! WE SHOULD STAY OUT OF IT!
YOU, HAMILTON, ARE A MONOCRAT!
A WHAT?
THAT'S A NAME I MADE UP FOR YOU THAT COMBINES THE WORD "MONARCHY" WITH THE WORD "DEMOCRAT."
IT MEANS YOU SECRETLY WANT A KING!

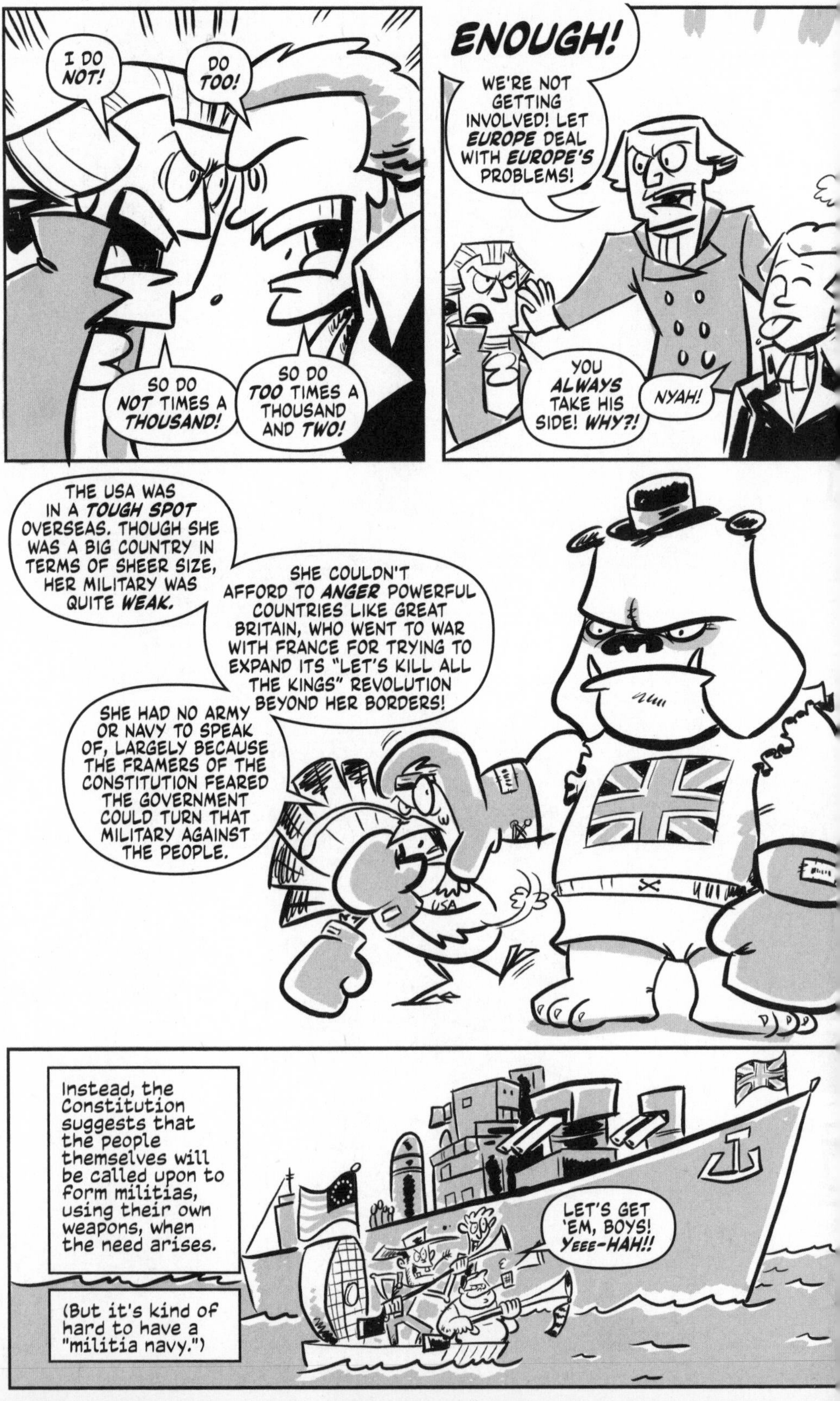

I DO NOT!
DO TOO!
SO DO NOT TIMES A THOUSAND!
SO DO TOO TIMES A THOUSAND AND TWO!
ENOUGH!
WE'RE NOT GETTING INVOLVED! LET EUROPE DEAL WITH EUROPE'S PROBLEMS!
YOU ALWAYS TAKE HIS SIDE! WHY?!
NYAH!
THE USA WAS IN A TOUGH SPOT OVERSEAS. THOUGH SHE WAS A BIG COUNTRY IN TERMS OF SHEER SIZE, HER MILITARY WAS QUITE WEAK.
SHE COULDN'T AFFORD TO ANGER POWERFUL COUNTRIES LIKE GREAT BRITAIN, WHO WENT TO WAR WITH FRANCE FOR TRYING TO EXPAND ITS "LET'S KILL ALL THE KINGS" REVOLUTION BEYOND HER BORDERS!
SHE HAD NO ARMY OR NAVY TO SPEAK OF, LARGELY BECAUSE THE FRAMERS OF THE CONSTITUTION FEARED THE GOVERNMENT COULD TURN THAT MILITARY AGAINST THE PEOPLE.
USA
Instead, the Constitution suggests that the people themselves will be called upon to form militias, using their own weapons, when the need arises.
(But it's kind of hard to have a "militia navy.")
LET'S GET 'EM, BOYS! YEEE-HAH!!

Still, in 1794 four states assembled a "**national militia**" of 12,950 men – more troops than George had at many times during the Revolution!

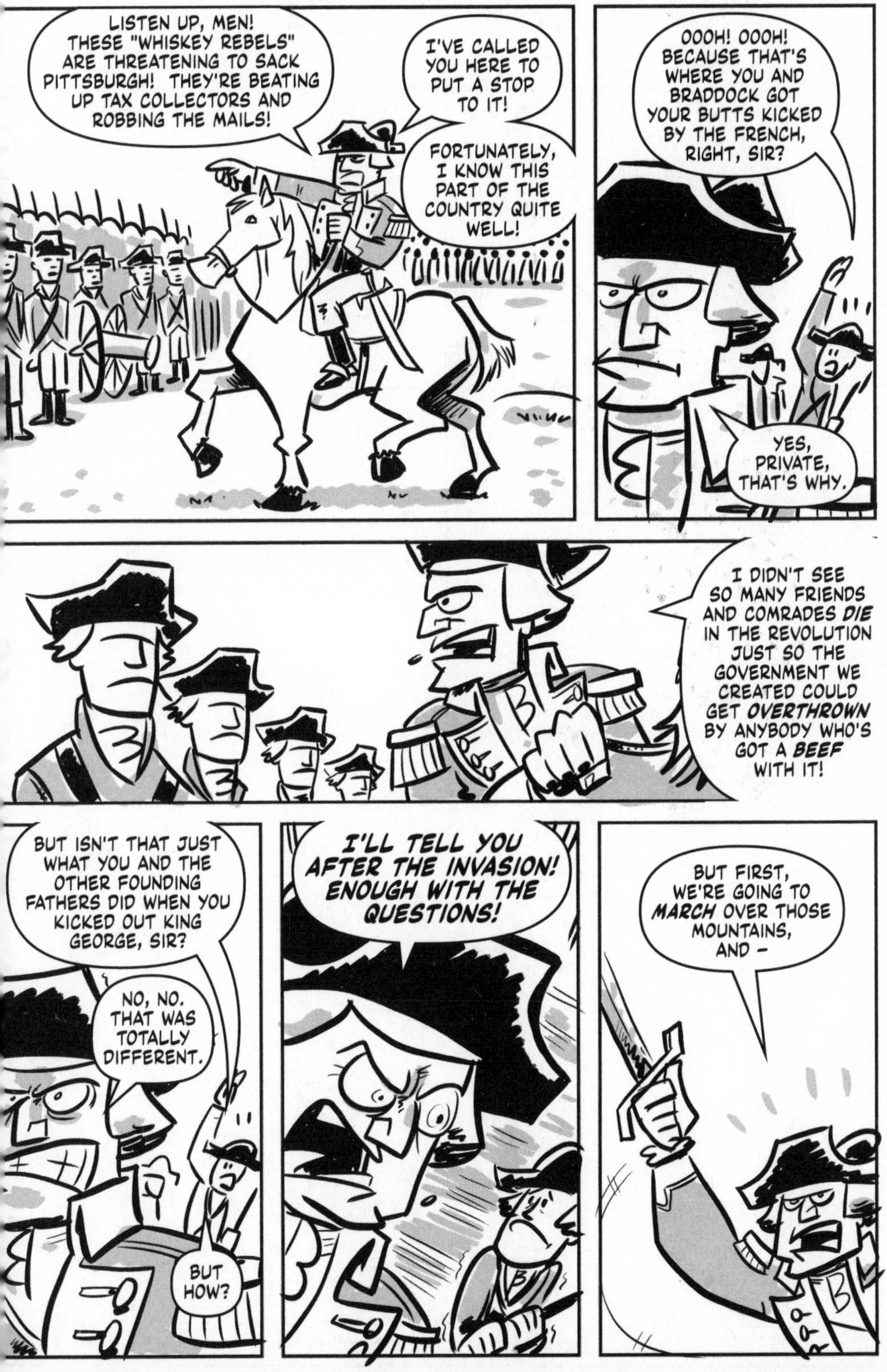

LISTEN UP, MEN! THESE "WHISKEY REBELS" ARE THREATENING TO SACK PITTSBURGH! THEY'RE BEATING UP TAX COLLECTORS AND ROBBING THE MAILS!
I'VE CALLED YOU HERE TO PUT A STOP TO IT!
FORTUNATELY, I KNOW THIS PART OF THE COUNTRY QUITE WELL!
OOOH! OOOH! BECAUSE THAT'S WHERE YOU AND BRADDOCK GOT YOUR BUTTS KICKED BY THE FRENCH, RIGHT, SIR?
YES, PRIVATE, THAT'S WHY.
I DIDN'T SEE SO MANY FRIENDS AND COMRADES *DIE* IN THE REVOLUTION JUST SO THE GOVERNMENT WE CREATED COULD GET *OVERTHROWN* BY ANYBODY WHO'S GOT A *BEEF* WITH IT!
BUT ISN'T THAT JUST WHAT YOU AND THE OTHER FOUNDING FATHERS DID WHEN YOU KICKED OUT KING GEORGE, SIR?
NO, NO. THAT WAS TOTALLY DIFFERENT.
BUT HOW?
I'LL TELL YOU AFTER THE INVASION! ENOUGH WITH THE QUESTIONS!
BUT FIRST, WE'RE GOING TO *MARCH* OVER THOSE MOUNTAINS, AND –

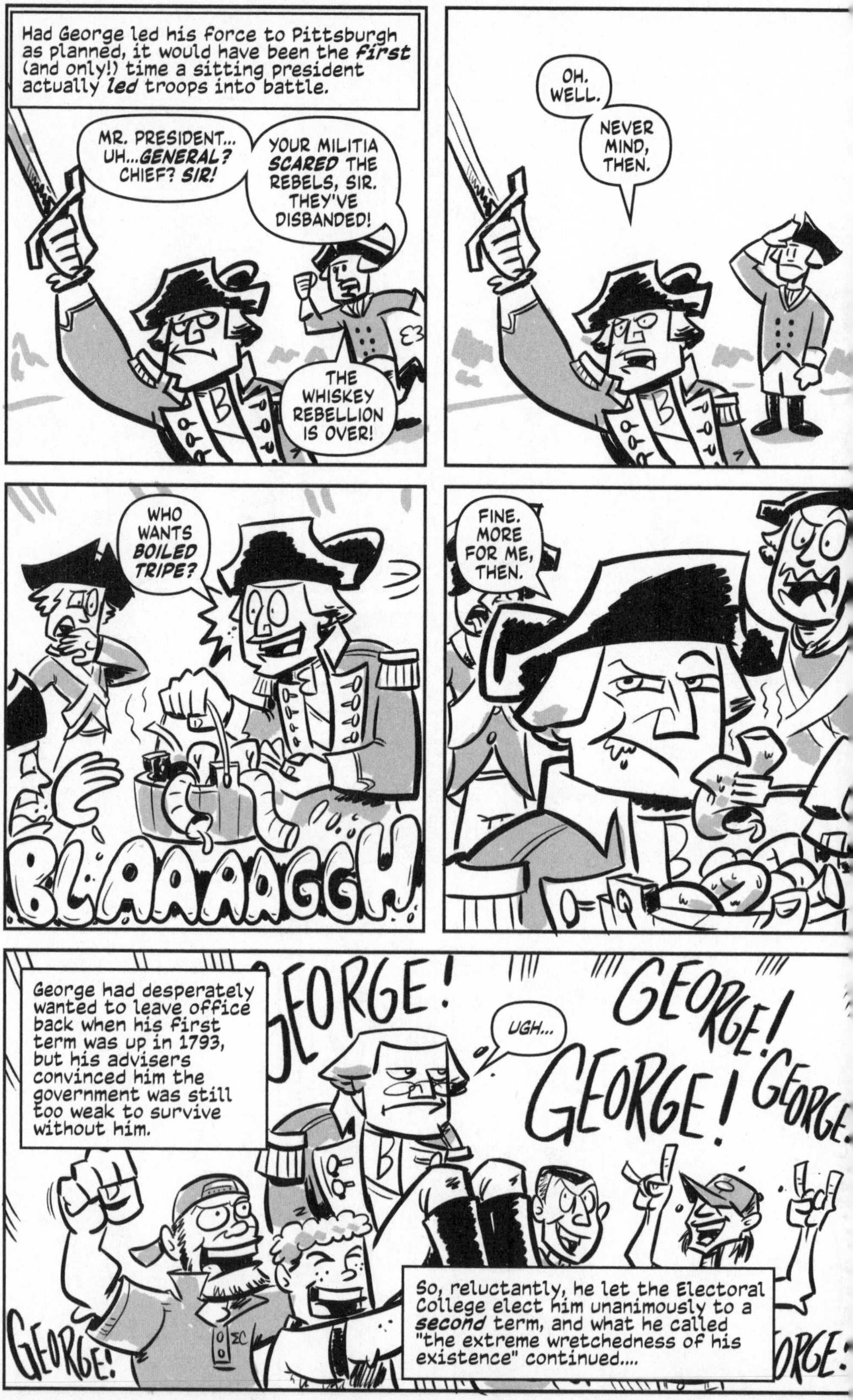
Had George led his force to Pittsburgh as planned, it would have been the *first* (and only!) time a sitting president actually *led* troops into battle.
MR. PRESIDENT... UH...*GENERAL?* CHIEF? *SIR!*
YOUR MILITIA *SCARED* THE REBELS, SIR. THEY'VE DISBANDED!
THE WHISKEY REBELLION IS OVER!
OH. WELL.
NEVER MIND, THEN.
WHO WANTS *BOILED TRIPE?*
BLAAAAGGH
FINE. MORE FOR ME, THEN.
George had desperately wanted to leave office back when his first term was up in 1793, but his advisers convinced him the government was still too weak to survive without him.
GEORGE!
UGH...
GEORGE!
GEORGE!
GEORGE!
GEORGE!
So, reluctantly, he let the Electoral College elect him unanimously to a *second* term, and what he called "the extreme wretchedness of his existence" continued....

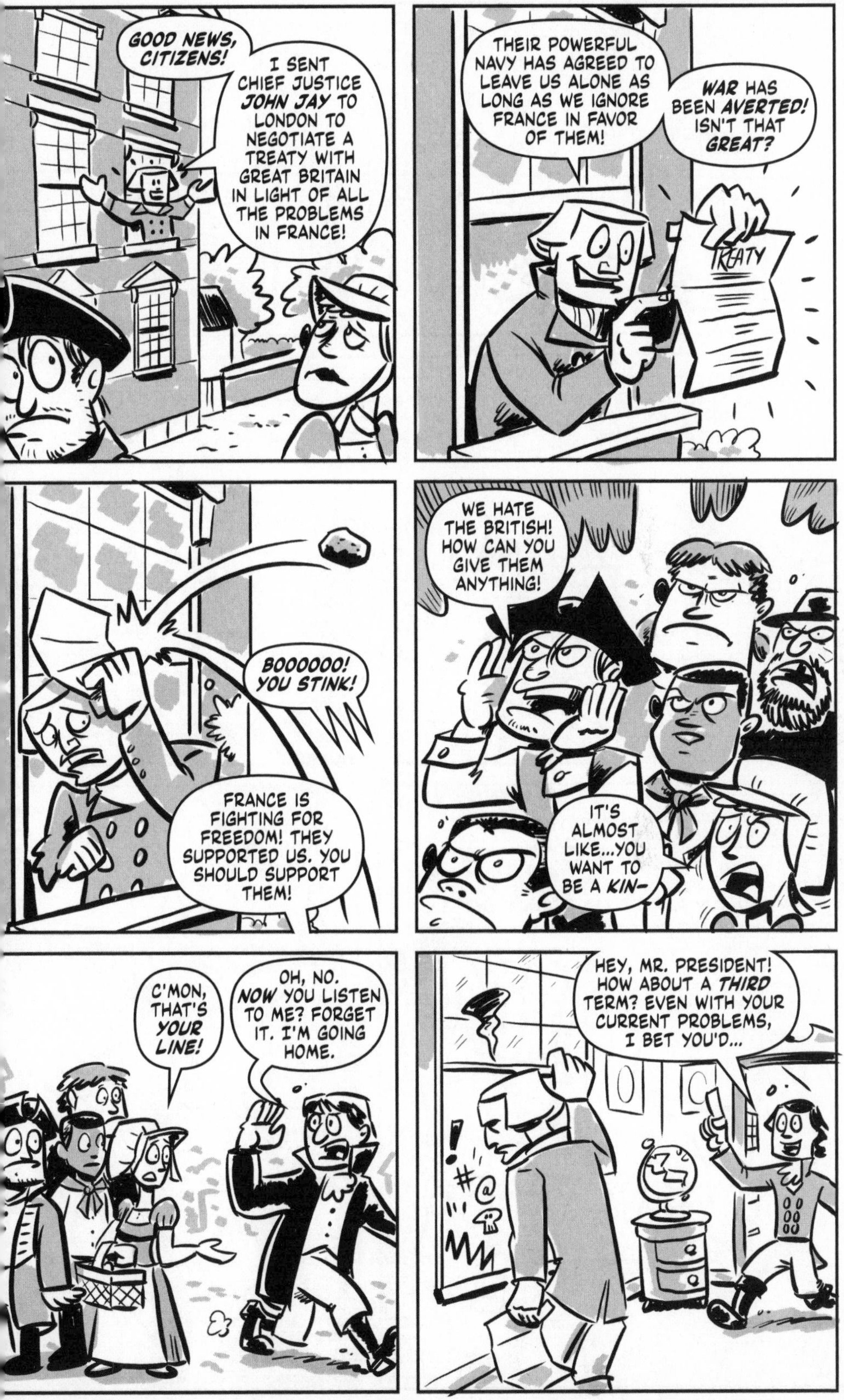

GOOD NEWS, CITIZENS!
I SENT CHIEF JUSTICE JOHN JAY TO LONDON TO NEGOTIATE A TREATY WITH GREAT BRITAIN IN LIGHT OF ALL THE PROBLEMS IN FRANCE!
THEIR POWERFUL NAVY HAS AGREED TO LEAVE US ALONE AS LONG AS WE IGNORE FRANCE IN FAVOR OF THEM!
WAR HAS BEEN AVERTED! ISN'T THAT GREAT?
TREATY
BOOOOOO! YOU STINK!
FRANCE IS FIGHTING FOR FREEDOM! THEY SUPPORTED US. YOU SHOULD SUPPORT THEM!
WE HATE THE BRITISH! HOW CAN YOU GIVE THEM ANYTHING!
IT'S ALMOST LIKE...YOU WANT TO BE A KIN—
C'MON, THAT'S YOUR LINE!
OH, NO. NOW YOU LISTEN TO ME? FORGET IT. I'M GOING HOME.
HEY, MR. PRESIDENT! HOW ABOUT A THIRD TERM? EVEN WITH YOUR CURRENT PROBLEMS, I BET YOU'D...

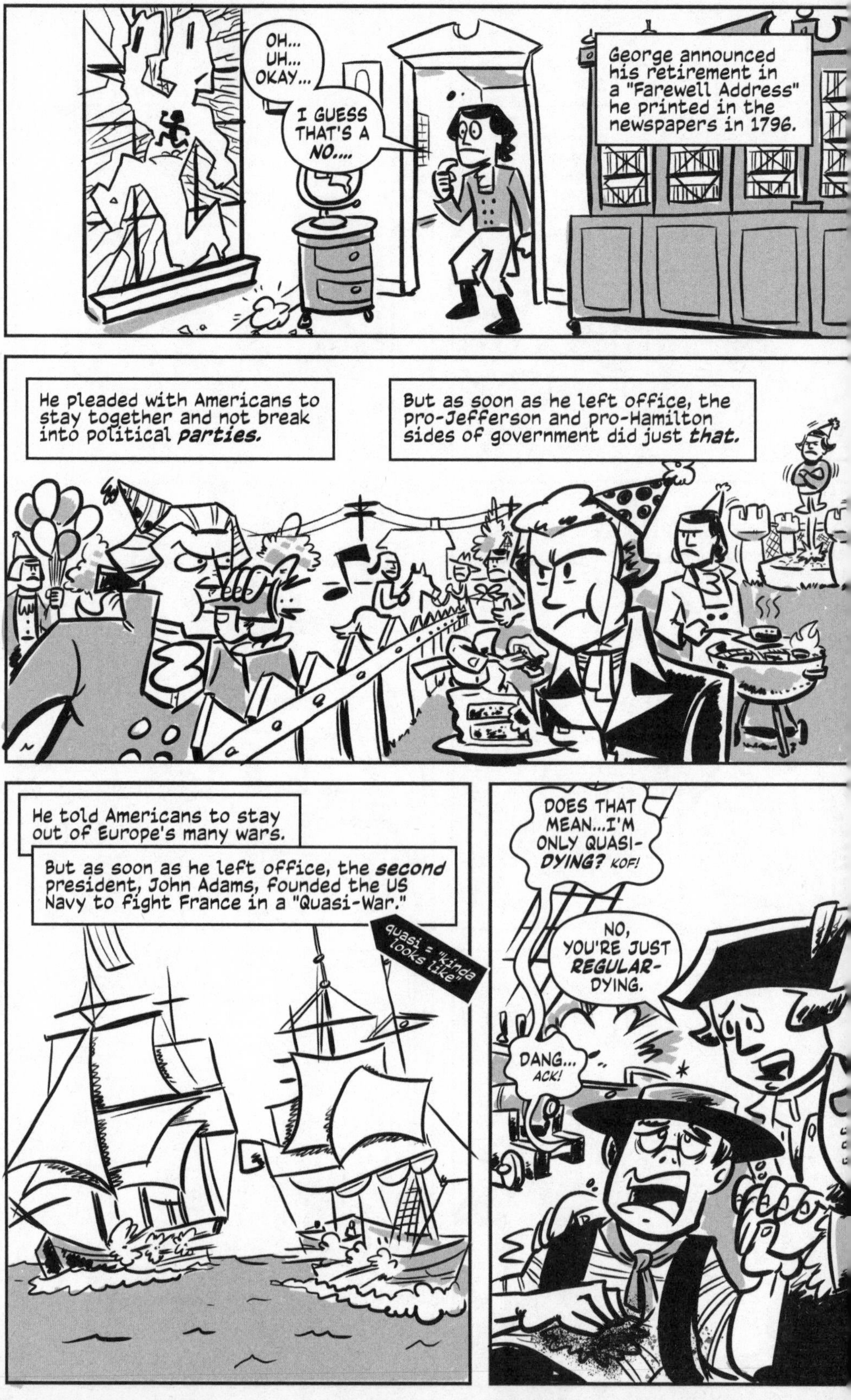
OH... UH... OKAY...
I GUESS THAT'S A NO....
George announced his retirement in a "Farewell Address" he printed in the newspapers in 1796.
He pleaded with Americans to stay together and not break into political *parties.*
But as soon as he left office, the pro-Jefferson and pro-Hamilton sides of government did just *that.*
He told Americans to stay out of Europe's many wars.
But as soon as he left office, the *second* president, John Adams, founded the US Navy to fight France in a "Quasi-War."
quasi = "kinda looks like"
DOES THAT MEAN...I'M ONLY QUASI-*DYING?* KOF!
NO, YOU'RE JUST *REGULAR*-DYING.
DANG... ACK!

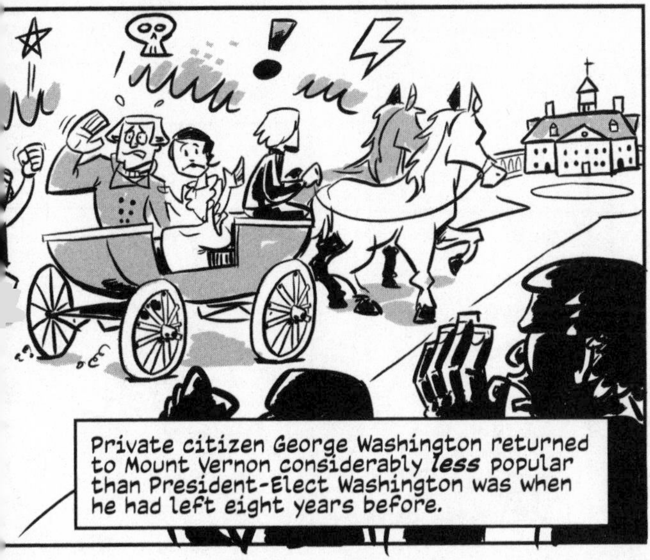
Private citizen George Washington returned to Mount Vernon considerably *less* popular than President-Elect Washington was when he had left eight years before.

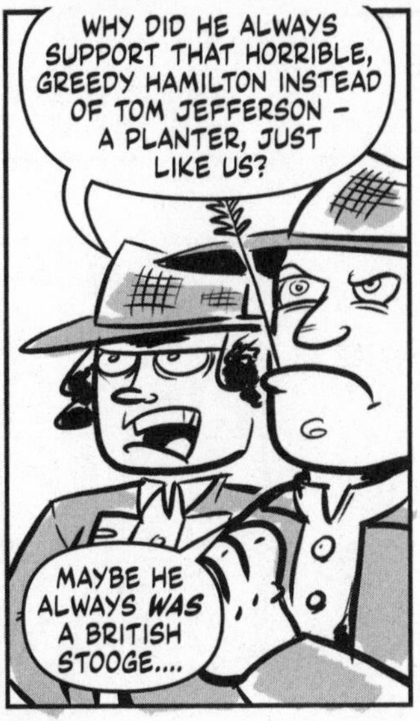
WHY DID HE ALWAYS SUPPORT THAT HORRIBLE, GREEDY HAMILTON INSTEAD OF TOM JEFFERSON – A PLANTER, JUST LIKE US?
MAYBE HE ALWAYS *WAS* A BRITISH STOOGE....

Few were the people George told about his reasons for siding with Hamilton – and it wasn't just because they had served together in the war.

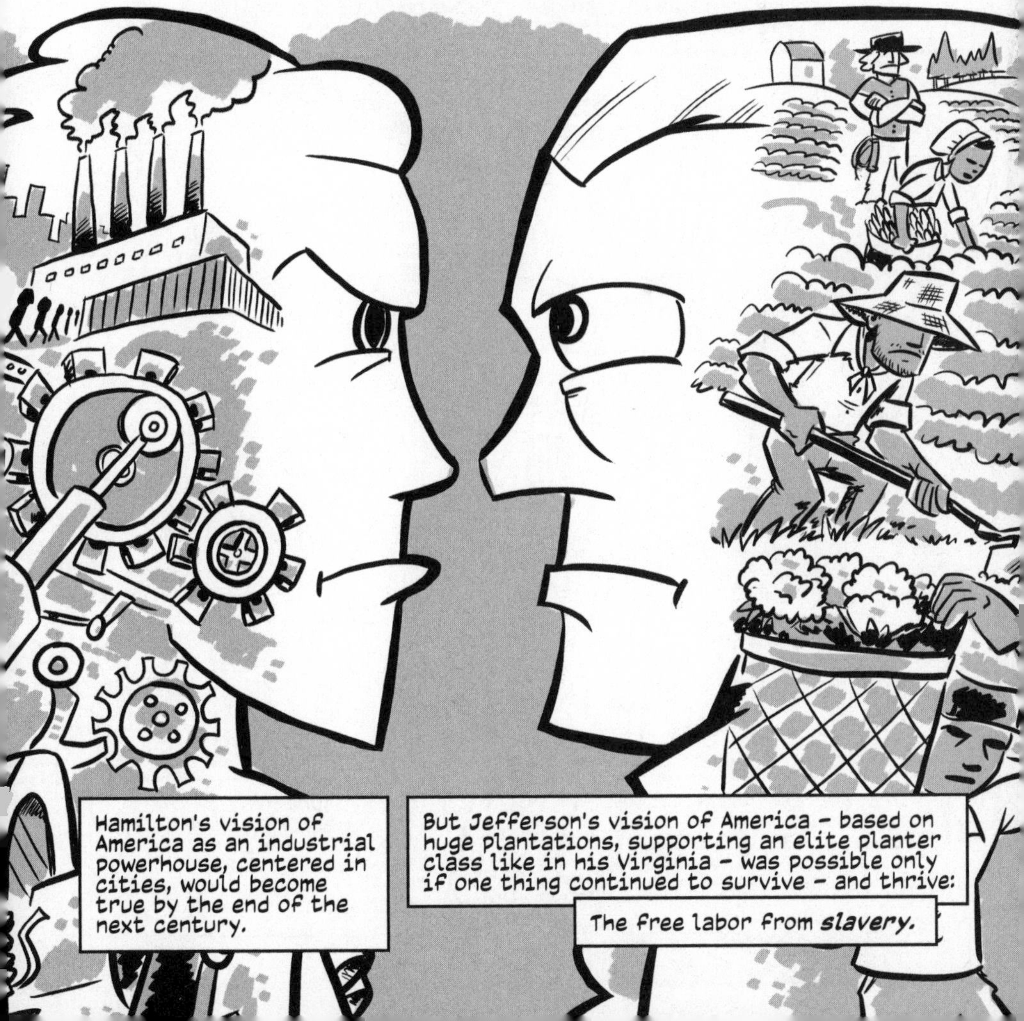
Hamilton's vision of America as an industrial powerhouse, centered in cities, would become true by the end of the next century.
But Jefferson's vision of America – based on huge plantations, supporting an elite planter class like in his Virginia – was possible only if one thing continued to survive – and thrive:
The free labor from *slavery.*

It's almost as if the outside threat of Britain kept Americans from fighting with one another over their differences.

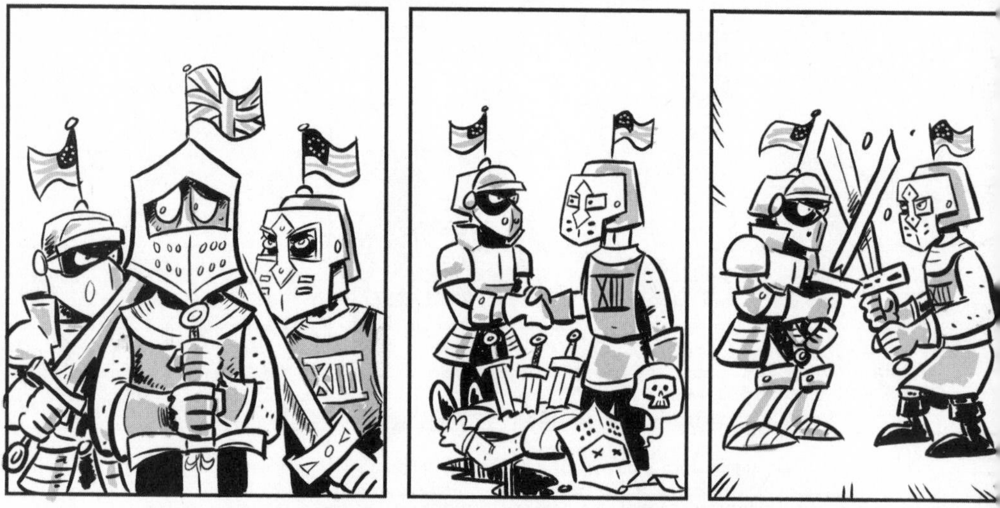
XIII
XIII

In many parts of the country, antislavery forces moved quickly. Pennsylvania passed a law in 1780 that said slaves who lived in the state six months or longer were automatically ***freed.***

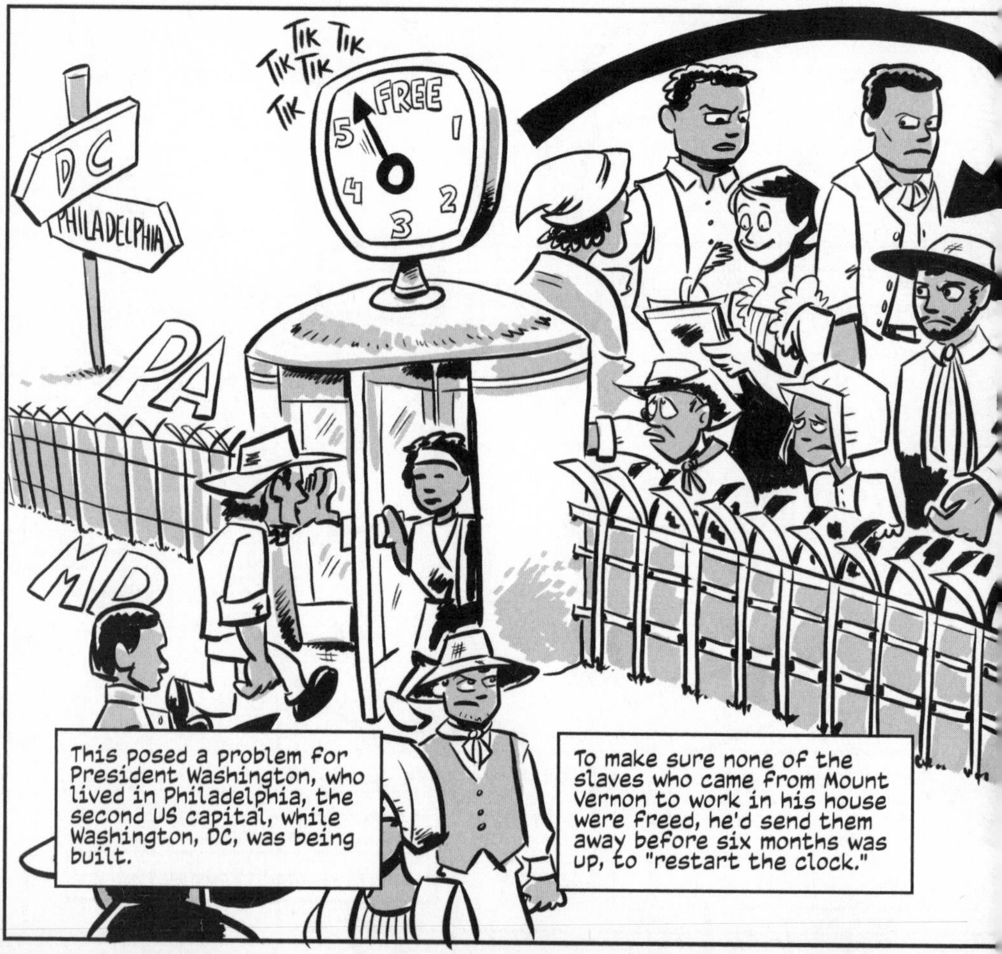
TIK TIK
TIK TIK
TIK
FREE
5
1
4
2
3
DC
PHILADELPHIA
PA
MD
This posed a problem for President Washington, who lived in Philadelphia, the second US capital, while Washington, DC, was being built.
To make sure none of the slaves who came from Mount Vernon to work in his house were freed, he'd send them away before six months was up, to "restart the clock."

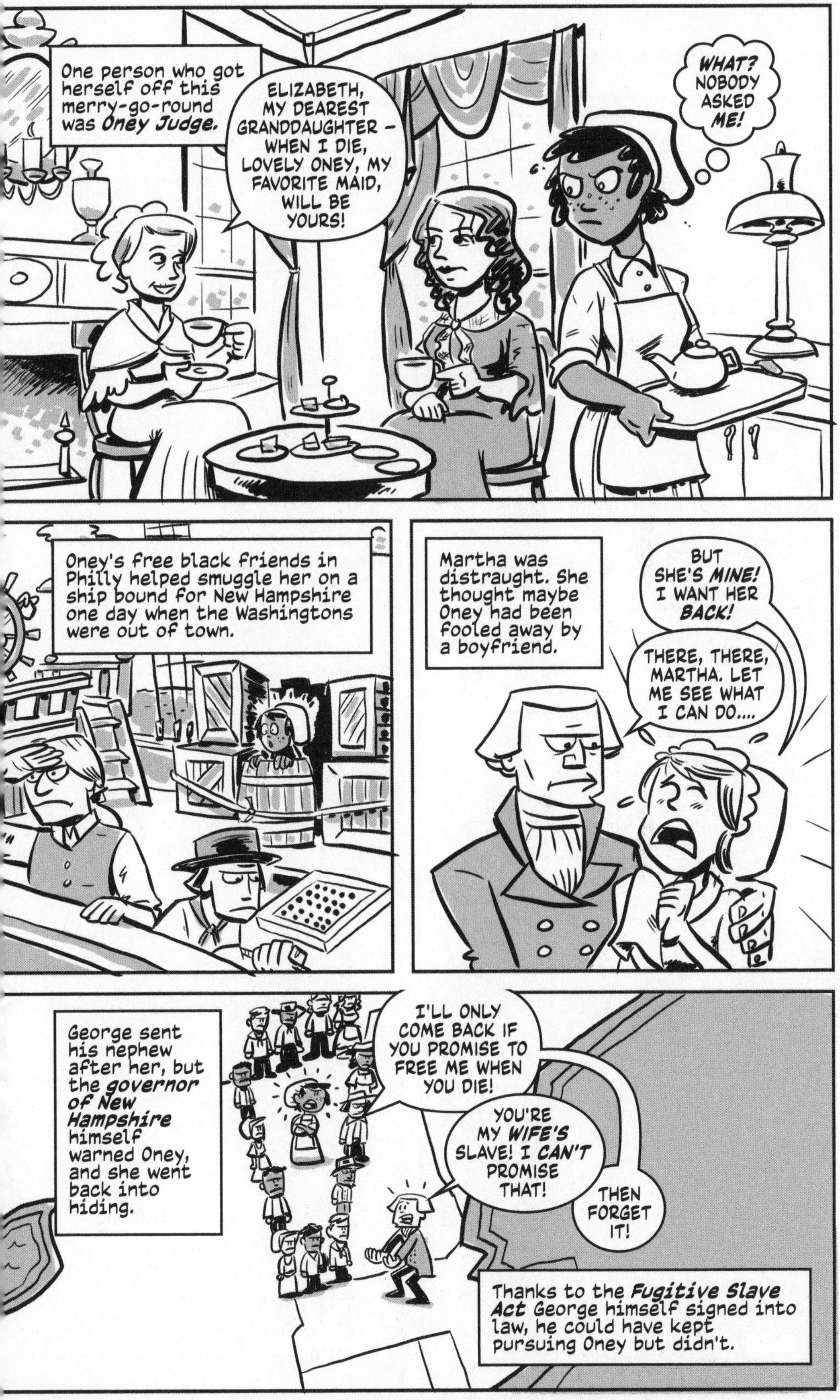

One person who got herself off this merry-go-round was *Oney Judge.*
ELIZABETH, MY DEAREST GRANDDAUGHTER – WHEN I DIE, LOVELY ONEY, MY FAVORITE MAID, WILL BE YOURS!
WHAT? NOBODY ASKED *ME!*
Oney's free black friends in Philly helped smuggle her on a ship bound for New Hampshire one day when the Washingtons were out of town.
Martha was distraught. She thought maybe Oney had been fooled away by a boyfriend.
BUT SHE'S *MINE!* I WANT HER *BACK!*
THERE, THERE, MARTHA. LET ME SEE WHAT I CAN DO....
George sent his nephew after her, but the ***governor of New Hampshire*** himself warned Oney, and she went back into hiding.
I'LL ONLY COME BACK IF YOU PROMISE TO FREE ME WHEN YOU DIE!
YOU'RE MY ***WIFE'S*** SLAVE! I ***CAN'T*** PROMISE THAT!
THEN FORGET IT!
Thanks to the ***Fugitive Slave Act*** George himself signed into law, he could have kept pursuing Oney but didn't.

George was willing to free his slaves, but only on *his* terms.

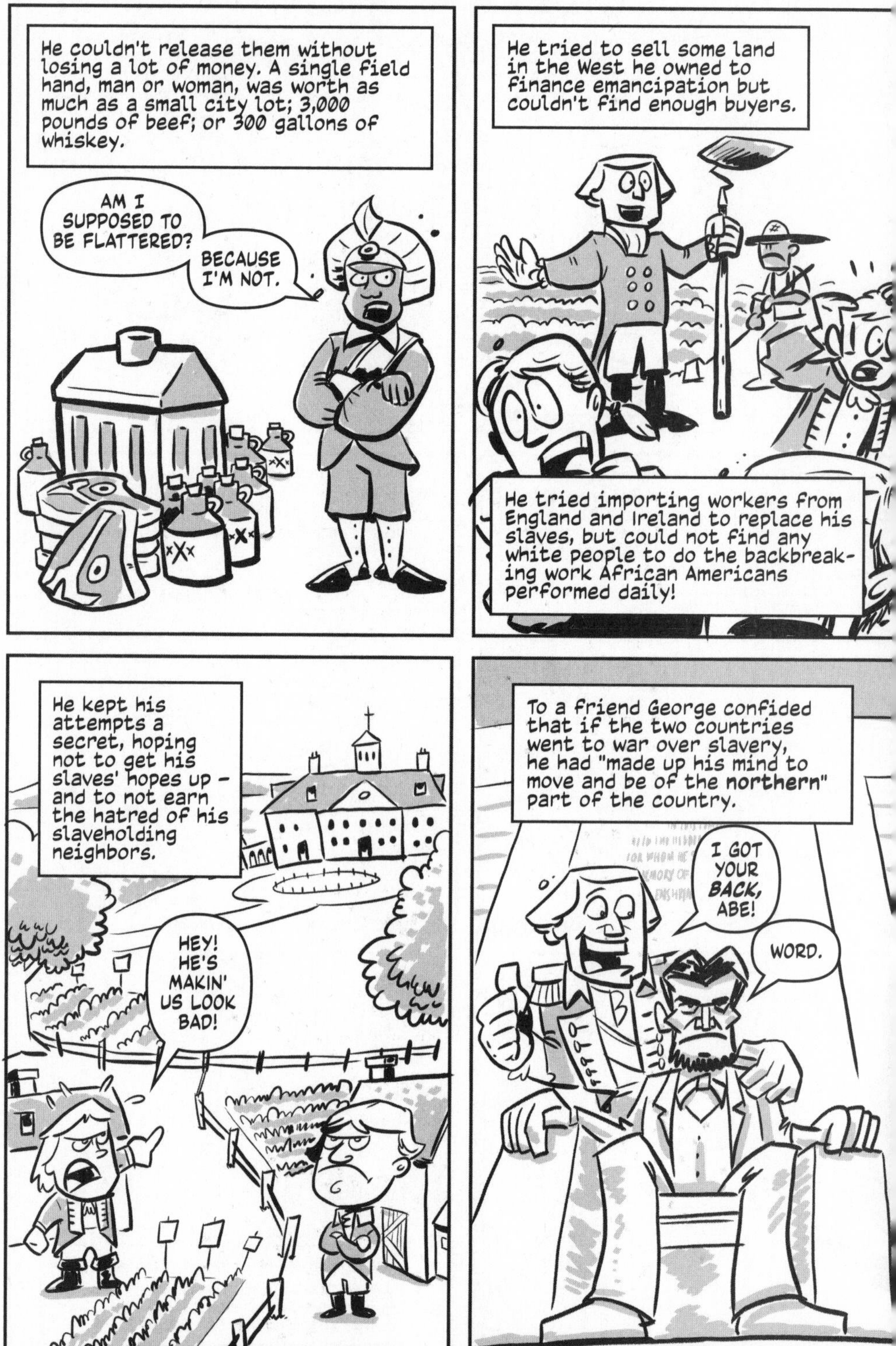
He couldn't release them without losing a lot of money. A single field hand, man or woman, was worth as much as a small city lot; 3,000 pounds of beef; or 300 gallons of whiskey.
AM I SUPPOSED TO BE FLATTERED?
BECAUSE I'M NOT.
He tried to sell some land in the West he owned to finance emancipation but couldn't find enough buyers.
He tried importing workers from England and Ireland to replace his slaves, but could not find any white people to do the backbreaking work African Americans performed daily!
He kept his attempts a secret, hoping not to get his slaves' hopes up – and to not earn the hatred of his slaveholding neighbors.
HEY! HE'S MAKIN' US LOOK BAD!
To a friend George confided that if the two countries went to war over slavery, he had "made up his mind to move and be of the **northern**" part of the country.
I GOT YOUR *BACK*, ABE!
WORD.

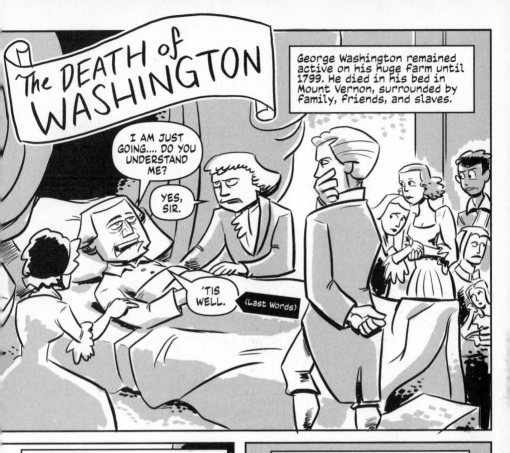

The DEATH of WASHINGTON

George Washington remained active on his huge farm until 1799. He died in his bed in Mount Vernon, surrounded by family, friends, and slaves.

I AM JUST GOING.... DO YOU UNDERSTAND ME?

YES, SIR.

'TIS WELL. (Last Words)

His will contained some surprises — it freed his longtime personal servant William Lee outright and freed all of George's own slaves upon Martha's death.

(Martha didn't wait that long, freeing *all* of George's slaves ten months after his death.)

This didn't apply to *Oney Judge,* who was one of *Martha's* slaves.

BUT THIS WAS *MY* IDEA IN THE *FIRST PLACE!!*

Fortunately, Martha's family left Oney alone. She married, had kids, and spent the rest of her life in New Hampshire.

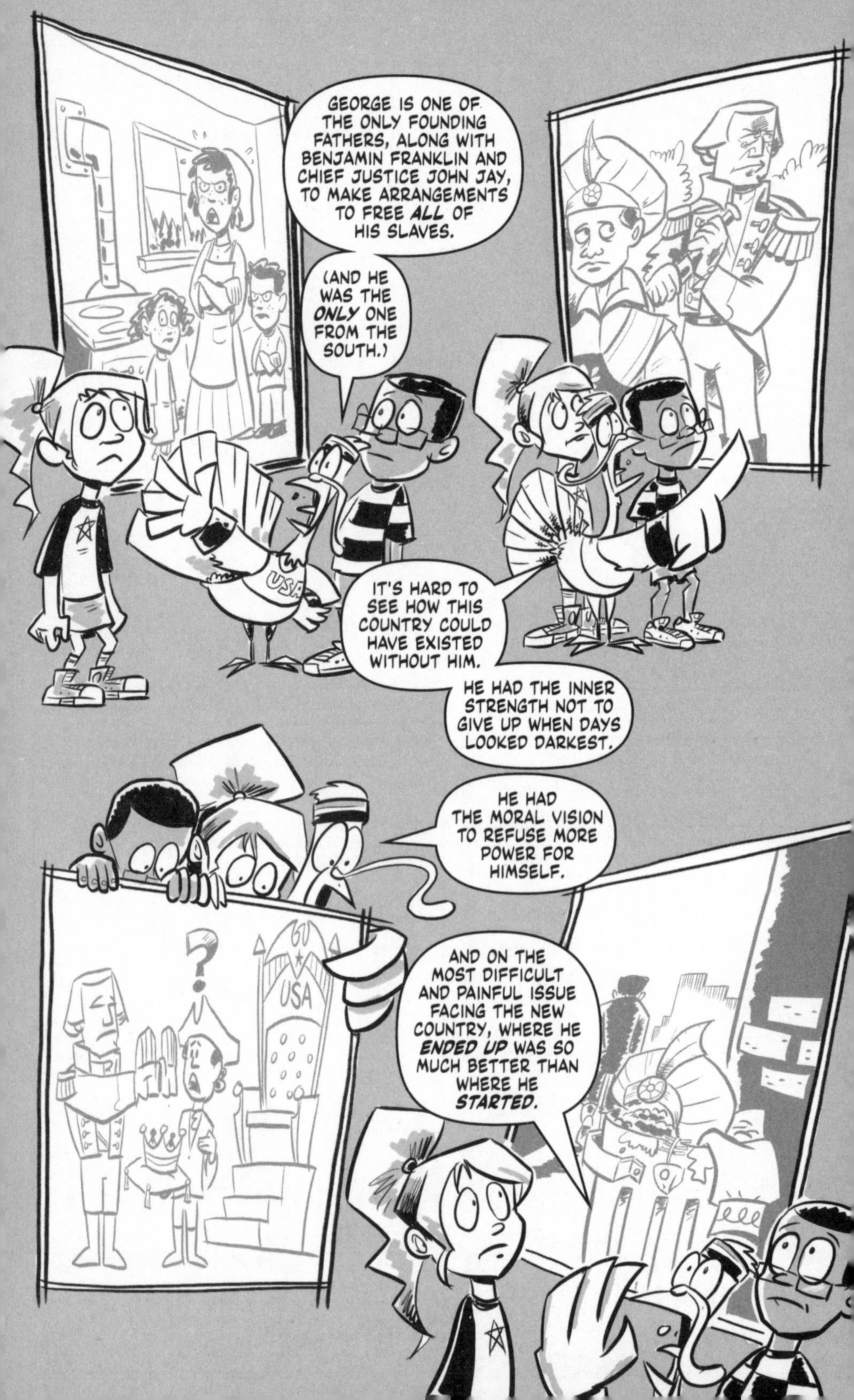
GEORGE IS ONE OF THE ONLY FOUNDING FATHERS, ALONG WITH BENJAMIN FRANKLIN AND CHIEF JUSTICE JOHN JAY, TO MAKE ARRANGEMENTS TO FREE *ALL* OF HIS SLAVES.
(AND HE WAS THE *ONLY* ONE FROM THE SOUTH.)
USA
IT'S HARD TO SEE HOW THIS COUNTRY COULD HAVE EXISTED WITHOUT HIM.
HE HAD THE INNER STRENGTH NOT TO GIVE UP WHEN DAYS LOOKED DARKEST.
HE HAD THE MORAL VISION TO REFUSE MORE POWER FOR HIMSELF.
?
USA
AND ON THE MOST DIFFICULT AND PAINFUL ISSUE FACING THE NEW COUNTRY, WHERE HE *ENDED UP* WAS SO MUCH BETTER THAN WHERE HE *STARTED*.

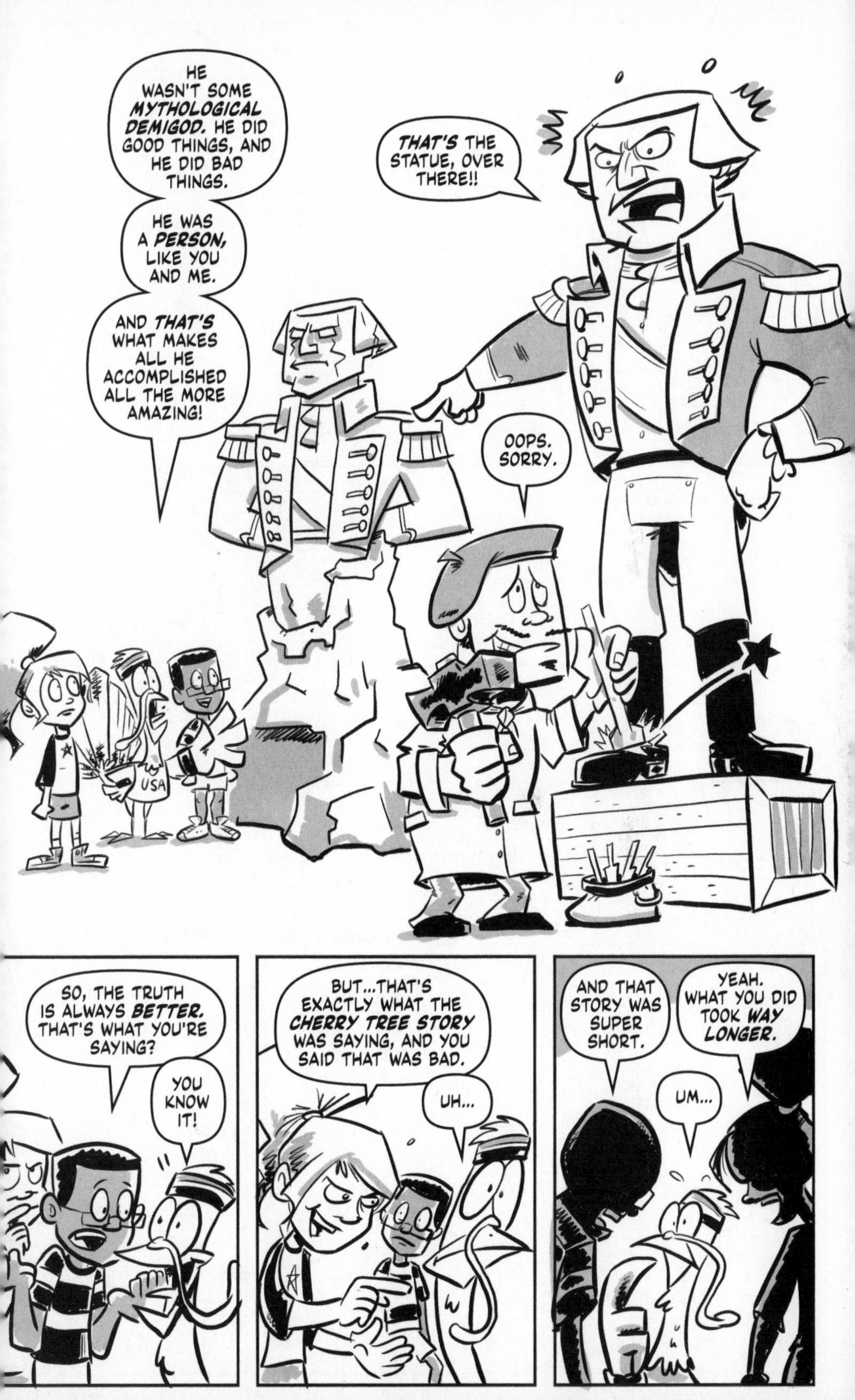
HE WASN'T SOME *MYTHOLOGICAL DEMIGOD.* HE DID GOOD THINGS, AND HE DID BAD THINGS.
HE WAS A *PERSON,* LIKE YOU AND ME.
AND *THAT'S* WHAT MAKES ALL HE ACCOMPLISHED ALL THE MORE AMAZING!
THAT'S THE STATUE, OVER THERE!!
OOPS. SORRY.
USA
SO, THE TRUTH IS ALWAYS *BETTER.* THAT'S WHAT YOU'RE SAYING?
YOU KNOW IT!
BUT...THAT'S EXACTLY WHAT THE *CHERRY TREE STORY* WAS SAYING, AND YOU SAID THAT WAS BAD.
UH...
AND THAT STORY WAS SUPER SHORT.
YEAH. WHAT YOU DID TOOK *WAY LONGER.*
UM...

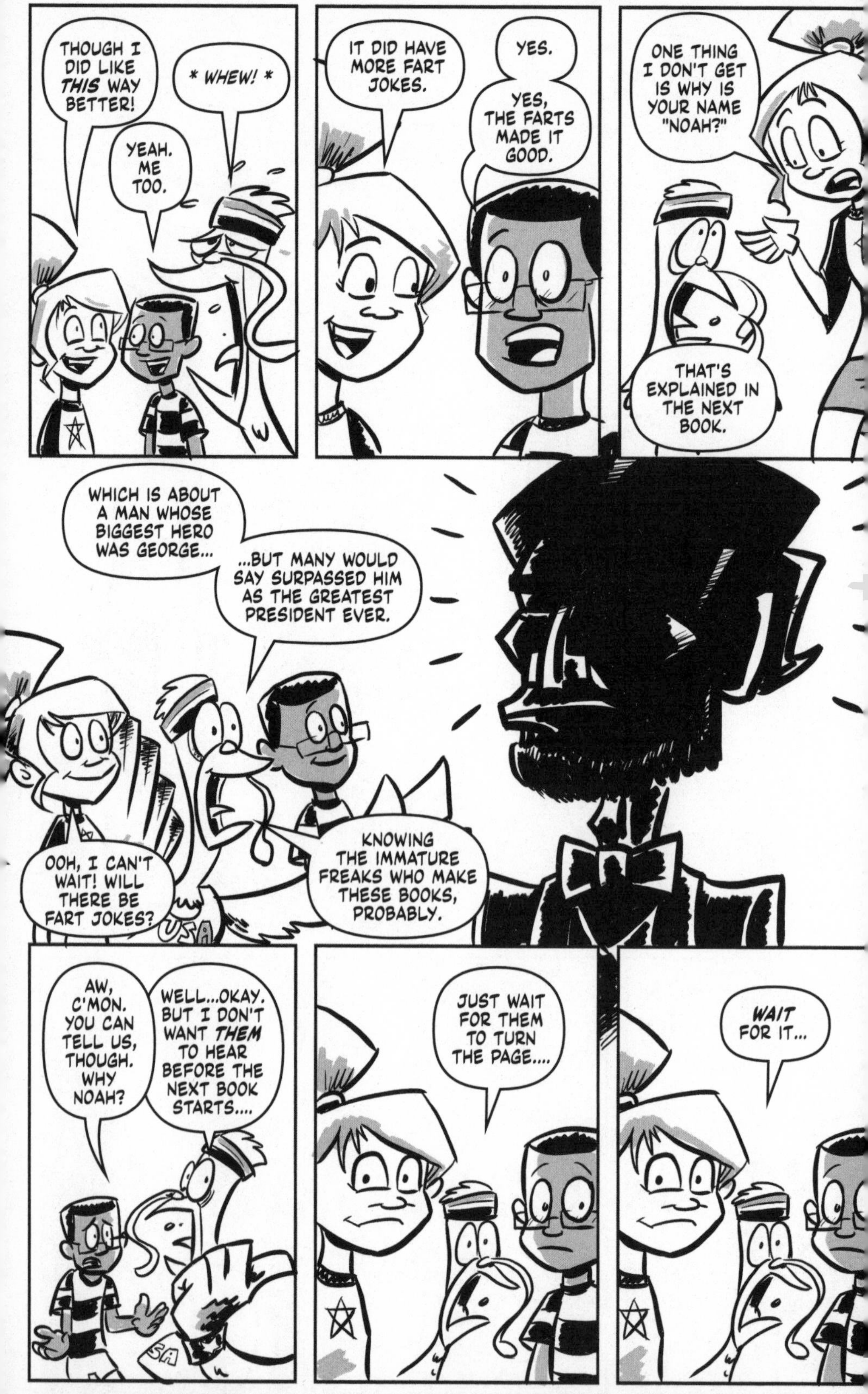
THOUGH I DID LIKE *THIS* WAY BETTER!
YEAH. ME TOO.
* *WHEW!* *
IT DID HAVE MORE FART JOKES.
YES.
YES, THE FARTS MADE IT GOOD.
ONE THING I DON'T GET IS WHY IS YOUR NAME "NOAH?"
THAT'S EXPLAINED IN THE NEXT BOOK.
WHICH IS ABOUT A MAN WHOSE BIGGEST HERO WAS GEORGE...
...BUT MANY WOULD SAY SURPASSED HIM AS THE GREATEST PRESIDENT EVER.
OOH, I CAN'T WAIT! WILL THERE BE FART JOKES?
KNOWING THE IMMATURE FREAKS WHO MAKE THESE BOOKS, PROBABLY.
USA
AW, C'MON. YOU CAN TELL US, THOUGH. WHY NOAH?
WELL...OKAY. BUT I DON'T WANT *THEM* TO HEAR BEFORE THE NEXT BOOK STARTS....
JUST WAIT FOR THEM TO TURN THE PAGE....
WAIT FOR IT...

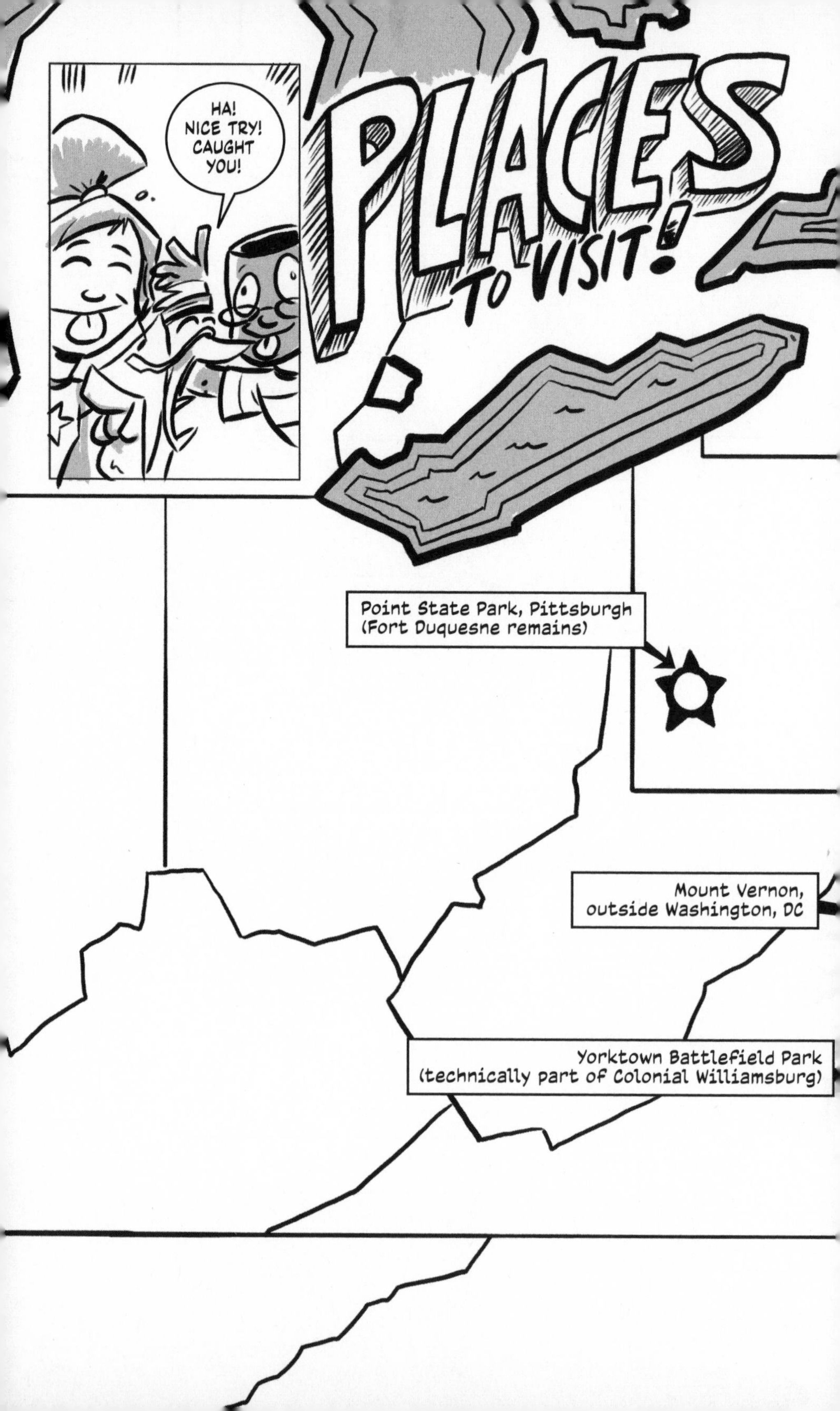
HA! NICE TRY! CAUGHT YOU!
PLACES TO VISIT!
Point State Park, Pittsburgh
(Fort Duquesne remains)
Mount Vernon,
outside Washington, DC
Yorktown Battlefield Park
(technically part of Colonial Williamsburg)

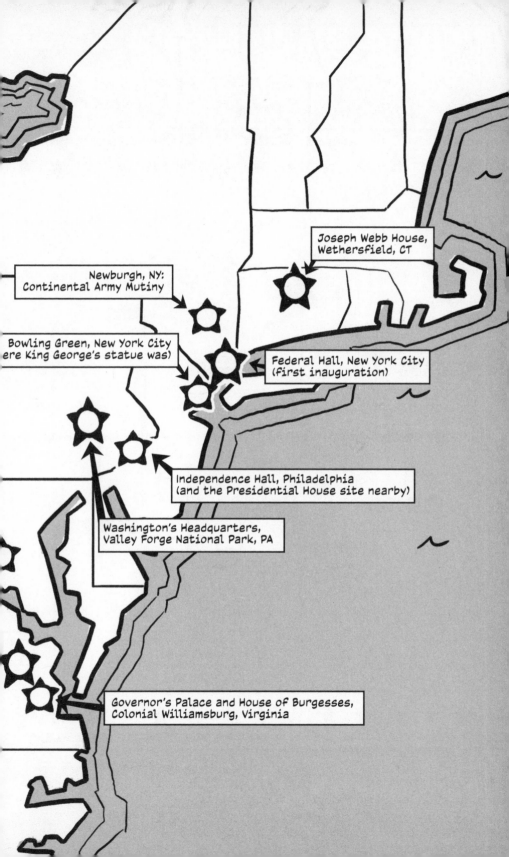

Joseph Webb House,
Wethersfield, CT

Newburgh, NY:
Continental Army Mutiny

Bowling Green, New York City
(where King George's statue was)

Federal Hall, New York City
(first inauguration)

Independence Hall, Philadelphia
(and the Presidential House site nearby)

Washington's Headquarters,
Valley Forge National Park, PA

Governor's Palace and House of Burgesses,
Colonial Williamsburg, Virginia

GEORGE WASHINGTON

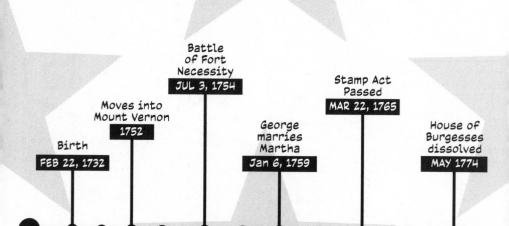

Battle
of Fort
Necessity
JUL 3, 1754

Moves into
Mount Vernon
1752

Stamp Act
Passed
MAR 22, 1765

George
marries
Martha
Jan 6, 1759

House of
Burgesses
dissolved
MAY 1774

Birth
FEB 22, 1732

APR 12, 1743
Father's death

MAY 1755
Braddock's
expedition

DEC 1753
Dinwiddie
Mission

FEB 10, 1763
French
and Indian
War ends

DEC 16, 1771
Boston
Tea
Party

19, 1775
tles of
ington
and
ncord

JUN 15, 1775
Second Continental Congress chooses George to lead army

JUL 9, 1776
Declaration of Independence read to George's troops

AUG 27, 1776
Battle of Brooklyn

NOV 16, 1776
Fall of Fort Washington

DEC 26, 1776
Battle of Trenton

SEPT 19, 1777- OCT 7, 1777
Battles of Saratoga: French-American alliance

DEC 1777- Jun 1778
Valley Forge

JUN 28, 1778
Battle of Monmouth

OCT 19, 1781
Surrender at Yorktown

MAY 14, 1787
Constitutional Convention

DEC 10, 1788- JAN 10, 1789
Election of 1789

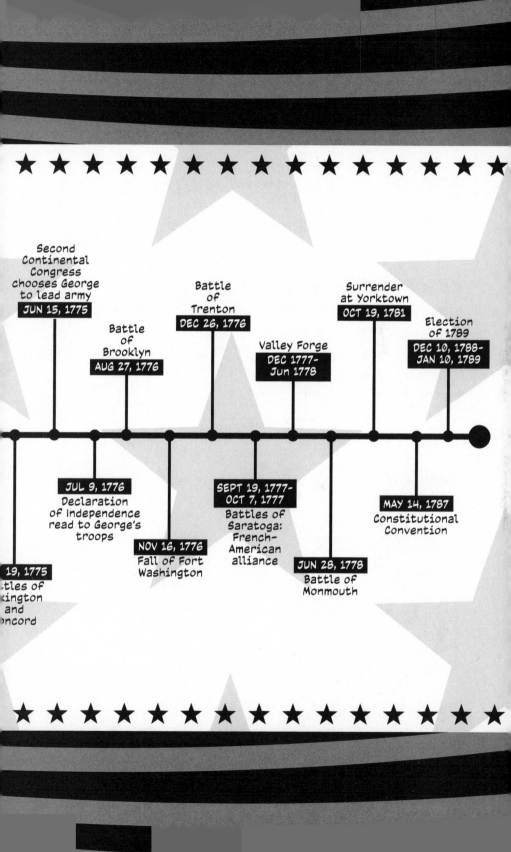

GLOSSARY

AMBUSH (v): to attack unexpectedly from a hidden place

ARTILLERY (n): the troops charged with the use of mounted guns

ASSUMPTION (n): the act of taking ownership of something, specifically here of the colonies' debt (see below)

BAYONET (n): a small sharp sword attached to the end of a rifle's muzzle, used for hand-to-hand fighting

CAMPAIGN (n): a military operation with a specific goal or objective

CANISTER (n): a can filled with a whole bunch of little cannonballs that can be shot from a cannon in lieu of cannonballs

DEBT (n): something that is owed to another person or entity

EMANCIPATION (n): the act of freeing someone from slavery

HIGHLAND (n): a mountainous region

INAUGURATION (n): the act of installing a person in a position of power, usually during a formal ceremony

LEGISLATURE (n): a body of people who are charged with drafting and changing the laws of a country and/or state

LOOT (v): to steal, especially in times of war

MILITIA (n): a group of citizen soldiers, usually not employed full-time in military service and often not professionally trained

MUZZLE (n): the end of the barrel of a gun

REINFORCEMENTS (n): an additional supply of personnel for military service

REPUBLIC (n): a country in which the leader is not a king or queen

SECEDE (v): to withdraw from membership in a group or union

SLOOP (n): a sailing vessel with a single mast

TYRANNY (n): an unjust government ruled by a tyrant or dictator

WITHDRAWAL (n): in war, the act of retreating

STUFF NAMED AFTER WASHINGTON

9 colleges

WASHINGTON UNIVERSITY
18 91
17 82
UNIVERSITY OF WASHINGTON
1861
WASHINGTON STATE UNIVERSITY
1890
WASHINGTON UNIVERSITY

7 mountains

10 lakes

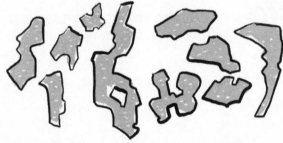

8 streams

The first ballistic submarine

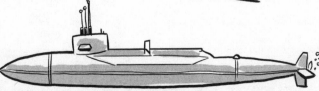

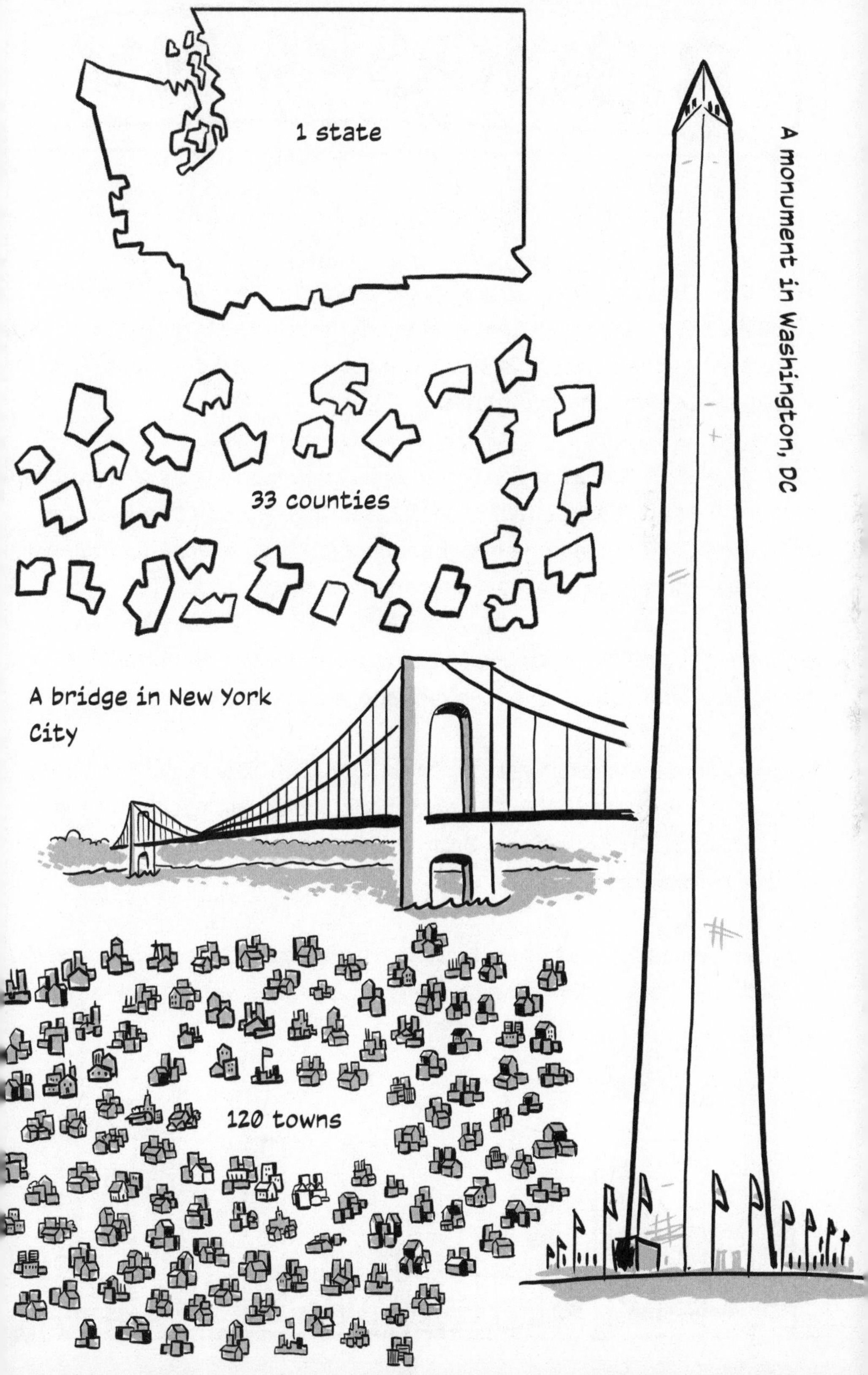
1 state
33 counties
A bridge in New York City
120 towns
A monument in Washington, DC

BIBLIOGRAPHY

Cook, Don. *The Long Fuse: How England Lost the American Colonies, 1760–1785.* New York: Atlantic Monthly Press, 1996. There's two side to every story, and this is a very good look at how Great Britain saw the American Revolution.

Ellis, Joseph J. *Founding Brothers: The Revolutionary Generation.* New York: Vintage Books, 2002. The classic look at how the Founding Fathers influenced one another; an excellent source to understa the two terms of the Washington presidency.

Finegan, Sr., Jeffrey E. *Colonel Washington and Me.* Siegle Books, 2012 picture book about the life of George's slave valet, William Lee.

Fischer, David Hackett. *Washington's Crossing.* New York: Oxford University Press, 2004. The best book about the Battle of Trentor it looks at the American, British, and Hessian sides – and reads like a movie thriller!

Flexner, James Thomas. *Washington: The Indispensable Man.* New York: Back Bay Books, 1994. The lavishly illustrated version of a classic biography of our George.

nnedy, Frances H., ed. *The American Revolution: A Historical Guidebook.* New York: Oxford University Press, 2014. A great guide to places (that you can visit!) and battles (with maps!) with views from many different historians. Proceeds from the book go to the Conservation Fund's efforts to preserve historic places.

rison, Samuel Eliot, ed. *Sources & Documents Illustrating the American Revolution 1764–1788 and the Formation of the Federal Constitution,* 2nd ed. New York: Oxford University Press, 1965. All the famous documents of the time period, plus selections from the debates that shaped them.

gy, John A. *Invisible Ink: Spycraft of the American Revolution,* 2nd ed. Yardley, PA: Westholme Publishing, 2011. If codes, ciphers, and devious doings are your thing, then this is the book about America's beginning for you!

ashington, George. *George Washington's Rules of Civility & Decent Behaviour in Company and Conversation.* Carlisle, MA: Applewood Books, 1988. Well, George didn't write this, he copied it from a French book on etiquette, but it's still an interesting historical curiosity.

ABOUT the AUTHORS

Fred · Ryan

Fred Van Lente is the *New York Times* bestselling writer of comic books like *Cowboy & Aliens* and *Marvel Zombies.* His previous funny nonfiction comics with Ryan were *Action Philosophers!* (named a YALSA Great Graphic Novel for Teens by the American Library Association) and *The Comic Book History of Comics* (which Fred's mom really likes).

Full-time award-winning cartoonist and part-time scout leader **Ryan Dunlavey** spends every day and most nights drawing cool and fun stuff for the world's most charming and attractive art directors. He's also the artist of the graphic novels *Action Philosophers!, The Comic Book History of Comics* (both with Fred Van Lente), *Dirt Candy: A Cookbook* (with chef Amanda Cohen), and the comic strip *Li'l Classix* (with Grady Hendrix). He can often be spotted with his wife, Liza, as they wrangle their two children on various adventures throughout the wilds of New York City.